ADVANCE PRAISE

If you read only one memoir addressing the Holocaust and victim resilience in the face of unspeakable horror, this should be the one. Hymie Anisman's account of the Holocaust experience from its victims' point of view, postwar displacement including governmental obstacles preventing the admittance of refugees, and the development of Israel as a safe haven for Jewish people is absolutely riveting. These historical events come alive with descriptions of the ordeal as experienced by individual family members who did not survive the Nazi regime, as well as those who did miraculously survive, some of whom dedicated themselves to ensuring we never forget how authoritarianism can take hold and ultimately destroy millions. This compelling memoir builds on Anisman's own research in neuroscience that has sought to improve understanding of post-traumatic stress disorder and illuminate how intergenerational transmission of vulnerability in descendants of survivors may occur. This is a unique mixture of science and history, delivered using a first-person narrative. It is hard not to see how the lessons of the past reverberate today. By guiding us through the Holocaust and its aftermath, Anisman tackles the big existential questions, without supplying easy or trite answers. Lurking in this timely memoir are warnings of growing fascist movements around the world, including the 'big lies' they disseminate, putting democracy and the future of us all at risk. — **Nyla Branscombe, University Distinguished Professor, University of Kansas, Kansas, USA**

This is not a comfortable read – but it is a compelling one, refocusing on historical and personal events of the Holocaust through the lens of survival – who, how, and most elusively (and critically) why. Anisman selects the events told here bravely, wisely, and compassionately – from the legacy with which he has been so painfully gifted.

The book presents the events not just in their terrifying immediacy but also through the reflections of those affected, as they try to make some sense and to find some meaning. The later chapters focus on the dance between the memory, or even imprint of the events and the critical, then scientific reflection on them, in the lives of the players – and outside analysts. – **Aviva Freedman, Professor Emeritus, Carleton University, Ottawa, Canada**

Professor Anisman has given voice to a panoply of survivor narratives, each more vivid than the next. The Shoah shadows and colors the lives woven together through fiction, memoir and genuine historical context. The reader is invited into disparate worlds ranging from Canada to Israel and the USSR, each vivified by the author's empathy and careful research. Among works written by second generation authors, this book excels with fulsome characters who do not shy away from the difficulties of starting afresh after the Holocaust. – **Vera Schwarcz, Mansfield Freeman Professor of East Asian Studies; Emerita Professor Wesleyan University, Connecticut, USA**

Many books have enriched our understanding of the horrors of the Holocaust through tragic personal testimony and probing historical analysis. Anisman's book adds to this important body of writing but does so in a uniquely powerful way. This is because as well as being the son of a Holocaust survivor whose family died at the hands of the Nazis, Anisman is also a world-leading neuroscientist. He draws on both identities to drill deeply into questions not only about the worst of human nature but also about the human capacity for resilience. This gives the book an unparalleled breadth of relevance that enriches our understanding of the past and, in the process, provides answers to some of the most pressing issues of our time. So while the reader will read and weep they will also read and grow. – **Alex Haslam, UQ Laureate Fellow, Faculty of Health and Behavioural Sciences, Brisbane, Australia**

Hymie Anisman's lightly fictionalized *Before the Beginning and After the End* is a beautifully crafted, intergenerational trauma narrative embedded in a richly layered, devastatingly factual account of the Shoa; a collective testimony demanding the reader to bear unflinching witness and grapple with existential tensions surrounding post-genocidal themes of silence and shame; meaning, justice, redemption, resilience, and ultimately, love. – **Stephanie Fagin-Jones, Ph.D.; Columbia University Teachers College; Holocaust Heroism Scholar, International Association of Heroism Science, USA**

BEFORE THE BEGINNING AND AFTER THE END

HYMIE ANISMAN

ap

ISBN 9789493322257 (ebook)

ISBN 9789493322240 (paperback)

ISBN 9789493322264 (hardcover)

Publisher: Amsterdam Publishers, The Netherlands

info@amsterdampublishers.com

Before the Beginning and After the End is part of the series Holocaust Survivor True Stories

Copyright © Hymie Anisman 2023

Book Cover Design/Illustration: Barış Şehri

All Rights Reserved. No part of this publication may be reproduced or transmitted in any form or by any means, electronic or mechanical, including photocopy, recording or any other information storage and retrieval system, without prior permission in writing from the publisher.

CONTENTS

Preface   xi

  Prologue   1
1. In the Beginning   5
2. From the Ashes   39
3. Is this the Promised Land?   83
4. Zosha: The Reckoning   127
5. A Dream Unfulfilled is like a Book Unread   175
6. Yossi and Sasha: The Kindertransports   213
7. Rachel: Mystery of Fate   249
8. Motti and Elie: Reemergence   277
  Epilogue   301

About the Author   311
Amsterdam Publishers Holocaust Library   315

For Yankele, Benyamin, Edgga, Reza, and Moshe.
May their memories and that of the six million be blessings.

PREFACE

How does one come to grips with the idea that members of the Third Reich engaged in killing more than 20 million people? Among them were six million Jews that were murdered in an effort to "exterminate" every member of that group of *Untermenschen,* subhumans, not because of anything that they had done but because of who they were – they were Jews and that was sufficient. What made this so much more abhorrent was the cruel and sadistic ways in which the Nazis did so. All the while, many of the people in the Fatherland cheered them on, assisted by their antisemitic henchmen in numerous countries that had allied themselves with the Third Reich. Even now, with all that we know about the horrors, it still seems unimaginable. But, as one of the characters in this book states "... the unimaginable became imaginable, and the inconceivable had become conceivable."

This book is, in part, a memoir based on experiences that were recounted by several survivors of the Holocaust (the Shoah). Prior to the Shoah, both my parents had large extended families within Poland and Ukraine, few of whom survived. Most who did had emigrated prior to the outbreak of the Second World War. My mother, who came from the region of Przemyśl, survived thanks to Righteous Christian families who hid her at their own peril.

Unfortunately, her first husband and three children were murdered. My father, who had lived in Lodz, was abducted within the first days of the Nazi invasion and spent the war in work camps, as did one of his daughters. His first wife and his other two children had been taken away; it isn't known when and where they died. My parents met after the war – I'm the product of their union. My parents' stories and that of my half-sister are included in this recitation. While my mother repeatedly spoke of her Shoah experiences, my father rarely spoke of it; part of the 'conspiracy of silence' that many survivors adopted, perhaps as a way of coping. Thus, much of what I know of his history has come from my half-sister. As well, my aunt and two of her children survived, and some of their history is described in this book, as are those of more distant cousins on both sides of my family.

Family friends who lived in Montreal, New York, and in Israel would occasionally describe or briefly comment on how they survived. I incorporated some of their experiences in this book. It was not uncommon for our family and friends to recount the experiences of several other survivors, only some of whom I met. I allowed myself to imagine how their lives might have played out, which was included in this book.

My intention in writing what I have wasn't simply to recount survivor experiences before or during the Shoah – there are numerous memoirs that do precisely this, each adding immeasurably to our collective memories of the Shoah. Instead, my intent was to show the resilience of survivors and how they were able to reconstruct their shattered lives. None of the survivors I've met have attributed their survival to their cunning, instead, as my father often said, "it was better to be lucky than smart." To be sure, what facilitated their resilience following the Shoah often involved a degree of luck, but there was much more that provided them the strength to flourish. A few survivors maintained that God must have had a purpose in allowing them to survive; many others found meaning in their lives, which allowed them to move forward. Several characters in this book dedicated themselves to the well-being of their families, particularly their children and grandchildren, with the hope that history wouldn't repeat itself. For others, meaning was obtained through their resolve and actions to prevent Jews from ever again being victimized. Several survivors found meaning by engaging in a purpose greater than themselves, much as Viktor Frankl described. This could be attained not just by exposing the atrocities committed by the Nazis but to document how and why many officials in other countries did so little to help Jewish people when it was so desperately needed. Regrettably, in contexts unrelated to Jewish people, these same pusillanimous behaviors continue to play out worldwide; far too often those who can't help themselves are abandoned. We need to keep in mind Elie Wiesel's assertion that "to remain silent and indifferent is the greatest sin of all' and the view expressed by Reverend Martin Luther King, "In the end we will remember not the words of our enemies, but the silence of our friends."

Those of us who were born after the Shoah, the second generation of survivors, carry both a burden and a blessing. Although we hadn't experienced the Shoah, it has often affected us to our core. In her brilliant book, *After Such Knowledge: Memory, History, and the Legacy of the Holocaust*, Anna Hoffman vividly describes the impact of living in a home haunted by memories of the Shoah, and how these embedded themselves in the minds of the children. We have inherited what Marianne Hirsch refers to as "Postmemory" – through the stories, images, and behaviors (as well as the silence in the home) that we witnessed, memories developed that comprised events that were stitched together, gaps often filled in, to create cohesive narratives.

The blessing is that my generation represents the linchpin, the hinge generation as Anna Hoffman put it, who can transmit not just the memory but the lessons of the Shoah to ensuing generations. This is not to say that there is a desire to create Postmemories in our children. However, it might be beneficial to remind them that the unimaginable can become imaginable, and the inconceivable can become conceivable. More than anything, the transmission of our experiences and that of our forebears may imbue our children and grandchildren with hope, kindness, and resilience. To paraphrase a comment of French theologian Hyacinthe Loyson's, "These trees which he plants, and under whose shade he shall never sit, he loves them for themselves, and for the sake of his children and his children's children" who will enjoy the shadow of their spreading boughs.

The narratives provided here are obviously just a few of those that survived. The voices of those who perished can't be heard. We honor them and pray that their memory be a blessing.

PROLOGUE

Then take me disappearin' through the smoke rings of my mind. Down the foggy ruins of time, far past the frozen leaves. The haunted, frightened trees, out to the windy beach. Far from the twisted reach of crazy sorrow. Yes, to dance beneath the diamond sky with one hand waving free.
– **Bob Dylan**, "Mr. Tambourine Man"

She hadn't considered she would spend years hunted and imprisoned by predators who wanted nothing more than to kill as many of her kind as they could. Chaviva had been aware Jews were in jeopardy. Still, she considered it unimaginable the hatred would become a coordinated effort to eliminate every Jew. But the unimaginable became imaginable, and the inconceivable became conceivable.

"In retrospect," Chaviva said, "I was simply naive. The hatred of Jews wasn't something new. It had been common for centuries. When it wasn't overtly present, it rested only slightly beneath the surface, waiting for the opportunity to emerge. But I wasn't among the most foolish. Many of our people believed they had been accepted by the citizens of the countries in which they lived. Of course, they did, and why wouldn't they have felt this way? In the late 19th century, Jews in Austria and Germany weren't any more threatened than those in

France and Britain. They were allowed the freedoms and rights that were common among German and Austrian people and frequently adopted the customs, conventions, and culture of their Christian neighbors. They could be found in every aspect of life; they were well-educated and well-represented in medicine, law, and teaching professions. Many had become business owners, whereas others were farmers or laborers. In the end, it didn't matter a whit. Irrespective of how assimilated they had become, even those who had married non-Jews were lined up together for extermination."

The contagion of hate wasn't restricted to Germany and Austria. She frequently heard that in many countries, the neighbors of Jews had turned on them, facilitating the heinous acts committed by the Nazis. The concentration camps were used to imprison and exterminate Jews from Poland, Ukraine, Estonia, Ukraine, Hungary, Lithuania, and Czechoslovakia, and even in countries that cherished their democratic principles, such as France, Belgium, and Holland, large segments of the population were content to rid themselves of their Jews.

"Like the Austrian psychiatrist Viktor Frankl had experienced, upon being imprisoned I initially felt utter shock. Soon afterward, this morphed into despondency, followed by apathy, and ultimately detachment from reality. And, I often wondered whether a quick death would be preferable than a drawn-out ordeal that comprised continued physical suffering and intense humiliation that stole my soul. How I eventually came to terms with my situation still eludes me, but I was determined that my life wouldn't be wasted in a hell that had been created for me. As Frankl indicated, survival was dependent on being dedicating to something greater than myself.

"Over the months after being liberated from the camp, the emotions I felt could easily have turned to bitterness and anger, especially when I learned that so many Jews could have been saved if only the Allied countries had done more to prevent the Nazi aspirations. Countless books would be written describing the trauma experienced by Jews who had survived the Shoah, while the voices of those who had been murdered would never be heard. Politicians would certainly investigate the abysmal behaviors of the Nazis and their many collaborators, and there would be no shortage of academics who would attempt to understand what motivated the Nazis and their followers to behave as they had. As far as I was concerned, the answers to these questions were intuitively obvious; it was enough to know that Jews were hated, and given the opportunity, haters were ready to participate in the brutality.

"The past couldn't be undone, and I focused on the future, wondering about the fate of those who had survived. Did they carry the baggage of their experiences so that they would forever be haunted by them, and would the trauma be passed on to successive generations? Alternatively, would Jews find safe places where they could flourish, and might the traumatic experiences somehow promote resilience, allowing them the luxury of moving on with their lives, as difficult as that might be?"

Chaviva was nobody's fool and was aware that for a while non-Jews would take some interest in helping Jews, although it might manifest itself in the form of tangible support. Moreover, whatever empathy they expressed for Jews was time limited. Eventually, the old hatred would emerge again throughout Europe and North America, facilitated by political and economic considerations.

Thus, she would say, "If nothing else, the multiple experiences of Jews before, during, and after the Shoah, ought to make it clear that for Jews to survive they couldn't rely on others and had to be masters of their destinies." With these thoughts in mind, Chaviva focused on discovering what led to some trauma survivors falling into despair while others thrived. As for their children, she wondered, how would the trauma experienced by their parents and grandparents affect them?

1

IN THE BEGINNING

A grief so deep the tongue must wag in vain; the language of our sense and memory lacks the vocabulary of such pain.
  – Dante Alighieri, Inferno

The morning of Tuesday, November 9, 1938, was the same as many in the past few weeks, hovering around 15 degrees Celsius, although the days had become notably shorter and the sun's trajectory had been lower in the sky as it passed his window. Lethargically, Asher got ready for school, washing up, brushing his curly brown hair, and getting into his standard-issue tan-colored uniform, which had become uncomfortably tight from growing somewhat over the spring and summer.

He had no appetite but sat slouched at the kitchen table and reluctantly ate the butter-smeared bread and drank the warm milk his mother had prepared. As usual, his stomach began to tie in knots as he readied for school. He dreaded every day, wishing classes would end so he could steal away to the privacy of his room to brood over his miseries.

Sunday was the worst day of the week, as it presaged Monday. A frightening, cold, creeping shadow would cause overwhelming apprehension as Monday loomed. His head swam and his jittery hands felt permanently clammy. At times, panic would overcome him and his chest would tighten so much he could hardly breathe, and his heart would pound as if trying to escape the confines of his chest. Far from being comforted by the company of others, even having his closest family or friends around was terrifying because he might suddenly experience one of these panics, which could lead to further shame and humiliation.

At first, the other children in the class acted as if he didn't exist. The feeling of being invisible was hurtful enough, but his foreboding reached new heights when they seemed to identify him for what he was. These vicious rats had sniffed out a frightened tiny mouse with no way to escape. He had become the butt of pranks and nasty remarks and felt helpless in the face of the incessant bullying. Now, every morning triggered the despair of the day before. If his former friends weren't avoiding him now, it was because they had joined the others in mocking him, pushing him, or spitting or throwing dirt at him. He was small for his age and had a thin frame. It was hardly possible to protect himself from the larger apple-faced children, who all seemed ready to mob him.

He counted his steps to school: 2,235 steps from home. The walk gave him far too much time to think, building up to a crescendo of trepidation. More recently, the number of steps had increased to 2,320, then to 2,390 as his stride shortened, perhaps in an unconscious effort to avoid getting where he had to go. With every few dozen steps, a new memory from a previous day assailed him, each more painful than the last. This morning, he thought back to a particularly horrid day. When he unpacked his lunch in the schoolyard, he found the chopped egg in the sandwich his mother had prepared had been replaced by excrement. He almost retched when the vile smell hit him, and upon lifting his head, he felt humiliated as he realized the other children were mocking him and laughing mercilessly. Several of the larger, stronger boys – the group leaders – had approached and encircled him, then tried to make him eat the sandwich. The rest stood around clapping and chanting *Fresse Jude, fresse Jude, fresse* – eat Jew eat, eat Jew, eat.

The teachers monitoring the schoolyard had done nothing to

help, instead watching and smiling mirthlessly at his dilemma. Only Fraulein Metz, his teacher from a year earlier, a brown-haired, young woman, perhaps 30 years of age, always conservatively dressed and usually carrying a welcoming expression, seemed shocked by the events, or so it seemed as he glimpsed her. But even she was of little help. She only lowered her head and turned away. The senior teacher, *Herr* Braun – Rudy, the other teachers called him – had joined in the general laughter. Herr Braun, a slightly overweight, round-faced man of about 35 or 40, already showing the ruddy skin of a drinker and a purple hue on his nose owing to broken blood vessels, seemed to delight in Asher's misery. Herr Braun was his homeroom teacher and often singled him out in class, mercilessly criticizing him in front of the other children, who laughed at the degradation experienced by Asher and his friend Josh, the only other Jew in the class.

On the poop sandwich day, as everyone called it, when the students returned to the classroom, Herr Braun drawled out with cruel humor: "Perhaps, in addition to their pencils and notebooks, some students should, in the future, consider bringing a toothbrush with them to class." Asher had wanted to cry from this humiliation on display for all to see. The hatred directed toward him wasn't a result of anything he had done but of who and what he was. As he walked along, reliving recent events, he wondered, "Why do they hate us?" This thought, more than the threats or actual beatings, became ingrained and assailed him when he was alone from when he awoke to when he went to bed.

Nights were the worst. He couldn't sleep, constantly replaying his public shaming. The repeated self-recriminations for being the target of the torture, and dwelling on what was, and what could never be. Why was he born a Jew? Why couldn't he have been a Christian like Friedrich? If he had, he wouldn't experience this daily abuse. Maybe then, Trudie, the prettiest girl he knew, might walk home with him, rather than shunning or taunting him along with the others. He painfully recalled how she had called him *schmutzig ... ekelhaft* [dirty, physically repugnant, and nauseating.] The expression of disgust smeared across her face as she said it stayed with him as much as he tried to erase it. He desperately wanted to be accepted and liked, especially by her. But he was less than dirt. He was a subhuman, an *Untermensch*. While a snake could shed its skin, his defects were permanent. His incessant brooding would last long into each night until fatigue allowed him to sleep. He could never shed his Jewish identity since everyone would still know him for what he was: *Ein ekelhafter Jude*.

How much better it would be if he were dead. He didn't know whether death was just a long sleep, or whether he would burn in hell for being a Jew, but he thought either way it would be better than what he was living through now. Would anyone miss him? Well, his Mutti and Papa would. But this would be their fair punishment for being Jews, or, he thought, for not leaving Austria years earlier when it hadn't been difficult.

He knew suicide was a sin, but he also knew from hearing hushed whispers between his parents that other Jewish children had died this way. The Holtzmans' eldest son, David, who had just had his bar mitzvah, had died a few weeks earlier, and Enga Teitlebaum, only 12, took her life by jumping into the Wien River. Her family had searched the riverbanks for weeks without assistance from the police, who ignored their pleas for help. Ruthy Gold, who had been a vibrant 14-year-old, became increasingly morose, unable to sleep, and lost much weight from her already slight body. People thought Ruthy had run away until her devastated parents found her hanging in their coal cellar. Ruthy had left a note to her parents telling them how sorry she was, but the misery of her life was too much to bear. He wished he could die, too, but he wasn't as brave as these other children, or maybe he hadn't yet suffered enough.

He wanted to ask his father why God – the God they prayed to every day – wasn't intervening on their behalf. Had they done something to offend God, or had God discovered he'd made a mistake in choosing the people of Moses and had now abandoned them? Simply moved on to find another set of Chosen People? Could God be so fickle?

"*Abba*," he had said, using the Hebrew term for daddy, wanting to ask his father whether suicide was a sin when children suffered.

Before he could ask his question his father interrupted sternly, "Asher, how many times do I have to tell you the same thing? I am Papa, and *Eema* is Mutti. Get used to calling us that."

"But Abba …"

"*Oy, Gott in Himmel*," he said emphatically. "Not Abba, call me Papa. Why is it so difficult for you to do as I ask? You'll be sorry, we'll all be sorry, if you're overheard. Your persistence will cause us grief. More grief than anyone deserves."

"But it's not a secret. Everyone knows we're Jews."

His father sighed. "Don't ask so many questions and don't argue with me. They may know we're Jews, but we don't need to throw it in their faces. If we're quiet, if we stay low, if we don't attract their attention, they might not notice us."

"Every day I try to stay low, and every day I'm unsuccessful," he replied emphatically and then abruptly stopped speaking so his father wouldn't become aware of his daily struggle. Yet, in not asking more questions, he would never be able to find out why God had abandoned them. Besides, even if he had asked, his father would probably say something like, "You're too young to understand."

Tension had been mounting for several years and the Jews of Austria collectively attempted to lay low to try to wait out the increasing contempt directed at them. At every turn, the Austrian government, encouraged by Germany, sought to segregate and humiliate Jews. In March 1938, the Austrian people voted in favor of the *Anschluss*: the annexation. Some would claim they were coerced, although judging by the excitement among his schoolmates surrounding the vote, Asher thought most had been enthusiastic about the *Führer's* wishes. Afterward, the situation for Asher and his parents grew progressively worse.

Wherever he went, he saw the German Wehrmacht had entered Austria to enforce the Anschluss. Soldiers in their crisp uniforms and officers with their tunics bedecked with medals strutted the streets and made themselves visible in the cafes and restaurants. The most fearsome were those dressed in black uniforms, referred to as the *Schutzstaffel,* or SS, as well as those who were dressed as civilians but carried themselves with an unusual sense of authority. Irrespective of rank, the Nazis sauntered about as if the city belonged to them, or they arrogantly rode about on their motorcycles or whizzed by in black sedans with small red flags imprinted with a black swastika fluttering just above the headlights. The Wehrmacht's presence seemed to energize the Jew-baiters, including the children, and the bullying he had been experiencing moved to unbearable levels. In recent months, the undisguised hatred expressed toward him and other Jewish children had increased exponentially, even though most of their tormentors had no idea what made Jews so repugnant. They didn't have to know. They simply followed the other children, who parroted the behaviors of their parents and teachers.

Those Jews who sensed the early winds of hatred before the full-on gusts blew in were able to leave Austria if they had the finances and connections to do so. Those who hadn't believed it could become so bad were now excruciatingly bound in place. Asher's family was among those who had rejected the idea of leaving, or at least his father opposed it. As hostilities increased, Asher's father changed his mind, but by then there was nowhere to go. Several family friends who had left during the preceding year were forced to return after discovering they were disliked or unwanted and were turned away by other countries. Several years earlier, future Israeli President Chaim Weizmann, who at the time had been a leader of a Zionist organization, forewarned that "the world seemed to be divided into two parts – those places where the Jews could not live and those where they could not enter." This is the world where Asher and his family now found themselves.

School had been canceled for eight days after the Anschluss, although it wasn't clear to Asher whether it was a precaution of some sort or a celebration. Either way, it made him happy, even ebullient. Unfortunately, the reprieve was only temporary; once he was back at school, it seemed it had never occurred. On the first day back, it was made clear to him that Jews were thought of as Bolsheviks and as such were mere guests in Austria – ones who had long outlasted their welcome. Jewish children were subjected to the pain they supposedly deserved for being who they were. Asher and his friend Joshua tried to make themselves invisible, as their parents had instructed them repeatedly. It might not have been so difficult for Asher, but for Joshua, it was nearly impossible. Tall and ungainly, pale, and prematurely growing dark hair on his exceptionally thin arms and legs, Joshua seemed to have a penchant for bringing attention of the worst sort to himself.

After the Anschluss, the Jews and their alleged communist friends were blamed for every problem Austria or Germany experienced. This morning, eight months after the Anschluss had taken place, was no different. The cooling temperature did nothing to diminish the fires of bigotry that had sprung from the embers that had simmered for so long.

Arriving at school on the morning of November 9, Asher surreptitiously made eye contact with Joshua. This was their usual greeting, as it didn't arouse the sneers of "Jews stick together" from the other children. Despite the precaution, he had a boding premonition this day was going to be especially bad. As if it had been planned, he and Joshua were almost instantly herded together and surrounded by a group of older boys and girls. From the sneers and smirks of these otherwise innocent-looking boys and girls, he understood his intuitions were correct. As usual, there was nobody to whom the two boys could turn. Certainly not the teachers who seemed willfully oblivious to the growing commotion.

After being pushed from behind, Asher and Joshua were thrown to the ground amid cries of "Let's see the Jew's *Schwanz*." Their arms and legs were restrained by several of the older children as their clothes were torn from their bodies and they were then pulled to their feet. The boys tried to cover their exposed genitals with their hands, but that only fueled the laughter of the children surrounding them. Asher and Joshua could offer little resistance as they were firmly tied to the chest-high ornate metal rods of the fence surrounding the schoolyard. Their humiliation at standing naked on display soon turned to abject terror as a chant rose: "Cut it off, cut it off, cut it off entirely ... here today, here today, totally gone tomorrow."

Standing at the edge of the schoolyard, *Fraulein* Metz grabbed Herr Braun's arm, her eyes beseeching him to do something. She was disgusted by this oily and malodorous man who rarely showered, but she knew that unlike her, he would have the strength and authority to stop the brutality.

"Please, Herr Braun. You can't simply stand here and let this go on. Have some empathy for those poor children."

He shrugged, removed his pipe, and smirked at her, showing his smoke-stained teeth. "Relax, Fraulein Metz, it's just boys being boys. The two Jew boys will likely escape with their schwanzies intact, if perhaps a bit bruised."

Using belts and tree branches, each of the older boys and a few of the girls took turns whipping Asher and Joshua across their chest, stomach, and face. Occasionally, purposely errant blows hit their penises to the hysterical delight of the children. They were then turned around and whipped on their backs, buttocks, thighs, legs, and the back of their necks. Welts erupted across their bodies, Asher's lip swelled to twice its normal size and his left eye was blackened. The boys grimaced in pain, but they refused to scream or cry, not because of stoicism, but because it would encourage the children to continue the barrage.

At the height of the frenzy, Walter, the leader of the older boys, accompanied by the pretty little blonde, Trudie, approached them. The whipping and lashing stopped while everyone looked on with expressions of mocking derision on their faces. Using a hankie, Walter lifted Joshua's penis while Trudie, sweet pretty Trudie, tied a red ribbon on it, complete with a bow. Then they moved to Asher and repeated this, except that Trudie tied the ribbon on more tightly, all the while glaring hatefully directly into Asher's eyes. Then they turned and walked away as Trudie waved to the now-enlarged cheering crowd. She then stopped and turned to look at the two bound Jewish boys with an expression of satisfaction, as a cat might look at an eviscerated mouse.

Hoping to take advantage of the situation, Herr Braun moved closer to Fraulein Metz and, putting his hand around her shoulders said, "Come, Erica, we should rescue these Jews." He knew full well it was too late to play the role of savior for today, and for now, his lascivious dreams would not come to fruition, but as the expression went, "hope sprang eternal."

Fraulein Metz shrugged his arm off her shoulders and glared at him contemptuously before walking off. She rushed to the boys and untied the bonds wrapped around their arms and legs. She passed them their shredded clothing and led them through the gauntlet of laughing children into the school building. The two boys attempted to cover their genitals, but it didn't stop a new chant: "Nothing to hide, we've seen it all, what little there is, is thin and small." Once they reached her cramped office, she gently urged them to put on what remained of their clothing as she turned her back to offer privacy. Once they were dressed as best they could, she had them sit while she brought each a glass of juice. Although sitting caused intense pain from the welts on their thighs and buttocks, their shame and humiliation were far more excruciating.

She came close to them, lowered herself so she was at eye level, and put a hand lightly on each of their arms. "Boys," she said in a soft solemn voice, "I am very sorry about what happened to you. Unfortunately, it's done and can't be undone. Now listen to me very carefully and do what I tell you. You are to go home and never return here. Understood?"

Receiving a nod from them, she added: "Tell your parents what happened, and tell them that no matter how, they must leave Austria as soon as they can."

She then turned to her desk and pulled out two sheets of unlined paper, and on each, she scribbled a brief message. She then passed the folded notes to the two boys and instructed them "Children, this is a very hard time for everyone, but more so for Jewish people. I'm afraid things will not get better soon and will probably get much, much worse. When you get home, give your parents the note that I'm giving you now. Do not forget. Impress them that they must follow my instructions to the letter, to the punctuation. The note warns your parents to stay hidden tonight and all day tomorrow. Emphasize that it is essential you all stay hidden. Do not venture out under any circumstances. They will need to have hiding places ready for your entire family. Children, this is a dangerous time, so please remember to do as I've instructed."

After looking directly at them, she rose, which was their cue to do likewise. To avoid other students or teachers, they left her office and took the back stairs to the outside. They circled the building, and she walked them to the edge of the school's fence and lightly squeezed the back of their necks, saying, "Go, quickly, children. Above all, be sure you give the notes to your parents, along with what I've told you." She then softly patted their backs and nudged them to go. The boys walked together, silent in their thoughts until they reached the point where they went their separate directions. They stopped and wordlessly studied one another's faces until they both teared up, unable to speak because of the lumps in their throats. They embraced, and when they let go, eyes reddened, Joshua said to Asher, "See you soon."

He never would.

Hannah had been proud of Shimon's achievements in his economic ventures and for his activities within the larger Jewish community. In most respects, Shimon was an ordinary Austrian man. With dark hair and average height, he didn't stand out in a group, nor did he carry himself in any distinguishable manner. But she understood he was extraordinarily brave and determined when it was necessary, although too often he was equally stubborn. Hannah was his perfect match. Soft-spoken but determined, she, too, was of medium height and dark hair, wouldn't stand out in a crowd, and certainly couldn't be mistaken as a threat to anyone. They were just a perfectly ordinary Austrian couple who desired to get along with their neighbors and help others within their community.

As Asher climbed the stairs to their apartment above his father's shop, he stayed close to the wall to preclude the creaks that would emerge if he stepped on the centers of the steps. He was concerned about the reaction his torn clothes and welts would elicit from his parents. Eema, he knew, would be at the edge of hysteria, while Abba wouldn't know what to do. Furtively, he entered the apartment, and as he slowly made his way to his room, he could hear his parents talking softly in the dining room. With proper timing and some luck, he might get past the dining area without his parents seeing him.

As he stood in the hallway where he was out of the line of sight, he heard his mother say, "Shimon, we must leave, we have to go … it's too dangerous to stay here. With every day, the risks increase. If you won't agree to save yourself, then think of Asher and me."

"Hannah," he replied, "it might have been possible earlier, but no longer. Besides, do we simply leave everything behind? Our friends, our business? Tell me, where do you suggest we go?"

"It doesn't matter, Shimon. Let's just go. Anywhere is better than here. If we stay, we'll be killed."

"Oh, Hannah, you're overreacting," he said gently, taking her hand. "I agree the situation here isn't good now, but it will become better. We just have to wait for people to find their senses. We are Austrians as much as anyone else is in this city. Surely, our neighbors and fellow Austrians will protect us. Besides, what do you think the Germans will do, kill us all? There are hundreds of thousands of Jews in Austria and Germany. They can't kill us all!"

"Yes," Hannah said emphatically. "that's exactly what I think they'll do. Worse than that …" and her voice trailed off.

"That's ridiculous," he declared emphatically. "At worst we'll be expelled from the country, which is what seems to be happening in Germany. That won't happen here. Trust me on this. Our fellow Austrians won't stand for it despite the annexation. This is a civilized country with civilized people. We aren't dealing with barbarians."

Yes, she thought, and these "civilized" people willingly subjugated themselves to Hitler, kissed his bottom, and went about their business maligning Jews in every way they could. She wanted to express these feelings of disgust, but the words were stuck in her throat, feeling like bile. Instead, she nodded, seemingly accepting his certainty, knowing any further argument would only escalate the debate.

In several ways, he was more capable than she was, but in many more, she was far cleverer and wiser. She knew it, and he probably knew it, too. However, she let him feel as if he was the smart one: the planner, the organizer, and the head of the household. In her mind, she would say, "If you want to feel you're the smart one, then fine, feel like the smart one. But in the end, we'll do what I suggest."

Having peeked into the dining room, he saw their backs were to the door, and it was then Asher who tried to steal by. He had almost succeeded, but sensing something, his mother turned and saw him. When she did, her mouth opened to scream, but no sound emerged. She ran to him, as did his father after recovering from his initial immobilizing shock. As Asher described what happened, his mother put a wet cloth on his eye that was swollen closed and smeared with chicken fat she had been saving for cooking over the dozens of welts spanning his body. With each stroke of her gentle hand, Asher winced as tears slid down his mother's face.

When Asher finished telling them everything, including the experiences leading up to today he had been hiding, he concluded by saying, "Pappa, why did we have to be Jews?"

Hannah and Shimon glanced at each other for a moment and then looked down to avoid each other's eyes. Instinctively, Shimon withdrew into himself, a poor imitation of a threatened turtle. Not only was he ashamed for having done so little to protect his family, but he was also seeing what was in Hannah's eyes. The humiliation of his failure to see what was happening overwhelmed him. Nothing, absolutely nothing, had ever made him feel so diminished.

It was then Asher remembered the note that Fraulein Metz had told him to give to his parents. After a brief recounting of what his teacher said, he passed the note to his father, who shared it with Hannah.

Upon reading the note, his father got up resolutely, nodded his head, and went to the front door, saying, "I'll return in an hour or two."

"No," Hannah implored. "You know what his teacher wrote."

He nodded again. "In an hour, more probably two," he said and quietly slipped out. Sitting and waiting, doing nothing yet again, was no longer an option for him. Not when his entire world had just been turned upside down. He couldn't handle the uncertainty of what these events meant for his family and he needed information to diminish his anxiety, to know what could be done, regardless of the danger he faced.

Time drew out excruciatingly, each minute longer than the one before. As he said he would, Shimon returned punctually two hours later. He seemed unlike himself, nervous and somewhat frantic, muttering he was worried he had been followed home. He paced about like a caged animal, periodically shifting the window curtain ever so slightly, looking in each direction until satisfied nobody was following him.

In a desperate whisper, he implored them, "Please, both of you, we need to go up to the attic quickly. We'll need to take some food and water with us and prepare hiding places up there if things are worse than I fear."

"Shimon! What is it? What did you learn? Keeping us in suspense isn't helpful. This is unbearable, so tell us what you learned," Hannah implored.

"I'm sorry," he replied. "Everything is uncertain and exceptionally confusing. I've heard many different things, each more disturbing than the last, but there are gaps in the stories. So much so that I don't know what I know, and I don't know what I don't know. Franz says we can expect a pogrom tonight or tomorrow, but no later than the day after, while Henig indicated that's an exaggeration. The hooligans will come, he says, but only to collect money. They will call it a safety tax, a newly legalized form of extortion. Every person I spoke to seemed to have a different story. I also learned that the Sobel brothers, along with their wives and children, left the city very early this morning. Those two are connected to several city councilors, and their leaving suggests the situation is very grim. Far worse than most of our friends have accepted."

They hesitated, staring at him uncomprehendingly, but in response to his anxious look and a slight nod of the head, they set about gathering food and filling containers with water. They lowered the ladder from the attic and climbed up, passing their bags and containers to Shimon, who had gone up first. Hannah had the sense to find their most valuable possessions, including her few pieces of jewelry and valuable heirlooms, and placed them in a cloth bag. She also placed the German Reichsmarks that had become the new currency after the annexation of Austria in the bag. Only when they settled in the attic did they realize how dark it was in the windowless space. Shimon went down again and returned shortly with some candles and matches. He had the foresight to bring a bucket they could use to relieve themselves.

Once they felt they had everything they needed, Shimon pulled the ladder up and stored it next to the trap door through which they had climbed. Even with two candles lit, the attic was very dark, although a minuscule shaft of light shone through the vent at the roof. The air was thick with dust. Perhaps there was mold, too, that had gathered with years of nonuse. After looking around and getting their bearings, they slid an old steamer trunk in which Asher could fit near the trap door in the hope nobody would think to look inside something left so obviously open to inspection. A second trunk was placed next to it, the idea being if the first was inspected and found empty, the second might be ignored. They bunched summer clothes, blankets, and even some old diapers in several piles in two corners. If necessary, Hannah would hide beneath one of the piles of these discarded items, although even a cursory search would reveal her presence. Shimon climbed to the top of the attic and found a few cross beams where he could perch comfortably and be safe as long as no one thought to look up. Shimon thought from this vantage, should anyone begin to look in the second trunk, he would jump down and hope it would distract anyone intent on inspecting it.

Having made the best plans possible under the circumstances, they gathered at the center of the attic to await their fate. Many hours passed, and the tiny shafts of light that had penetrated the attic disappeared as dusk arrived. Several hours later, they heard what they feared would lie ahead. A hoard of people, chanting and screaming, was marching down the street. The mob drew closer. Shimon, Hannah, and Asher could hear the crash of breaking windows, and they could smell smoke wafting slightly through the small opening in the attic. They took to their hiding spots and remained motionless as the hours crept by.

While comforted to be together, the waiting was unbearable. But they had no other options and could only hope for the best. They tensed when they heard the windows of their store shatter and the shouting, smashing, and looting of merchandise two floors below. After what seemed an interminable time, the commotion quieted as the mob moved down the street, vandalizing homes and shops as they went. Shimon and Hannah feared the building might be set on fire and waited for the smoke to reach them.

They remained in their hiding spots throughout a largely sleepless night. Even during brief periods of sleep, their minds didn't rest, remaining in a state of high vigilance. Finally, as the first wisps of morning light entered the attic, Shimon stiffly climbed from his perch atop the room, soundlessly tiptoeing to the corner of the attic to urinate in the bucket. Shimon then drew Hannah and Asher from their hiding places, ready to return if necessary, and they, too, dealt with their bodily needs.

They spent most of the day in the attic sitting tightly together, taking comfort in the physical contact. When dusk came, Shimon said, "I have to see what's happened. I can't stand not knowing what's going on, not for another moment."

Despite the objections of Hannah and Asher, he opened the loft hatch and lowered the attic ladder. From below, he assured them he would be careful and be back soon. "No more than two or three hours, depending on what I see." Used to such vague statements, Hannah simply nodded and said, "Go. Go see what you need to see." With Asher's help, she pulled the ladder back up into the attic, where they remained, listening for sounds from the outside.

When he finally returned two hours later, he was pale and

shaken. "Every window of Jewish-owned shops has been broken and the shops have been looted. Many houses have been torched. The synagogue has been burned to the ground. I met Motte and he said the same thing occurred in many cities throughout Austria and Germany. A few people were killed, and many, many more were dragged away. He had no idea where they were taken or what would become of them."

He paused before speaking again. "They broke into the synagogue before burning it and defaced the Torah scrolls by urinating on them. Rabbi Shmuel tried to intervene, and for his efforts, they beat him mercilessly. For good measure, they cut off his beard. The rabbi's wife ran to him, but they grabbed her and beat her as fiercely as they had the rabbi. Motte says they are both alive, but only barely. They suffered many broken bones and severe cuts. The Rabbi has a fractured skull and is in a coma. His wife is conscious but so weak she can't lift her head. It's appalling an elderly couple would be abused this way. These hooligans aren't humans. They're monsters."

Again, he paused before continuing. Then, sighing heavily, he said, "This wasn't a spontaneous event. It was well-planned and orchestrated. You were right, Hannah. I should have listened to you long ago. We should have left."

"You did what you thought was best," Hannah replied. "We can't go over the past. Instead, we need to look to the future. I don't have any idea what we can do, but we should find out what others are planning and then figure out a strategy for ourselves."

As they continued to discuss their options, they heard the front door squeak open. They immediately stopped whispering and waited, hardly breathing. They could hear the light footsteps of a single person below them, and after a few minutes, a muffled whisper called out, "Asher. Are you here, Asher? It's me, Erica. Fraulein Metz. Are you here?"

His father's strong arm held him back from answering her call. "It's my teacher," Asher whispered. "The one who warned Joshua and me."

His father then let Asher move to the hatch that had been left open and softly call down to Fraulein Metz. She appeared moments later, and once the ladder was lowered, she deftly climbed into the attic and introduced herself to Hannah and Shimon, who thanked her repeatedly.

She shushed them, saying, "The mob may be coming back for a second round of looting, although they likely won't be back this evening. Last night was a terrible night here, as it was in Germany. The violent, destructive behavior was encouraged by the Nazis, and I've heard Jews are being held responsible for the events and will have to pay for reparations. Aside from the many businesses and synagogues looted and burned, thousands of people were taken away, but I have no idea where they will end up."

"That's terrible," said Hannah, entirely dispirited. "I wouldn't have expected this to be so widespread and violent."

"We may have a brief reprieve as the hooligans drank themselves under the table last night and will need a day to recover before revisiting," Fraulein Metz said. "Still, it would be best for me to get you out of here quickly. Their next search may be more systematic, and what they do to Jews they find will be merciless."

"What do you mean when you say you will get us out of here?" Hannah asked in a shaky whisper.

"You certainly can't stay here," replied Fraulein Metz. "They will eventually be back, and even if they aren't tonight or the next night, they will eventually return and they will find you."

As they looked at her incredulously, she stated, "Tomorrow morning I will come for you. I don't think I need to say you shouldn't pack a suitcase. Take the money or valuables that fit in your pockets. Where you will be going it will be cold, so wear a coat and a second shirt under that as well as a sweater. Put on your heavy socks, and if you can, fit two pairs of socks into your shoes. Make sure you have very comfortable shoes, or boots if you have them, which should be tucked beneath your pants."

Turning to Hannah, she said, "Wear your skirt but bring along heavy pants, perhaps a pair of your husband's wool or corduroy pants. Be ready in the morning. When we go, it will have to be quick."

"In the morning. So soon?" Shimon asked. "Where will we go?"

She nodded and said, "You'll go with me. That's all I can tell you at the moment. Tomorrow at 8:30 when people are going to work. We'll be safe in plain sight."

"I'd like to say goodbye to Joshua before we leave. Can we stop by his house? It's not far from here," Asher said.

"That won't be possible. They have already left," she answered, stealing a glance at Shimon, who imperceptibly nodded his head in understanding.

Shimon then asked Fraulein Metz directly, "Why are you helping us? We've never even met you before. You're risking your safety in helping us."

She simply said, "The less you know, the safer I'll be." Putting her hand on Asher's cheek, she added: "He's a wonderful boy who has already been through enough. He needs to have a good life, a happy life. I was his teacher, and this is my gift to him. Truthfully, being able to ensure his safety is also a gift to me."

The second night in the attic again passed slowly. There were none of the sounds from the mob that previously horrified them. But even the silence in a world that had just teemed with horror was disquieting. When the sun finally rose, they began to prepare for their departure, dressing as instructed, sharing the valuables, and hiding them in their various pockets. Moments before 8:30, when people were beginning to be heard on the street, Fraulein Metz returned, and the four of them furtively entered the street, mixing with others who were moving toward the city center. Fraulein Metz, with a gold crucifix boldly hanging on her sweater, had one arm through Shimon's, while the other held Asher's hand. Together they calmly walked down the street. Hannah, like a dutiful nanny, walked, head bent, two paces behind them. Piles of glass had already been swept to the curb in front of Jewish-owned shops, and the aftermath of the looting was apparent inside them. The pedestrians moving along the street hardly gave these scenes a glance.

They had gone no further than two blocks when Hannah stopped suddenly. "I can't go," she said. "I can't go without seeing my brother Levi. I'm sorry. I just can't leave this way."

She and Levi had been very close, seeing each other almost every other day, and the two families were often together for Friday evening dinner. The thought of leaving him and his family behind was more than Hannah could bear, and no amount of quiet coaxing from Shimon and Fraulein Metz altered her feelings. Levi lived only five minutes away, and they resignedly headed there. As they approached the house, Hannah moved more and more quickly, almost breaking into a frantic run, while the others fell back to avoid causing suspicion.

Levi had been peering through a crack in the curtain when she ran up to the door. He immediately opened it just wide enough to let her in and then just as quickly shut it behind her.

He hugged her, saying, "I'm so glad you're safe. I was terribly worried. But what are you doing here?"

"We're leaving this place, Levi," she said, firmly holding both his hands. "As bad as it is now, it's only the beginning. Their hatred for us will become stronger, and the future will be much worse. If we wait, there may not be a way out. Come with us now. It has already been arranged, and we want you, Rachel, and the children to come with us. Hurry! Take only a few things and come quickly."

He was stunned. "I don't understand," he whispered. "Where are you going? You can't simply leave. There's nowhere to go. You know that as well as I do."

"I don't know. I don't know where we're going. Wherever it is, it will be better than staying here," she said, panic rising in her quiet voice. "Come quickly and don't ask so many questions. There's no time."

"Hannah, calm yourself, please. This will all pass. Pogroms in Russia passed, and this will, too. The Austrian people aren't the Nazis we've heard about. What we're seeing now is the work of a small number of thugs."

"Levi, please, don't you see the danger that's roiling in front of us? This isn't a new antisemitic wave that will simply pass. Have you forgotten the difficulties our parents, may their names be inscribed in heaven, endured during the time that Karl Lueger was mayor of Vienna some 30 years ago? As ferocious as the hatred for us was then, the current situation is far worse. Believe me, believe your own eyes, it will become much, much worse for Jews. What the German Nationalists are doing now, they learned from the Austrian Jew haters."

No amount of cajoling and pleading on Hannah's part diminished Levi's resolve. Hurriedly, with tears streaming down her face, she whispered, "All right, Levi. I have to go, but wherever we end up, I'll write to you. With God's help, we'll be together again."

They embraced with a pang of heavy sadness. Kissing her forehead, his farewell words "I miss you already" resounded in her ear. Before she left, she ran over to the cabinet, removed a picture from its frame portraying her worldly brother and his family, and put it in her coat. "This way my thoughts will be with you every day," she said.

Before she could leave, Levi's wife, Rachel, appeared in the doorway to the hall that led to the rest of the house. After embracing Hannah, she turned to Levi, and said, "Levi, I know your thoughts, like mine, are entirely consistent with those Hannah expressed. Yet, with the children and us, there are too many to be smuggled out safely. I'm not prepared for our fate, but I'm still less prepared to jeopardize Hannah and her family."

Realizing that further objections would be pointless, Hannah, hugged her bother and Rachel, and squeezed out through the slightly opened door.

Hannah rejoined the group and they walked in formation as they had earlier, but she could barely stifle her tears and her heart felt empty. A few blocks before Graben, a main street lined with stately historical buildings, they turned off, and after half a block, Fraulein Metz directed them to a small store that sold artwork. Inside, they met a graying older man wearing rimless glasses who was all business. Fraulein Metz introduced them as friends, revealing no names. After delivering them, she indicated she would be leaving them now. Before she did, she pulled Asher to her, bent and hugged him, kissed his cheeks, and then hugged him again and said, "Go with God, your God or my God, it's all the same," and quickly left the shop.

The nameless elderly man led them to the back of his shop and then through a half-empty adjoining studio. After moving a table and rolling back the carpet beneath it, he removed several planks of wood from the floor, which revealed stairs that took them to a basement beneath the studio.

"Stay down there and remain absolutely still no matter what you may hear," he said. "Later, in perhaps ten or eleven hours, once it is properly dark, someone will come to take you on your journey." He handed them some black bread and a jar containing water, which they took down with them. In a well-practiced fashion, he covered the entranceway with the wood planks, and they heard the movement of the carpet and the table being dragged back into place.

The waiting was intolerable, but at least they were together even if danger surrounded them. Asher leaned into his mother in exhaustion, but given their heightened vigilance, the best any of them could achieve were periods at the edges of sleep, leading them to believe they hadn't slept at all. Finally, after anxiety-ridden hours, they heard muffled footsteps above them, and soon the table and carpet were moved and the boards lifted. Two tall men, both in their late thirties or early forties, motioned for them to come out of the cellar and wordlessly beckoned them to follow. Silently, they went through the studio and out a back door. From there, they moved through an alleyway that opened onto a small street, and one by one they were quietly hustled into the back of an open lorry. Tarpaulins that smelled of oil were used to cover them, and beneath the tarpaulins, they discovered another family of Jews whom they knew. After brief, hushed greetings, they settled in.

The older of the two men whispered they would be on the road for many hours, after which they would transfer to another lorry. He then hopped into the cab, and the truck slowly started to depart Vienna and onto the highway, which Shimon knew went to Switzerland but could also take them to Italy or Germany. Nobody told them what the plan was, which he knew was for security purposes. What they didn't know, they couldn't tell.

Once on the highway, the lorry moved more rapidly, approaching its top speed, which was still tediously slow as automobiles passed them, including elegant black sedans and several trucks carrying either soldiers or munitions. None took any interest in the lorry, which had pulled close to the edge of the road to let other vehicles pass. The monotonous rolling of the lorry eventually put most of the hidden passengers to sleep, and they only awoke as it pulled off the main highway and onto a small side road that led to a lane where it stopped. Peering from under the tarpaulins, they could see the sun was just beginning to rise. They remained in place until they heard another lorry pull up less than 30 minutes later. Soon after, the two families were led out and transferred onto the second truck of similar dimension and design, but not before they were pointed to some bushes and advised to use the "facilities" before they headed off. Once again, they were covered with tarps and provided with water and black bread that was more than a couple of days old. It tasted wonderful.

The second lorry had a few additional passengers, whom they politely greeted, cautious not to use names. They traveled for hours, much of it uphill, with the lorry's motor straining at the challenge. Often it was necessary to swallow to unblock the pressure on their eardrums. After many hours, they pulled off the highway onto a side road, and then onto a still smaller dirt lane, until they came to a stop. Two trucks were parked in a small clearing lightly covered with snow. Waiting for them were families of Jews from various parts of Austria. It was noticeably colder than in Vienna, supporting Shimon's suspicion they were in the foothills of the Alps. Nobody spoke, knowing the need to remain silent.

A delegate of each family was ushered to a common area. A guide said, "From here we have a very long walk that will take several days."

"Over the Alps?" asked a middle-aged man. "It's not possible."

"No, of course not," answered the guide. "There would be no possibility of that. We'll be skirting the Alps, but there will be a few climbs and descents, and we will be at a higher altitude than we are now."

"So, it will be colder than it is down at this level," said the middle-aged man.

"It certainly will be cold," the guide replied, before adding, "But not unbearably so. The temperature is on the warm side for this time of year, and the forecast is good. Once we're moving, the cold temperature will affect you less. I believe you all can make this journey. Your lives depend on it." He added, unnecessarily: "If you fall behind, you might have to be left on your own as otherwise our entire group might be endangered." Each person nodded and expressed their thanks.

After a brief meal of cheese, bread, and cold tea, they were each given strips of tarpaulin that they were instructed to wrap around their shoes to help maintain a grip on snowy or icy patches. They then headed off in single file along a narrow trail, led by one of their nameless rescuers. At the start of their trek, they were surrounded by a dense forest of stately, leafless oak, beech, and elm trees. As they climbed higher, the trees were replaced by fir and spruce, as well as by the sharp Alpine cold that penetrated the little protection offered by their inadequate clothing. A cold front had unexpectedly moved in and the temperature continued to decline as they moved upward. The walking that had earlier provided some warmth no longer did so. Every hour or so they rested for a few precious moments and the children were given candies in hopes the sugar would provide them with the energy needed to keep going.

Despite the fatigue and excruciating pain in every muscle, they moved onward. Their guide was unrelenting, keeping them moving, occasionally looking over his shoulder to be sure the group was still with him. Only when they were spread too thinly on the path did he relax his pace, allowing the stragglers to catch up.

One of the men stumbled, falling to the ground, unable to get to his feet. Hannah was instantly at his side, pushing and cajoling him to rise, finally telling him he had to go on for the sake of his two children. He eventually did. So it went, march for a while, rest, march again, and rest once more. As the sun began to set, they were exhausted. For a few of them, their city shoes left them with painfully blistered, cold feet. Finally, they reached a dilapidated wooden structure where they could shelter from the wind, but the cold was still bitter. The shack contained several old blankets and some dried fruits that were preserved in the cold, as well as biscuits wrapped to protect them from moisture. The cabin had been prepared for those who would be making the trek, and no doubt it had been used previously and would be again. It wasn't comfortable by any means, but it was better than sleeping in the open.

At dawn, after eating some of their meager food supplies, they began to march again. At one of their periodic rests, they could see open meadows in the distance, which they longed to head for if only to expose themselves to the sun's warmth. Despite their chattering teeth, they followed the instruction to remain in the forest. Their guide encouraged them, indicating they soon would reach a protected region where it would be warmer. As he promised, after further painful trekking, they came to a group of boulders that seemed to have arranged themselves to form a cavern. The boulders had likely been part of a rockslide from eons earlier, creating a large chamber against the side of the mountain. Entering, they immediately felt slightly warmer, which was made more comfortable after the guide made a small fire using small sticks and moss that had been left by its previous occupants. The children were seated closest to the fire and the adults sat behind them. Later, each family found a comfortable spot where they would remain until sunrise when they would set off again.

These city dwellers had never imagined they would be sleeping in a cave or even be able to do so, but the fatigue was intense, their eyes closed readily, and they slept heavily. Families were wrapped around one another to share warmth, children laying between parents. The guide woke them just before sunrise. They groggily stood, their bodies stiff and muscles aching from the previous days of walking, and they readied themselves for the next leg of the trip. After a hurried meal of bread, raisins, and water, from which parents provided their children with parts of their portions, they made off. Again, the same routine – walk, rest, walk, rest. This portion of the climb was more arduous than that of the preceding two days, made worse by adults frequently having to carry children. Asher was as brave and determined as the adults, so Hannah and Shimon were able to help others carry their young children. Once more, when any member of the group faltered, Hannah was there to encourage or harass them until she successfully had them moving again.

During the next two days, they repeated their slog, and when it seemed there was no possibility of being able to go much further, they gathered strength from one another and continued on. On the fifth day, they were awoken by their guide earlier than before. He informed them they would begin their walk in the dark as this was a treacherous part of the trip. They had been traveling for three or four hours when the guide alerted them they were coming to the dangerous section he had mentioned earlier. To enter Switzerland, they would have to go through more heavily patrolled areas, and it was essential they remain silent and that children hold tight to their parents.

Over several hours, staying low, one small group at a time crossed the expanse separating them from the border. As they crossed open areas, the gusting wind seemed to find new ways to punish them. They saw and heard occasional patrols, including some with dogs. At one point, as they waited on the Austrian side of the border, two Wehrmacht soldiers in heavy coats, along with their dogs, strode by on a wide trail 50 meters below. The dogs suddenly began barking and pulling on their leashes as the families hidden in the woods froze in terror. They heard the soldiers try to calm their dogs, which relentlessly continued their ferocious barks and strained to climb the hillside. The younger of the two soldiers began climbing the steep hillside, but the other, who was disinclined to stray from the road, called him back.

"Don't go up there," he muttered. "Otto and Franz simply caught the scent of a hare. There's nothing to see up there. Besides, if we show up at the barracks with our uniforms and coats ruined by the mud and the brambles, we'll be worse off than the hare."

With this, they dragged the Dobermans off, despite the dogs' protestations. The dogs periodically looked back toward the huddled refugees.

With care, the caravan of trekkers breached two sets of fencing. Their guide then announced they were now in Switzerland. He led them into a nearby forest where they were to remain until someone came for them. He accepted their thanks and communicated through eye contact and hugs.

"Ah, this was easy," he said. "There is not an official war yet. This is just practice for the greater danger that will come not long from now. When war breaks out with other countries, as we believe it will, the passes we went through will be watched more carefully, and so the danger will increase." He dispensed food from his pack to each family, and like a ghost, he disappeared into the forest.

Before they had time to fully rest their strained muscles, a strong, confident, young man soundlessly appeared, motioning for them to rise and follow him, which they did. They continued their diligent single-file hiking on a slight downward grade. Without any warning, and close to giving up hope after several hours of trekking, they emerged into a small clearing where a lorry waited for them. A single family of two parents and two children was loaded on board, while the rest were told to wait. Not long afterward, perhaps a half hour, a second flatbed truck arrived, which Shimon, Hannah, and Asher, along with another family, boarded, covering themselves with tarps that were provided, and they quickly departed. The truck carried several crates of produce, including two labeled as pork products. The ironies just didn't cease.

They moved along for several hours until the truck pulled over to the side. The driver came around to the back and, through a space in the tarp coverings, he softly said, "We are not in imminent danger here in Switzerland, but one never knows what might be encountered. In a while, we will come to the border with France. When we get there, you must be very quiet and motionless. The guards, most of whom I know, won't give us any problems, but occasionally new guards are rotated into these positions, and they may be highly motivated to impress their bosses. If you're found, then you will likely be sent back to Austria, and I will pay a dear price." Almost as an afterthought, he added: "Oh, yes, the border is also watched by Nazi soldiers, probably members of the SS, who are exceptionally keen to find Jews. These Germans have no authority in Switzerland, but they have ways of interfering and can press the Swiss to send illegal immigrants back to Austria or Germany, or from wherever they came."

Within less than an hour, they reached the border crossing where the driver jumped down from the lorry, stretching his body as if he had been driving for hours. As he had told them, he seemed to know the guards on the Swiss side of the border and engaged one in a laughing conversation as they shared stories while smoking strong Gauloises cigarettes the driver had provided.

The second guard fit the description of a new recruit, as he slowly walked along the sides of the lorry. He diligently inspected the undercarriage from back to front and then walked to the back again where he shined his torch onto the truck, all the while watched by SS guards on motorcycles at the side of the road. Enthusiastically, he hopped onto the lorry, perfunctorily assessing the pork-laden crates, and then began to look beneath the tarps. In short order, he discovered what was beneath them, making eye contact with Hannah, who was holding Asher close. Their pleading frightened eyes met his, and after a confused moment, he said under his breath, "*Au revoir, et bon chance,*" and then descended from the truck, joining the other guard and the driver. Hannah had no idea what his words meant but was relieved by his brief, seemingly kind eyes.

Crossing the border didn't immediately allay their anxiety. Could they really be safe? Was the gut-wrenching turmoil at an end? As the truck carried them across the mountainous countryside, the growing relief Shimon and Hannah felt was immense. The feeling of safety increased with time and distance, and their anxiety ebbed. It had been a long time since they could breathe with the anticipation of achieving freedom. It had been so long they had forgotten what it was like to feel normal again. Shimon looked down at Asher who was sleeping with his head on his father's lap.

Softly, he whispered, "Now you'll be able to call me Abba."

At the time, Shimon and Hannah didn't realize how lucky they were to leave Austria when they did. Only later did they learn that aside from the thousands of Jewish-owned stores looted or destroyed during Kristallnacht [Night of Broken Glass], there were several hundred Jewish cemeteries vandalized, hundreds of synagogues destroyed, and about 30,000 Jews arrested and sent to Dachau, Buchenwald, and Sachsenhausen. The official death toll was 91 Jews, although the actual number likely exceeded several hundred. For the 200,000 Jews who lived in Austria, this had marked the beginning of their elimination. About 130,000 were either expelled or escaped and 65,000 were killed.

France wasn't what Shimon and Hannah had imagined or expected. "Do you feel it, Hannah?" Shimon asked. "There is a sense of freedom and joy in Paris we never felt in Vienna."

"Absolutely, it's less conservative, less oppressive, and the people are more full of life than those in Austria," she replied. "Yet there's a percolating tension beneath the surface. An uncomfortable anticipation seems to exist, possibly prompted by uncertainty over the threat of a war with Germany, what their leaders were up to, and the persistent question of what might come next."

"I've had that feeling, too, although I've attributed it to the lasting effects of our living in Austria," he said.

Hannah was more concerned than Shimon and wouldn't speak about her anxieties in front of Asher. However, when they were alone, she said, "Most often, antisemitism isn't openly expressed here, although there have been various fringe newspapers that have fomented this attitude. I believe under certain conditions the latent bigotry could emerge and some people might readily collaborate with the Nazi regime."

"This isn't a new phenomenon in France, and injustices have been directed toward us for several centuries in France," Shimon replied pessimistically. "I can't help thinking about the Dreyfus case of the late 1800s when a Jewish artillery officer was falsely accused and found guilty of sharing military information with the German embassy in Paris. If not for the public outrage that emerged following Emile Zola's open letter entitled '*J'accuse*,' he would have remained imprisoned on Devil's Island in French Guiana. If an honorable French military officer could so readily be thrown to the wolves, what would it take for illegal immigrants like us to be treated much worse? Indeed, where is the outrage regarding the current Nazi behavior toward Jews in other European countries?"

Their foreboding worsened with rumors about the intentions of the Germans, who seemed to be readying for battle against France. Every day the radio reported further moves by the Nazi regime, which Shimon's friends in the Jewish community translated for him since he couldn't speak French. Yet he was repeatedly told not to worry. France was bordered by water on two sides. Spain on the third side wouldn't dare attack, and the Maginot Line to the east was too well entrenched to be breached by the German army.

Despite these assurances, which Shimon passed on to Hannah, her feelings of insecurity continued unabated. "I've begun feeling the same looming dread I had in Austria, which increased markedly when Hitler annexed parts of Czechoslovakia, the so-called Sudetenland, allegedly to protect the enslaved ethnic German population in the area," she said. "The Nazis have made no secret of their intentions. They demonstrated this when they invaded Poland, and eventually, Hitler may decide to occupy France."

Seeming forlorn, Shimon said, "What's puzzling me, even without having knowledge of political intrigues, is why France and England have repeatedly tried to appease Hitler. Perhaps they were chastened by the horror and tragedy of the Great War and are reluctant to confront the Nazi regime. For his part, Hitler is relentlessly testing France and Britain, believing the British are wary of war and weak in their commitments. If anything, efforts at appeasement might be taken as signs of weakness, which only embolden him. For that matter, the little that France and Britain have done in Poland's defense has informed the National Socialists they have a free hand to do whatever they like with few repercussions."

After pausing to collect his thoughts, he added: "If they wouldn't come to Poland's rescue, is there any possibility they would take steps to protect the Jewish population anywhere?"

With these realizations, Hannah and Shimon decided to leave Paris and go to Marseille, where they hoped to board a ship to flee the country. They fully believed Chaim Weizmann's view "there was no place safe for Jews in this world, save a place of our own," and so they chose to try reaching *Eretz Yisrael*, the land of Israel that God had promised to Jacob that was then known as Palestine.

The British government, which had colonized much of the Middle East just as it did so many other countries across the globe, had recently restricted the immigration of Jews to the Holy Land. Still, there were Jewish organizations that continued to smuggle Jews into the region, and shortly after arriving in Marseille, Shimon was able to form contacts within one of them: the Jewish Agency. However, it was difficult enough to obtain a single spot on a boat, let alone three. Jews still living in territories where their lives were in imminent jeopardy were the top priority, and those in seemingly safer locations such as France were at the bottom of the list. The number of Jews in France attempting to get out was immense and, given they only arrived recently, Shimon and his family were at the bottom of the list.

Driven by his continued self-recriminations for having delayed leaving Austria, Shimon relentlessly pursued safe passage for his family. Marseilles was one of the few places through which Jews could leave France, but he believed this refuge might ultimately become a trap. He sensed government officials were not fond of their own Jews, let alone Jews who immigrated illegally.

Hannah was even more ill at ease. "If the Germans successfully invade France, every Jewish life will be in peril, and we may be offered to the Nazis as sacrificial lambs," she said.

Given their fears, they always had their packs ready so they could depart quickly. Every day, Hannah or Shimon visited the Jewish Agency offices, haranguing officials to obtain berths. Even one berth, she had pleaded, would be enough so her young son could emigrate, and God willing, both she and Shimon would follow afterward.

They had expected that for each departing ship, for whatever reason, several people might fail to show up, so they impatiently waited to take a spot if it became available. Their persistence finally paid off. One family could not board as their child developed a serious lung problem, so Hannah, Shimon, and Asher obtained their spots, feeling both relief and guilt for this unexpected event. On May 3, 1940, several families, including theirs, boarded a ship headed circuitously for a port in Tel Aviv under the pretense of delivering farming materials and equipment.

The old rusting ship was crowded, loud, and reeked of human stench. The engines strained, and everyone aboard silently wondered whether the ship would get them across the Mediterranean. Each cabin was overcrowded, the halls carried a mix of a thousand scents, and the sea was unkind to digestive systems. Despite the discomfort, the anticipation of a new blessed life was tangible every moment. Not only were they escaping danger, but they were going to what they felt was their real home, even if the occupying British troops didn't want them there.

As the ship neared the end of its extended voyage, excitement on board was palpable but mixed with disquiet. They had been warned the ship could be stopped by the British and forced to return to France or diverted to Cyprus, where they would be held in internment camps. Rumors abounded they might have to wait at sea for smaller boats to come out to smuggle them ashore. The relationship between the Jews in the Holy Land and the British soldiers and officials was a tense one, especially since the British White Paper of 1939 had placed stringent restrictions on the immigration of Jews as well as their ownership of land. Of course, some of the passengers couldn't imagine they would be prevented from entering what they considered their own country, especially as Great Britain was opposed to the Nazi government in Germany. They didn't think Britain could conceive of sending them back to Europe under those circumstances. These passengers, working-class people with a few professionals thrown into the mix, had little understanding of the duplicity and immorality that pervaded politics at all levels, and international politics was no different.

As it happened, their entry into Eretz Yisrael was far easier than anticipated. No British patrol boats approached them, and they reached port without incident. Oddly, the port area was in chaos, with soldiers running about in disarray. Few officers seemed to be present to control the situation, and immigration officials seemed to have disappeared entirely. On shore, they learned the news Hitler had invaded France on May 10, 1940, the day before the ship docked.

The Jewish organization within Palestine found them temporary housing while a suitable home on a kibbutz, a collective agricultural community, could be found for them based on their skills and aptitudes. While they waited, Shimon engaged in a new task. Although he had not been a particularly orthodox Jew, he took it upon himself to teach Asher about Jewish history. Not so much the religious tenets, which would be left to others, but the history of the Jews and their multiple travails over centuries. He told him about the slave times in Egypt under the pharaohs. The many wars between the children of Moses and various groups, the loss to the Babylonians and the Jewish enslavement that followed, the fall of Jerusalem to Nebuchadnezzar, and the subsequent destruction of the temple constructed so assiduously about 400 years earlier. He told him stories about the Persian era of control, the Roman conquest of Judea, and the destruction of the second temple that had stood for about 600 years, followed by the subsequent diaspora across multiple countries and the persecutions and slaughters that occurred in many of these places. What Shimon emphasized was that for a time the Jews were a unified people, but over time, arguments and divisions among subgroups had weakened them to the point they proved unable to withstand the numerous, repeated assaults against them.

It was especially significant to Asher that the mistreatment of Jews had continued for centuries and occurred across countries, including those in Europe. The Crusades resulted in the slaughter of tens of thousands of Jews and Muslims. He also heard of the expulsion of Jews from France on several occasions in the 14th century, their subjugation and maltreatment in England, and worse still, the Spanish Inquisition initiated by Queen Isabella and King Ferdinand. Repeated pogroms had been experienced at the hands of Ukrainian Cossacks and Russians, and even closer to their new home, repeated attacks against Jews occurred in the areas of Jerusalem, Hebron, Safed, and Tiberias.

To be sure," Shimon said, "Jews eventually experienced freedom and a degree of acceptance in many countries. Yet, when times are hard, we seem to be the first scapegoat. It was true historically, it's true now, and it will be this way forever. We need only look at what we experienced in Austria to know the dangers our people face. I can only imagine the situation in Poland, Austria, France, and other countries Hitler's armies have overrun. I keep wondering what's happening to the Jews there now and how few had the opportunity to escape before the invasion. My only question was how far Germany would go in their quest for world domination. Since Stalin and Hitler signed a nonaggression pact and invaded Poland, allowing them to share the spoils, other European countries have been cowed and resistance to Hitler has become negligible."

"I agree with you," Hannah replied, "although I believe Hitler's greed and hatred of communism, or perhaps his fear Stalin would strike first, will eventually cause him to turn on Russia."

Overhearing their conversation, Asher asked, "Abba, can Hitler's armies reach us here, or will they be satisfied to occupy all of Europe?"

"Who knows what's in the head of a madman or the heads of his inner circle?" Shimon answered. "Europe is far away, so I expect that crazy man will limit his ambitions, but it's hard to predict what he'll do. When the wild beast has a taste for blood, it looks for more."

Sighing heavily, Shimon added: "God in heaven looked after us before, and in our own land we can only hope we won't face war again. Here we're safe for the moment. But just for the moment."

"Abba, from the stories you've told me, God let the Jews down many times over many centuries. So why do you believe God will help us now?"

Lacking a logical answer, Shimon could only shrug and say, "What else can I believe? Your Eema and I continue to marvel at how lucky we were in escaping the Nazis, and always by a hair. We can only thank God for the mercy."

Hannah and Shimon didn't speak of it, but their gratefulness for having survived was tempered by their certainty Levi and his family hadn't been as lucky. Gazing at Levi's picture lovingly, every day she would silently, tearfully, mourn him.

Asher was coming to his bar mitzvah, at the age of 13 when he would officially become a man, even if he didn't need to shave yet. He had absorbed everything from the stories of the collective, historical traumas his father told him. They made him both sad and angry, and he wished in some way he could do something to make a difference for his people. Yet what could an almost 13-year-old do? He wasn't alone. Many other children who were learning about Jewish history, including what was happening in Europe, had conscious and unconscious screams emanating from their collective brains and psyche. Whether or not God was merciful became irrelevant. It was more important for Jews not to rely on others and instead take control of their destiny so the horrors would not recur. Never again.

2

FROM THE ASHES

> The guardianship of the Holocaust is being passed on to us. The second generation is the hinge generation in which received, transferred knowledge of events is being transmuted into history, or into myth. It is also the generation in which we can think about certain questions arising from the Shoah with a sense of living connection.
>
> – Eva Hoffman, *After Such Knowledge*

The emotion of landing in Eretz Yisrael, their biblical homeland, was overpowering for Shimon and Hannah, who could hardly believe their dream had materialized. As they walked along Rothschild Boulevard, Shimon said, "For the first time in ages, I feel as if I'm in a place where we belong with our people in our own land. This is the land of pomegranates, honey, wheat, barley, figs, and olives, and I want to taste them all, as well as see the places where they're grown."

They had little savings to help them become established and build a new life. Fortunately, within several months, the Jewish Agency assisted again by finding them a place on a kibbutz in the northeastern part of the territory, close to the Syrian border.

As the bus took them toward their new home, Shimon couldn't help but fret. Whispering to Hannah out of Asher's earshot, he said,

"We're city people – what do I know about planting and tilling? What skills does a shopkeeper have that are useful here? More than that, I'm uncertain I'm up to the challenge of handling the rigorous life of the kibbutz and afraid to fail and embarrass myself."

Fortunately, his worries were diminished by the warm and celebratory welcome they received upon arriving. Although neither Shimon nor Hannah was politically inclined – and indeed they were frightened of socialism – they were somewhat relieved when one of their welcomers quoted Karl Marx: "From each according to his ability, to each according to his need."

Asher and his parents weren't used to living in close quarters. But this was the norm on a kibbutz, and they adapted quickly and began to appreciate the advantages of the lifestyle. They even got used to the oppressive heat enveloping this semiarid region, whereas other dangers that were ever-present kept them on edge. Nomadic Bedouins would sometimes attack settlements, burn crops, and undermine the workings of farms. The collective nature of the kibbutz afforded a degree of protection from such attacks.

Another advantage was by pooling their resources and efforts, members of a kibbutz could accomplish far more than they could individually. What was most rewarding was the sense of belonging. Despite the difficulty of kibbutz life, it was highly popular, with more than 20,000 living within the dozens of such communities established throughout the region. Hannah felt this lifestyle might not be ideal once the country was more mature and populated, but for the moment, it was the best strategy for happiness and, indeed, survival.

Their kibbutz had been established a dozen years earlier and, among other things, had a school, health and dining facilities, administrative offices, and warehouses as well as several buildings that served as sleeping quarters. It also had daycare for infants. Based on the design of other settlements, the kibbutz comprised concentric circles, with public buildings in the central core, homes in the innermost circle, then farm-related buildings further out, after which were the gardens and fields, as well as training areas where agricultural expertise could be learned and practiced.

"I discovered most of the 180 people here had migrated from various parts of Europe," Hannah said to Shimon. "Some are relatively recent arrivals like us, escaping antisemitism, whereas others are the children of parents who had arrived in the country a generation earlier, often escaping the pogroms in Russia or coming here simply to find a new life in the ancient Jewish homeland. For everyone, the greatest desire is to make a better life, work hard, and raise our families in the best possible way. And most of all, to never again have to experience blatant antisemitism."

The school Asher attended was small, and there were only a few children in each class. Those Asher's age were taught mathematics, geography, languages, biology, chemistry, and agricultural studies, and as much as possible these topics were introduced by highly educated mentors, many of whom were experts in their respective fields. Much learning also took place outside the classroom, not only among the children but the adults. Most of the immigrants had not spoken Hebrew before arriving. Yiddish was the language of the diaspora, whereas Hebrew was the language of Jews who had lived in the Holy Land. Acquiring this new language came easily for children, whereas it was more difficult for adults. But they slowly picked it up as they worked and spoke with others and with their children, who had abandoned Yiddish entirely.

Asher's classes began early in the day and ended at noon. Being able to learn without the fear and constant bullying he had experienced in Austria allowed him to open his mind to explore new thoughts and ideas. He liked science-related topics, especially mathematics, which seemed like a puzzle game. After his classes ended each day, during the two-hour daily rest break, Hannah would take on the role of educating Asher further, primarily helping him develop his passions and imbuing him with the importance of having his own identity and how important social connectivity was to get through tough times.

Together with his father, Asher would do his share of work in the field: tilling, planting, watching the fruits grow, and, later in the season, picking the produce. Some of it went into the kibbutz pantries and some were destined for distribution elsewhere. The physical labor involved in achieving such tangible results provided Asher and his father with a therapeutic outlet that helped put the events of the past year behind them. It also had the effect of strengthening them physically. Asher, who had been slightly small for his age, grew like the fruit trees he was tending. In a matter of months, his arms and legs were noticeably muscular, and even though he was only in his early teens, he could easily pass for a young man several years older except for the peach fuzz on his well-tanned face.

Evenings were reserved for nonwork activities. Asher and others his age would play cards and chess, while the adults discussed plans for the kibbutz. Often bonfires would be lit and songs were sung. Folk dancing was remarkably effective in bringing everyone together, cementing their already-shared identity. Feeling accepted strengthened Asher, and during these evening activities, he felt a bond and camaraderie unlike anything he had previously considered possible. Women and men, young girls and boys, celebrated life as much as they could. Even so, Asher could see that during these better times, his mother's memories haunted her.

She wasn't alone. Overshadowing their daily lives on the kibbutz was the continuing war in Europe. Stories filtered in regarding the horrid fate of their brethren in Poland, Russia, Czechoslovakia, Hungary, France, Belgium, Austria, and Germany. During the evenings, men and women frequently congregated in the mess hall around the kibbutz's single radio, a sturdy German-made Blaupunkt. By creating an effective antenna, they were able to hear news from far away.

"I'm so excited when we occasionally hear good news regarding an Allied victory, but typically the news is of further defeats, which fills me with depression and anxiety," a kibbutz member said. "It's astonishing the Allied countries have been powerless in stopping Hitler. Their Nazi Panzer divisions rolled over whatever confronted them. The constant air bombardment of England, the lethal effects of the German submarine fleet, together with failures of the Allies to make any headway, makes me believe the Nazi war machine is invincible."

"I'm equally concerned about what has been happening in *our* region," Shimon said. "The fact Italian planes could bomb Tel Aviv speaks to our vulnerability. Moreover, the British army repeatedly failed to destroy the forces [Field Marshal Erwin] Rommel pitted against them. It seems *der Wüstenfuchs* [Desert Fox], is too adept and too cunning for the bumbling British forces."

Finally, despite achieving multiple victories, Rommel was defeated in November 1942, ending the possibility of the Egyptian city of Alexandria falling. Still, in other parts of the Middle East, Italian and the Vichy French soldiers combated the Allies, even bombing Tel Aviv and Haifa and causing problems in Acre and Jaffa.

Most concerning was the persistent rhetoric of the Grand Mufti of Jerusalem, Haj Amin al-Husseini, whose virulent hatred of Jews was well known.

"He's found it convenient to court the Italian and German leaders," Hannah said, "and their support has emboldened him to make every effort to prevent Jewish immigration to Palestine. He continues to write prodigiously in favor of the Nazis, his pamphlets are widely distributed, and his inflammatory statements are often quoted, particularly the exhortation that. 'The Day of Judgment will come when the Muslims will crush the Jews completely: And when every tree behind which a Jew hides will say, There is a Jew behind me, Kill him.' One day, when this war ends, I hope this viper will receive proper judgment. This is probably wishful thinking as he seems too important to Arab leaders."

The attitudes and behaviors of al-Husseini were hardly new, and unwittingly, he contributed to the development of a defensive force within the country. Beginning in the 1930s, he frequently encouraged violence against the Jews. As a result, each kibbutz had to have guards posted to assure they weren't raided, and military drills were conducted by men and women. Like most others, the kibbutz in which Asher lived had become a component of a broader defense force even though an army, in the usual sense, didn't yet exist.

"The many broadcasted reports of the war never mention the fate of the Jews within Europe," Asher lamented. "They're a nonissue. They're invisible. Defeating the Nazis is understandably the priority of the Allies, but shouldn't the violence directed at targeted groups also be on the agenda? Nobody seems to be lifting a finger to help homosexuals, Roma, political prisoners, and certainly not Jews."

"It's worse than that," Shimon said. "I've learned through word of mouth that not only are the Allied countries not trying to rescue Jews from the Nazi grip, but they have been complicit in the death of many. When Jews can find transportation by boat to distant countries, they are frequently not permitted entry. They have been turned away from Canada, Cuba, and various European countries, and the attitude within the United States has been apathetic. Sadly, many ships were intercepted, and they were forced to return to the hands of their tormentors. Even in 1939, when the threat in Europe was clear, the *St. Louis,* a ship carrying 937 men, women, and children left Hamburg destined for Cuba. However, it was turned away from the port in Havana and every other Latin American country. The United States wouldn't even consider requests from those on board even though the ship was close enough to the coast to see the lights of Miami. Politicians in Canada were no more sympathetic. After all, if this shipload was allowed in, then others would follow. Some of the passengers ultimately found refuge in European countries, but hundreds perished simply because they weren't allowed entry to countries that appeared safe. The Jews are outcasts – the unwanted. Nowhere to remain and nowhere to go."

Said Asher's mother, who was a realist, "If they behave this way now, at some time down the road, maybe in five years, maybe in 50, these same policies and attitudes will be seen again."

His mother's views weren't meant to teach any specific lesson, but her comments ensured Asher would be cautious in dealing with the British who had colonized the region and to be wary, always.

Zionist organizers continued their concerted effort to rescue Jews, and to an extent, they were successful as tens of thousands of Jews originating in Europe made their way to the promised land in less-than-seaworthy boats. Too often, however, these efforts had disastrous outcomes. In February 1942, the *MV Struma*, a 79-year-old ship bound for Eretz Yisrael carrying Jews escaping from the death in Romania was waylaid in Turkey because of engine problems. Since

Britain wouldn't allow it to proceed to Palestine, it was towed out to sea and left adrift, soon being sunk by a Soviet submarine, resulting in the death of all but one of the 791 people on board. Thereafter, the use of boats to allow Jews to escape to Eretz Yisrael was severely diminished and officially halted until the war ended.

Through a variety of means and subterfuges created by Jewish agencies, some Jews continued to be smuggled into Eretz Yisrael. The immigrants who reached the country shared their news of events within Europe. They reported that Jews were systematically being eliminated. They were shot in front of pits they had been forced to dig, asphyxiated in trucks that billowed poisonous gases, incinerated in temples and other buildings, and exterminated in camps constructed specifically for this purpose. The few lucky ones were in slave labor camps where there was the possibility of survival, however remote it might be.

"Eema," Asher asked plaintively, "if we're hearing about the fate of Jews here despite our limited resources, surely the British and Americans know what's going on. Why aren't they doing anything to help?"

Resignation permeating her voice, Hannah answered, "Earlier, Asher, when the Allies were losing, I thought they were unable to help. However, now, the Allies have been getting their planes through, the front is moving into Germany, and the Russians have largely defeated them in the East, but still, the trains carrying Jews to the camps keep on with their hideous business. Simply bombing the rail lines would slow things down and would, no doubt, save many lives. It seems that isn't a priority for the British, Americans, or Canadians. I could live as long as Noah and still wouldn't understand why."

As the war neared its end, the Allied forces were discovering one concentration camp after another, many of which functioned primarily as extermination centers – Auschwitz, Bergen-Belsen, Belzec, Buchenwald, Chelmno, Dachau, Janowska, Majdanek, Maly Trostenets, Mauthausen, Sajmište, Sobibór, Treblinka, and numerous others that served as slave labor camps and transit camps that were the last step before extermination camps. What they found was worse than anyone could have imagined. Word went out to those in the Promised Land, and Asher and his parents, like so many thousands of others, grieved for their lost friends and families. Only after the war ended was the full death toll calculated. The number was too high to be absorbed into the normal mind.

The kibbutz Jews, like those across the world, compulsively gathered news. They learned six million had been killed, perhaps more. Europe had been denuded of its Jews. The number hardly conveyed the brutality of the deaths, the horrors and abuses inflicted on men, women, and children alike. With deep sadness, Hanna concluded her brother, Levi, and his family were among those exterminated. The very word "exterminate" was enough to make her ill as it suggested what humans did to lice and other vermin.

Shimon exclaimed to Asher, "Six million! People won't understand this. Ten or twenty thousand deaths, the mind can grasp. Maybe the mind can conceive of 100,000 deaths of a single people. But six million – understanding the enormity of the catastrophe for individuals and their families will be lost on minds that were steps removed from this horror."

Every Friday evening, before sunset, Asher's mother would light the Sabbath candles, cover her face with her hands, and following tradition recite the Sabbath blessing. Then, with hands still covering her face, Hannah would quietly weep for her brother and friends who had likely been killed, and she would weep and weep and weep until she had no tears left. Each week the pattern would be repeated. And, every Friday evening, Asher's heart would break into a thousand pieces as all he could do was watch her from a distance.

Extended families, husbands, wives, children, and grandchildren had been wiped out from the face of the earth. Even the ashes that had spewed from the crematoria no longer rested on every leaf. For many, there was nobody left to say *kaddish* [the prayer for the dead]. It was as if they had never existed, and no gravestones marked their passing.

In one of their afternoon conversations, sitting on the ground next to the orchard, his elbows resting on his knees, Asher again wanted to reflect on why people in Germany and Austria were claiming they didn't know what was happening in the camps. "How could they not have known? They saw their neighbors taken away, never to return. They witnessed the demolition of ghettos. They moved into the homes of Jews and took their belongings. Is it even remotely possible they didn't know?"

"They most certainly knew, Asher, just as the Allies did," his father responded bitterly. "Now that all is done, it's just convenient not to have known. As early as 1942, they were told in multiple ways what was happening. The Polish diplomat Jan Karski told British and American officials, and even President [Franklin] Roosevelt knew of the crisis for the Jews in Poland and elsewhere. Karski witnessed it firsthand and warned the Allies that if nothing was done, the Jewish population in Poland would cease to exist. So what did anyone do? Nothing, nothing at all."

"It doesn't help, Abba, and it won't bring back the dead, but people should know the truth."

"There will be many witnesses to the horrors who will speak out for decades. But don't fool yourself, Asher. How many will listen, and how many will remember? Apologists for the Nazis and their more-than-willing henchmen and followers will find any number of creative ways to revise history. Soon there will be those who claim the number of six million is greatly exaggerated. Some will even deny the extermination camps existed at all. Some collaborators will go so far as to say they protected the Jews from the Nazis. Even in countries where collaboration with the Nazis was rampant, half the population will claim they were in the underground fighting the fascists. You can count on some countries, especially those with the most Jew-baiters and Nazi accomplices, enacting laws to punish anyone who criticizes their actions against Jews during the war."

As Asher would learn in years to come, some major figures did exactly what his father predicted. Numerous historians attempted to revise history by denying, minimizing, or ignoring facts that should have been obvious to anybody. In France, where 125,000 Jews were deported and the French police vigorously rounded up Jews, the Vichy government may have been trying to curry favor with the German occupiers, but just as likely they were motivated by antisemitism. Stunningly, in his later defense, Pierre Laval, Marshall Philippe Pétain's prime minister, stated he was convinced the Jews were deported to Poland with the intent of establishing a Jewish state, not exterminating them.

Not surprisingly, many people and governments were only too keen to accept warped versions of history. "The Holocaust never happened." "The gas chambers were a fiction." "Typhus was what killed the Jews." Such denials included historians, so-called pacifists, politicians, and presumably educated professors. Some Holocaust deniers even claimed Hitler hadn't known of the extermination of the Jews, and if he had, he would have opposed it. Remarkably, some neo-Nazis maintained Hitler supported Zionism.

Shimon was appalled by what he heard in the years after the war, that many Germans attempted to portray themselves as victims of the Nazi regime, much as others had been persecuted.

"This is tantamount to the arsonists complaining about too much smoke!" he said. "How could they insist on their innocence? The university professors and students, who lit pyres of books before proceeding to burn the Jews themselves, arguing they weren't guilty of any crimes?"

They were the intelligentsia, so nobody could dare insinuate their complicity in acts of barbarism, he realized. Even the members of the Gestapo, the SS, the *Sicherheitsdienst* [SD; the intelligence arm of the SS], the *Ordnungspolizei* [uniformed police], the civilians who denounced Jews to the SS and Gestapo, the *Totenkopf* [Death's Head squads], the concentration camp guards who enjoyed torturing inmates, the cheering crowds that filled large stadiums, and the women infatuated by young soldiers in their Panzer uniforms claimed they were innocent of the vile Nazi behaviors.

As repugnant as the deniers were, Asher couldn't rid himself of the thought that explicit antisemitism wasn't the only ingredient that facilitated Hitler's Final Solution. The politicians in many countries stood by and did nothing to protect Jews and then adopted a collective denial. His mother would repeatedly remind Asher of the lines in Dante Alighieri's *Inferno*, "The darkest places in hell are reserved for those who maintain their neutrality in times of moral crisis." Likewise, his father would repeatedly say, "For a time, the collective guilt and the memory of the Holocaust will limit overt antisemitism. However, in time these memories will dim, and the old antisemitic canards will again emerge." The message to Asher was clear.

Throughout 1946 and for some time after, Asher and other young people like himself continually discussed issues related to the war and the fate of Jews. One evening, at a campfire with friends in an adjacent kibbutz, Asher raised a thorny issue. In some quarters, he noted, it was said the Jews of Europe hadn't done enough to defend themselves.

"This is twisted thinking," he said. "If country after country equipped with sophisticated war machines was unable to stand up to the Nazis, how could anyone expect weaponless Jews to defend themselves? Then again, no matter how hard I try, I just can't fathom how so many Jews were kept in concentration camps, and how rarely they attempted active resistance to escape their deaths. If resistance was possible in Warsaw, why wasn't it possible elsewhere?"

Angrily, he continued, "We counted on the British and the Americans to come to our aid. What a fantasy! How could we fool ourselves into such inane thoughts? Antisemitism isn't a new disease – it's been around for centuries, and its full-throated expression was heard in Britain, France, and even in America. Why would we expect it to change? Counting on others for our survival invites treachery. We must be able to defend ourselves."

Others around the campfire jumped in to fervently voice their opinions. Menachim Samuelson was especially resolute.

"When I think of the passivity of the Jews in Europe, it causes me fear," he said. "Yes, I feel afraid. Afraid that other Jew-haters will think we're weak and spineless and continue to see us as an easy target. If nothing else, there is a lesson here. We must act as a strong people, united in our purpose. We can't ever let this happen again. The words 'Never forget. Never again' need to be remembered always."

Miriam Zvi added: "Recently, I heard about the writing of a historian in the Riga ghetto, Simon Dubnow, who encouraged and begged *'Yiddin, schreibt und farschreibt,'* which means 'Jews, write it down, write it all down.' That was the right thing to do, for sure. The pen might well be mightier than the sword. But I don't believe for a heartbeat we should rely solely on the pen."

As the friends carried on their discussion, a young man Asher's age came around the campfire and sat cross-legged next to him. When the others turned to him inquiringly, the dark-haired newcomer shyly introduced himself as Aryeh. In the poor Hebrew of a newly arrived immigrant, he said, "In Poland, where I come from, my name was Pinchus. Pinye, my family used to call me, God rest their souls. But here I'm Ari."

"Shalom," Miriam greeted him. "We're pleased to meet you, Ari. How long have you been here?"

"Aaahh, I suppose my limited Hebrew gave me away as a new immigrant. I was able to find my way here two months ago, and learning Hebrew has not been easy. My Polish, Ukrainian, Russian, and Yiddish are interfering with learning yet another language."

"Well, you're speaking well enough for me to understand you," Asher said. "So are you a lion as your name implies?"

Ari laughed. "Usually I'm a rabbit, but hopefully someday I'll become a lion," he said. "In Poland and Ukraine, we were all rabbits, hiding from many wolves."

"Mostly hiding from the Totenkopf and the Einsatzgruppen [mobile killing squads]?" Menachem asked.

"Yes, they hunted us persistently, as did their Ukrainian allies led by Stepan Bandera, may his name be erased from history. Most people focus on the depravity of the Nazis, forgetting Ukrainian Nationalists went out of their way to hunt down and round up Jews, killing them in the most atrocious ways or sending them to the camps."

After a long silence, Ari continued, "Many Polish citizens, quite a number, were very good to the Jews, putting themselves at risk to hide us. But some took great pleasure in turning Jews in to the Nazis. Some of the priests even encouraged this, although many were very kind. So when you asked tonight why action wasn't taken in self-defense, ask yourself what we could have done. How could a fight be undertaken while taking care of children and babies and old people? The Nazis had guns, tanks, and every other means of destruction, while we had nothing. Tell me, what could we do? Stab them with the pencils of writers?"

With some embarrassment, Asher said, "You're right. Some of our comments were naive and unfair. It's too easy to say such things after the fact and from a great distance where we feel safe. Still, that is what some people are saying. And, as Menachem said, if our enemies think we're weak, then what will stop this from happening again?"

After a pause, Asher asked respectfully, "Forgive me if I'm being too intrusive. I'm wondering, with so many killed, how did you survive?"

During their conversation, others around the fire had drawn closer. There was no shyness or secrets among them.

"It's a very long story, a very sad one, and I'm not sure I should burden you with it," Ari replied. "The pain is deep and I'm not sure I'm fully ready to talk about the horror I witnessed."

Nobody spoke, and they all gazed at him sadly. Finally, he said in a voice so soft they had to lean forward to hear, "Mostly it was luck, Asher, although it could be argued I was the unlucky one. As I said, I was a rabbit, a young one. One day, soon after the war began in Poland, my little brother became very ill with a high fever. He was sweating and shivering and in a delirious state. My mother was reluctant to send me to the *apteyker* [pharmacist] in the adjacent village. She was afraid for me to wander the roads given the dangers. But I was 14 years old and believed I was as capable as any adult. So I was persistent. Eventually, in desperation given my brother's declining condition, my mother sent me off to get the medicine. It was a long way to walk, and when I arrived, it took the apteyker what felt like an eternity to prepare the medication. Once I had it, I ran most of the way back, as several hours had now passed, and I was anxious about my brother."

Ari broke off, once more withdrawing deep in thought, before he continued again fighting to keep his composure. "As I was nearing my village, a young Christian boy whose family we knew well ran up to stop me, warning me not to go further, and pushed me toward the forest just beyond the farmland. I hurried into the woods, which would force me to take a circuitous route to reach my house. But I knew the dense woods well, having walked every trail many times. Before long, my home was in sight across the field. But I stayed hidden in the trees, where I still had a good view of my village. Almost instantly, I could see why the boy had warned me not to continue. From the woods, I saw my entire family, my father, my two sisters, and my mother, who held my poor little brother. They were huddled with most of the people of our town, or I should say, the Jews of our town, who were being lined up on the street. The Nazi soldiers on either side of them forced the Jews to begin walking in a double line. Those who were slow, such as some of the old people, were hit with rifle butts, and women holding children by the hand were threatened in the same way.

"I had no idea what I could do, and I panicked to the point I couldn't think properly. Just then, I could see a Polish neighbor, a kind woman, Panye Dubzeska, boldly beckoning my mother and brother to follow her, and they disappeared into a side street. The soldiers, oddly, didn't interfere, although I have no idea why. Perhaps they thought Panye, being as brash as she was, had the authority to do so. Still hiding in the trees, as carefully as I could, I followed the line of people, able to see my father and sisters near the front of the group. At the edge of town, they were marched into the field, where a long ditch had been..." Ari broke off and couldn't continue. His eyes filled with tears, and he just kept shaking his head silently.

"It's okay, Ari," Asher said, putting his arm around him. "You don't have to talk about these painful experiences. Another day you can finish your story."

"No, I want to continue. I have to continue," he said. "There were so many intelligent, kind, and wise men and women in Poland who were slaughtered. My father and two sisters joined them that day. Children half my age who never... and here I am. A lucky rabbit. I've come to learn sometimes it's better to be lucky than smart."

The group around the campfire was silent. Hardly a sound could be heard except a slight breeze from the north that caused the fire to crackle. Muffled sniffles were audible. Several silently wiped tears. Asher knew this was not a good road of memories for Ari to travel further that evening, so he changed the conversation.

"Ari, are you living at a particular kibbutz now?" he asked.

"No, I thought I would travel around the country to see where I felt accepted. I like the idea of living and working on a kibbutz, but I feel at loose ends. No place seems quite right, and being on my own is very lonely. So, I'm not here and I'm not there."

Asher stood up, stretched out his arm, and pulled Ari up.

"Come, you're accepted here with us," Asher said. "I'll introduce you to my kibbutz."

Ari nodded, and after embracing their campfire friends with promises to see one another again soon, the two headed off in the truck Asher had taken from the kibbutz. After driving for about half an hour, they reached the edge of the settlement, where the security guard waved them in. After parking, they went to Asher's home and quietly entered the sleeping quarters, careful not to wake anyone. Both were asleep as soon as their heads were down. Asher slept dreamlessly, while Ari's brain gave him little respite. He dreamed of the horrors he experienced, just as he had almost every night.

Despite their late arrival, they awoke early the next morning, and after they washed up, Ari accompanied Asher to the dining hall, where he introduced him to others. They greeted him warmly.

Shimon and Hannah were introduced last, with Hannah laughing, "Ah, Asher has brought us a stray cat."

"Not quite, but close," Asher said. "This is Aryeh, a lion, but he goes by Ari."

"Wonderful, we need more lions, although oxen to till the field would also be appreciated," his father said.

Hannah appraised the two boys, noting how similar they appeared. Both were dark-haired, thin but muscular, and relatively tall.

"The two of you could pass as brothers," she said, then signaling Ari to sit next to her and pushing some food toward him. "Eat something. You need to put some flesh on your frame. You're too thin."

After breakfast, Hannah headed toward the infirmary where she worked, and Shimon, Asher, and Ari, together with a group of other men and women, headed for the orchards to gather the fruits of earlier labor. Ari continued to work alongside Asher and Shimon, and during the subsequent days and weeks slowly unburdened himself of the cumulative distress of the preceding years. Talking appeared to be therapeutic as he seemed more and more confident and less sad. Beyond this, the friendship of Asher and his parents was especially curative.

A bit at a time, Shimon and Asher learned what Ari had endured and how he came to be where he was.

"After watching my father and sisters, as well as friends from the village, shot and buried in a common pit, I was grief-stricken. I remained in the woods at the edge of the village, watching for Panye Dubzeska. After a while, she came out of a neighbor's house and saw me signal her from the edge of the woods. She glanced around cautiously and came over, making an effort to appear she was casually picking flowers. In a brief hushed conversation, I came to understand what was happening. She would hide my mother and brother from the Nazis, although it was very dangerous and couldn't promise how long she and her neighbors could do it. Still, she promised they would do their best, and after assuring him she would let his mother know he was safe, she continued to pick flowers at the edge of the woods before slowly making her way back onto the roadway."

This was how 14-year-old Ari found himself alone in the forest. Occasionally, Panye's daughter, who was also 14, would bring him food and messages from his mother. He was reluctant to move far from the village, so he remained in the nearby forests, hiding when things looked dangerous. With time, he wandered further, sometimes kilometers from the village. On one of these wanderings, he came across five boys roughly his age who had also been hiding in the woods. They joined in hiding from the Nazis and their Ukrainian henchman, as well as from Poles, some of whom despised Jews and took pleasure in turning them in. Some felt this hatred for no apparent reason, whereas others blamed the Jews for the war or maintained that the Jews were allies of the Russians, whom the Poles feared as much as the Nazis.

"Occasionally, we encountered 'Righteous Gentiles,' as they were later called, who risked their lives and that of their families to rescue endangered Jews," Ari said. "Yet, given the ever-present uncertainties and risks, it was more pragmatic to trust no one. With time, I became increasingly edgy, finally telling the other boys I had to return to visit my village, and the others decided to accompany me. We slept in the woods that evening as usual, and early the next morning we crept to a bluff near the edge of the village. I was in the lead and the others single file behind me. When I peered over the bluff, the sight stopped me. When the others came to my side and looked too, their reactions were the same.

"That," Ari choked out, his eyes never leaving the now discolored, purple, and blue corpses with swollen tongues protruding from their mouths, "is Panye Dubzeska, her daughter, and the neighbors who were hiding my mother and brother. Their bodies have been left hanging as a warning to others who might have thoughts of aiding Jews. I've no doubt that her death was the result of one of her neighbors snitching to the Nazis." Left unsaid by all but expressed by the gentle laying of hands on Ari's back or shoulders was the acknowledgment his mother and brother had been taken away by the Nazis.

The six teenagers spent almost all their time in the woods, occasionally sneaking out to help themselves to food from nearby farms, sometimes having to run for their lives when spotted by farmers who might inform the local Nazis of their presence. Once, they discovered an abandoned truck laden with provisions. They swiftly stuffed their pockets with as much as they could and used their jackets as sacks to carry still more. They were able to make two trips this way before having to retreat as armed Ukrainian *chuliganis* [hooligans], rifles in their arms, approached the truck. Fortunately, the chuliganis were more intent on helping themselves to the spoils within the truck than on killing a few Jews. One called out to the others, "Jan, we can kill Jews on any day, but finding a truck filled with this stuff doesn't come along often."

"The leader of our small band, Yankele, was only 16 but much wiser, cunning, and brave than would be expected considering his age," Ari continued. "He was dedicated to the group's survival, and he didn't shy away from taking revenge against the Nazis or Jew-hating Poles and Ukrainians. When word came to him that a Ukrainian husband and wife were being paid for turning in hidden Jews, he sneaked into their home, slit their throats, and cut out the man's tongue, replacing it with *zlotys* [Polish money]. Likewise, upon hearing a village priest was encouraging his congregation to keep a look out for Jews and to turn them in to the Nazis, Yankele took action. He and the boys abducted the priest and hung him upside down with his arms spread from the church steeple so he appeared as an inverted crucifix, signifying the devil. Yankele and the others were spotted as they left the village, and it wasn't long before word spread of the group's presence. The locals, as well as several Ukrainians, swore to avenge the priest. They especially wanted to mete out their wrath on Yankele, who had been recognized."

"I guess we were wrong about Jews doing nothing to protect themselves," Asher admitted. "Of course, we've heard about the Warsaw Ghetto, but evidently, there was resistance elsewhere we never heard about."

"That's true, but I doubt there were many such pockets," Ari replied. "At any rate, because of our excursions, we had to be more vigilant than before and rarely separated from one another. The exception was Yankele, who would leave us for a day or two, returning with provisions, sometimes a knife or a gun with a few bullets, as well as some warm clothes and blankets. He wouldn't discuss these expeditions, as he called them, and when asked, he would become evasive. On occasion, he would go see his mother, who was hidden by local Christians. Late at night, she would meet him based on prearranged signals, and she would pass on items the Christian farmers had given her. Other Poles also provided him with food and clothes, which they would leave for him in the forest. As much as we wanted to thank the donors, he never revealed where it all came from as doing so could endanger them. The sad fact was the Poles who were supportive, at least in that region, were far fewer than those who would have turned us in."

Shimon said, "It would have been difficult to stay hidden at any time of year, but less so in the summer and early autumn when the trees and bushes were full. How did you manage to hide during the barren winter?"

"We dreaded winter," Ari replied. "During the warm months, we could become comfortable, food was easier to come by, and it was certainly safer than in the ensuing months. Winters were hard on us not only because of leafless trees but because our tracks were easily visible in the snow. Sometimes the cold was unbearable. The clothes and blankets Yankele brought were sufficient to survive, although during particularly treacherous cold spells we had to find an abandoned barn or hut for shelter. Sometimes we stayed only a day or two, and on occasion we lingered longer, making sure to remove any traces of our stay before leaving."

Ari went on to tell them more information on several occasions.

"During the first year, four more stray boys who had escaped the Nazi and Ukrainian net joined us," he said. "The youngest, who was only eleven, turned out to be especially valuable. His small size allowed him to wriggle through small basement windows or squeeze between missing barn boards where others couldn't fit. In this way, he could smuggle the supplies we needed. On one of his forays into a basement, he was caught by a farmer, who immediately shot him. The farmer took the body to the village to reap a reward. When Yankele and a few of the other boys later caught the farmer returning from the village, he had a pocketful of zlotys he would never enjoy spending.

"So it went over years, and we would repeatedly say this existence couldn't last forever. But eventually, rescue would come. During the last year of the war, the Russian forces pushed the Nazis back. We continued to stay in the woods, however, believing that although the Russians were enemies of the Nazis, it didn't mean they were friends of the Jews. Once the Nazis were finally defeated, we came out of the forest and returned to our villages. Each of the boys was forlorn as they left the group, which was now their adopted family, but they were anxious to learn the fate of their families."

Ari later learned none of the boys found any living family members. All eventually found their way to other countries. A group of three, Yehuda, Kali, and Dov, somehow reached Greece and then boarded a ship headed for Eretz Yisrael. The ship was stopped by British naval vessels and, after a brief inspection, escorted to Cyprus. They remained in a detention camp for almost a year but eventually made it to their destination.

"Yankele and I stayed together, visiting a town near Yankele's home, when we were struck by a commotion on the streets followed almost immediately afterward by the appearance of soldiers, some of whom wore red stars on their lapels," Ari said. "The Russians were treated as if they were saviors, at least at first, but they soon displayed extreme paranoia and ruthlessness and the populace shied away from them. We were enlisted as forward scouts to root out the many Ukrainian and Polish collaborators who had aided the Nazis."

"The Russians were especially interested in capturing or killing Bandera, who was obsessed with ethnic cleansing. Bandera and his men had joined with the Totenkopf, who had constantly searched for Jews. History was already in the remaking as stories of Bandera made him out to be a Ukrainian freedom fighter. But we had dodged this group in the forests and knew they were nothing more than thugs – malicious, evil vipers whose bravery was fueled by alcohol and their hatred of Jews. So, Yankele and I were more than happy to aid the Russians in their search.

"Yankele had become notorious for his ability to taunt and thwart the Ukrainians throughout the war. The Ukrainian followers of Bandera had put a price on Yankele's head, but this only encouraged

Yankele further. Ultimately, Bandera was captured and executed, but during the search, which lasted months, Yankele was shot by a sniper and died quietly while I held him in my arms. I cried for the very first time in many years. Word spread among Ukrainian Nationalists in the area Yankele had been killed and they celebrated it as a victory over their conquerors."

Ari couldn't let go of the thought that Yankele had lasted through the war only to be shot from a distance by a cowardly hooligan.

"I had never met Yankele's mother, but I imagined her grief, especially as she had already lost her younger son and daughter," he said. "It made me realize that in an unspeakable way, it was good my mother hadn't survived a war that resulted in so many of her loved ones being killed. She didn't have to endure the deep pain of her losses, whereas Yankele's mother would carry this grief throughout her life."

"Without Yankele at my side, I lost the balance he provided and couldn't regain it readily. If nothing else, however, my time in the woods hardened me, and I learned to be resourceful. When the Russians moved on, I stayed behind and returned to my small town. It wasn't long before I felt the place in which I had lived for most of my life was no longer a home where I could feel safe. As far as I could tell, not a single Jew had survived besides me."

Ari felt the loss of Yankele deeply. Part of his healing process involved telling his new family about Yankele's past, as difficult as it was.

Yankele had told him his mother, Chana, who was called Henia by the local Polish people, was born in a small village near the town of Kłokowice, which lay in Poland or Ukraine, depending on the century, as it seemed to change hands often. She was born in 1908, 1910, or 1912. There weren't any birth certificates given out, and she claimed to be uncertain, but it was equally possible this was her way of maintaining a younger identity. She was the second of three children, with an older brother, Menachem, and a younger sister, Elisha.

Chana began school as a young child, but her education was cut short by the outbreak of World War I. During the war years, Menachem taught her at home. She was a wonderful student. Her appetite for books was voracious, and she could read in several languages by the age of ten. She dreamed of reading all the great novels, going to Warsaw to see the grand theaters and the Yiddish plays, and of one day entering the upper school – the *gymnasium* – so she could become clever and wise, just like her older brother. This was the dream, but it remained only a dream.

Through her father and brother, she learned the skills of a merchant.

"She has a head for numbers, and she has a good way with people," her father would say.

"She was exceedingly accomplished at the 'trading wheel,'" Ari continued. "For example, if she wanted to buy cows but farmer Padvorev only had chickens for sale, she wouldn't be deterred. Mr. Kreitz had cows but wanted wheat in exchange. So she bought Padvorev's chickens in exchange for cloth, then sold the chickens to Panye Galowsz for wheat, which she then used to buy Kreitz's cows. She ended up with the cows and a small profit from each transaction.

"A man named David Litwin was taken by her intelligence, and he soon approached Chana's father for permission to marry her. Soon the marriage was arranged, likely involving yet another trading wheel to provide everything needed for the festivities. Chana now had other dreams. Dreams of children, dreams of grandchildren, dreams of walks through the fields with the family, dreams of wading through the stream that bordered their farm. Soon these dreams began to form her reality. Yankele, the firstborn, was followed by a daughter, Edgga, and then another son, Benyamin. Wonderful dreams filled with possibilities, and the century wasn't even a third over."

Ari described Chana's family as happy, even though times were often hard. Despite antisemitism being common, violence was infrequent. Being in an isolated village, they had no idea that across the border in Germany, a disease was being spawned, and in 1933 a virus spread in the form of the National Socialist movement, which seemed to be rabidly infectious. The fascists became increasingly self-assured and felt so strongly about being the master race, they began conquering adjacent countries, and in 1939 they attacked Poland with apparent impunity as the rest of the world watched in wonder and horror. In a matter of a few months, the Germans, as well as their Ukrainian Nationalist followers, reached Chana's town in Poland on the Ukrainian border.

Ari repeated the words exactly as Yankele had said them: "When my parents, brother, sister, and I returned from visiting my grandparents, who lived near Lviv on the Ukrainian side, we came to the top of a ridge, where we saw a large group of Nazi soldiers rush into our village in armored vehicles, and then violently enter each house. We scrambled to the side of the road in total panic, and then hid among some low bushes and watched the scene unfold before us like a nightmare that seemed surreal but was tragically real. Can you even begin to imagine what it was like to witness the Nazis efficiently round up the Jews, including my mother's brother, his wife, and their children, beating them mercilessly in the street as they were hauled from their homes, and then shoving the stumbling collective to a field at the edge of town? They were lined up along the side of a long trench and then shot so the bodies fell directly into it, after which they were covered up with the loose earth surrounding the trench. We witnessed this from our hiding spot. As we watched, my mother bit into her hand so as not to scream, and we children, ever curious, were mesmerized as we peeked through the bushes and saw every bullet enter every single body. It seemed both endless and instantaneous at the same time. Imagine the abrupt loss of innocence and imagine as well that this horror was just the prelude to much worse."

Yankele's father, David, refused to leave the family for even a moment, so Chana sent Yankele to search for her sister, Elisha, who lived in an adjacent village, and bring her family to their spot in the woods.

When he reached their house, his uncle Gabriel was skeptical of what Yankele told him. "Don't be a donkey," he implored. "What you're saying is impossible. The Germans have no reason to run around killing people, even Jews. They won the war against Poland,

and now they simply want to take what they can, which doesn't include killing local people."

Yankele objected to his uncle's naivete, even though he knew from his father his uncle Gabriel wasn't particularly astute. His father occasionally referred to him as "someone who believed he knew more than anyone else did."

"Uncle Gabriel, I saw it with my own eyes," Yankele told him. "They made everybody stand before a ditch, and a large gun on three legs was placed about 20 meters from them. When it started shooting, everyone fell like wheat before a scythe. Please, you must come to the woods where we are hiding."

Elisha pleaded with him, as did their children, and he finally relented, saying, "Fine, fine. If it will make you happy, then we'll go meet Chana. I'll put some food in a bag, but I'm sure in a few hours we'll be back and have to unpack the food. As always, Chana is hysterical, causing trouble for everyone."

As they walked, they heard the loud sound of machinery coming along the road behind them and felt the ground rumble. They instinctively moved away from the road, crouching low in the bordering field. Soon, large tanks appeared, each with their guns pointed forward. Not one, not ten, but tens of tens approached, raising dust above the treetop, and creating noise more threatening than the most severe thunderstorm. Behind the tanks came lorries filled with soldiers and many large trucks with wheeled cannons attached to their back ends. This retinue of armaments seemed to continue forever, leaving the family with intense foreboding.

Once the army vehicles passed, the unnatural silence descended again. Cautiously, they rose from their hiding places and resumed their trek, eventually reaching the spot where they were to meet Chana. Although they could see nobody when they arrived, Yankele's mother, father, and siblings soon emerged and the group huddled on the ground to listen to the plan she had formulated. Chana knew a few families in the area that might take them in given their earlier friendship with her parents.

As quickly as they could, the families moved cautiously across the farmland that would take them to another village adjacent to Chana's farm. They presumed that since the Nazi tanks and soldiers had passed, they were relatively safe, particularly as they were so deep in the fields and away from the road. But suddenly, floodlights from many vehicles illuminated the field, turning night into day. Instinctively, they ran for the safety of the nearby woods. Behind them, they could hear several vehicles charging after them. As the wheat hadn't yet been harvested as it should have, they had some cover while running in a crouch. They were able to get into the dense woods where the vehicles couldn't travel, although occasional bullets came close to them, hitting nearby trees. They found an old trail, and as quickly as their feet would carry them in the dark, they continued to run for safety to the point their lungs hurt. But when they stopped to gather in a thicket, both Gabriel and Chana almost simultaneously realized Elisha wasn't with them. Gabriel wanted to go back to find her, but Chana wouldn't allow it,

"If she's still alive, she'll find us," Chana said. "And if she's been killed, then there will be nothing gained by you going back."

They stayed put, hoping beyond hope Elisha would catch up with them. She finally appeared at dawn, disheveled, her blouse and dress torn by the hands of the hoodlums who had pursued them. She was dirty and bruised. She didn't say a word and just sat quietly and sobbed. The children, of course, didn't understand what had happened, but Chana did, and so did Gabriel."

Later that day, Chana returned to the village alone, wearing her peasant smock and babushka, walking as confidently as she would have at any other time. Through a passageway at the back, she gained entry to the building that housed the shop she and her husband had owned. Once inside, she turned over the flour box, exposing a compartment that could be opened using a knife blade. From this hiding place, she withdrew a small sack that contained some jewels, a few diamonds, and some gold and silver rings, as well as some zlotys saved over several years. Having collected the potentially life-saving booty, she left as quietly as she had come.

From there she went to her brother's house, knowing he and his family were dead. She pulled back some rafters behind a wood pile and extracted another small sack. She and her brother shared every secret so they could act if one of them was in trouble. As much as she knew he couldn't come back and it was his wish to take the sack, her guilt was immense. Nonetheless, having the contents could help them survive. Before she left, she stood at the spot where he would ordinarily have said his morning prayers and quietly recited Kaddish to help his soul reach heaven.

When Mrs. Wincewicz saw Chana standing at her door looking distressed, she pulled her inside instantly, warning of spies everywhere. With tears streaming down her cheeks, Chana began to tell her what happened, but Mrs. Wincewicz gently cut her off.

"I know Chana, I know," she said. "But thank God you're alive. Bring me your family, especially the children, and I'll keep them here or put them with others who will assist us."

After dark the next day, Chana appeared at Mrs. Wincewicz's home, with the two families trailing behind her. They were taken behind the house and led to an opening to a cellar that stretched a few meters beneath the house. It was large enough to hold several people, although it was damp and cold. When Chana tried giving her money, Mrs. Wincewicz took only enough to cover the cost of food. She was a good woman, perhaps too good, and as the year progressed, the group she kept hidden in her cellar reached 14. Many months later, precisely eight months and two weeks, Elisha gave birth to a son and the total became 15.

The sheer amount of food being brought to the house, although typically late at night, should have cued informers who would alert the Nazis. The circumstances, coupled with the crowded conditions, led to Yankele choosing to hide in the woods, while Chana took her daughter and younger son, Nathan, to the home of Mr. and Mrs. Stronsky, another kind Polish Catholic family. Life at the Stronsky house was far less comfortable as the cellar was just slightly more than a meter high, so movement required the occupants to bend at the waist. But given the alternatives, nobody complained.

As fate would have it, only a few days after Chana and the children left Mrs. Wincewicz's cellar, the house was raided by SS troopers and Totenkopf. The fugitives hiding in the cellar were silent, afraid to breathe lest the sounds give them away. Moments before the raid, Elisha had passed the baby to Gabriel to hold, and he continued to do so, clutching him close to his chest, covering his mouth to prevent cries from alerting their hunters. The search was thorough, including stomping about to determine whether a basement was present. Fortunately, the earth between the floor and the cellar muffled sounds, so the cellar wasn't discovered. The search went on for more than an hour, but it seemed much longer. Once the searchers left, the Jews in the basement let out a collective breath.

It was only then Gabriel realized the child he had been holding so close hadn't let out its breath.

Elisha was forlorn and Gabriel felt immense guilt, and she added to his misery with her expression of contempt whenever she looked at him.

The loss of the baby, as bitter as it had been, one of many horrors. Their younger daughter, Mindy, having very light blond hair and looking like the prototypical Polish Christian child, was allowed out to play without fear of being identified as a Jew. After playing outside a few weeks after the raid, Mindy didn't reappear inside when she should have. After a time, with mounting dread, Elisha sneaked out to look for her, but her daughter was nowhere to be found. That evening, together with Mrs. Wincewicz, she went looking for Mindy, returning later with nothing to show for their efforts other than frustration and devastation.

The mystery was solved the following day when a neighbor reported she had seen two Gestapo men draw the blond-haired child into their car and drive away. They had no way of knowing it, but a black market existed for blond-haired children who were offered to German couples who could not have children of their own., Elisha was doubly distressed at losing her daughter so soon after the tragic loss of her son. Was this punishment from God for Gabriel accidentally smothering the baby?

As devastating as Elisha's experiences were, Chana's life had become far worse. Her husband was killed several days after they moved into Mrs. Wincewicz's cellar when he went out to determine what became of his parents. Not long afterward, her younger son died of liver failure from ingesting something poisonous he found in the woods while accompanying Yankele for a brief period. Her daughter, Edgga, was killed, but it was never clear to Yankele how it happened, and Chana would never speak of it. What could be so horrible to make her mute on this subject? No doubt the Nazis could find more and more monstrous ways of killing a young innocent child.

For the rest of the war, Chana would say, "I've lost two children, but I'm thankful to God he spared my third." After the war ended and she learned of Yankele's death, her world imploded. She could do nothing but wander for days in a dazed, bewildered state. She was an animated corpse who didn't speak and didn't hear but just kept on walking, one among a small army of other walking corpses.

With war's end, the 30,000 or so Jews who had survived the labor camps, and the 50,000 who lived in the forests or were hidden by Christians, began their own walk, trying to find their brothers, sisters, mothers, fathers, husbands, wives, and children. They scoured the areas where they had lived, desperately hoping to find them alive but knowing in their hearts it was a virtual impossibility. Chana heard the voices asking, "Have you seen my brother? What of his children?" And still others inquiring, "My son and daughter, are they still here? Are they with my wife? When was the last time you saw them?" But Chana couldn't speak and couldn't answer. An army of wandering souls roamed the countryside, slipping by one another with the constant refrain, "Have you seen …? Have you seen …?"

When Ari received word that Jews were gathering in Germany because the Allies were headquartered there, he headed off in that direction – it was the irony of ironies to have to go to the home of the oppressors. One way or another he would leave wretched Poland behind. With a small backpack and a blanket rolled on top of it, he left the village.

"It wasn't long before a lorry pulled up next to me driven by a kind dark-skinned American soldier. Even though I didn't understand a word he said, his gesture were enough for me, and smiling and nodding my head in thanks, I ran to the back of the lorry. What I saw astonished me, and I was only torn from my shock by the sound of the driver's voice asking if I was getting on. Men and women were sitting on the floor along each side of the lorry. A few seemed reasonably well, but most were barely recognizable as humans. They were skeletons, living skeletons – heads shaved, with bulging eyes too large for their heads, with arms and legs so thin their bones seemed to poke through nothing more than a layer of skin. They were all survivors of the camps, and as hardened as I had become, the pitiful scene before me was heartbreaking. I pulled myself together, climbed on board, and found a small spot into which I could squeeze along one side of the lorry."

Nobody spoke. Instead, everyone simply stared at him. Once the truck was underway, one of the women quietly asked in Yiddish, "Are you a Jew?"

"Yes, of course. I guess everyone here is a Jew."

She nodded. "We are a few of those who survived," she said. "Now, we'll get to see who is left, but I don't think there will be many."

As the lorry moved on, he learned Zosha's story of survival.

"For many years, I was moved from camp to camp," the woman said. "First, I was at Theresienstadt, and then for a reason I didn't know, I was sent to another camp, Sobibor. I was supposed to be exterminated, but when I told them I had been a cook, they put me to work in the kitchen. Perhaps because I was a good cook, or maybe because I was so cooperative, I didn't go to the gas chambers like the thousands and thousands that came through the camp for only brief periods."

She paused frequently in her tale, sometimes seeming to restrain tears, but then she would say, "There's no use in crying. Nothing can undo what's done. Even God in heaven can't bring back what we've lost," and then she would sigh and continue after another prolonged silence.

"They would round up groups of men and women, force them to undress, and tell them they had to be decontaminated so they wouldn't spread disease. They were led naked along a long path, perhaps 100 meters or more, which the prison guards called the Road to Heaven. They were then pushed into a large chamber by Nazi and Ukrainian guards. After everyone was inside, the doors were locked and gas from running trucks was piped into the chamber. When they were all dead, Jewish prisoners were forced to remove the bodies, and the chamber was readied for the next group, who would meet the same fate. Escape was virtually impossible, but even so, some tried. Mostly they were killed in the effort, even before reaching the fences around the perimeter. Of the few who were able to get past the fences, they were caught soon after and shot on the spot, where they were left to rot."

Again, she paused, her thoughts seeming to overwhelm her. But, needing to unburden herself, she would continue. "For some reason, I was transferred to another camp, Mauthausen-Gusen, in Austria. I was certain I would be killed there, but once again I was selected for work in the kitchen. Others were not so lucky and were worked to death, shot, pushed off a cliff within the camp, beaten to death, hanged, or starved to death, and some were injected with experimental chemicals. The Nazis seemed to get joy from finding new methods of killing Jews. I still don't understand how I survived. Nobody lasted there for any great length of time – a month or two, sometimes three if they were very unlucky. So, young Ari, tell me how come I'm still here?"

Ari didn't know how to respond and feebly ventured, "I frankly don't know the answer to that question, Zosha. Maybe God has a plan for you."

Before he could continue, she cut him off. "I don't think so," Zosha said. "I don't have anything that would make me capable enough for God to choose me for something like that. I'm not made like our matriarchs Sarah, Rebecca, Rachel, and Leah, nor do I have the vision of Miriam the Prophetess who pulled Moses from the bulrushes. To be frank, there are many times when I have questioned whether there is a God."

"Maybe not," Ari said, "but I prefer to believe there is. Then, at least, I have hope things will become better."

"I considered that maybe God is collectively punishing us for something we've done," Zosha replied. "Or perhaps he's testing us as he did Job to determine whether we would remain loyal to him. Surely he could have found a simpler and less destructive way of testing us." Then with a brief mirthless laugh, she added: "Like asking us to write a brief essay on religion and their love of God as we ask children to do at school."

This comment made Ari laugh. "Yes, Zosha, that would be a more humane test," he said.

"Oh, Ari," she continued, "it's good to see you laugh. Our people have always found solace in laughter and in telling stories. It reminds me of the Jewish inmates who told a story that was also a joke. One of the prisoners, after a day of hard labor, was forced to carry heavy stones up and down a set of stairs leading to the ledge of a quarry. After many such trips to the top, he finally dropped to his knees, whereupon a guard dragged him to the edge of the cliff and pronounced, 'You have a choice. I can shoot you here and now, or I can push you off this ledge and that will be the route to see your god. You choose.' The tired, winded Jew, hardly able to speak owing to his heavy breathing, replied, 'Sir, I've been working like an ox all day, and then you had me carrying rocks up and down repeatedly. I'm so exhausted I can barely think, and this choice is terribly difficult. Would you be kind enough to give me a couple of days to think it over?' I doubt this story is true, but when I heard it, I couldn't help but laugh."

Ari laughed with her.

"As I said, no matter what, our people love to laugh," Zosha said. "I suppose such morbid humor is a way of helping us through hard times.

"I'll tell you another story, which has a funny element, but a sad message, too," she said. "The concentration camp Mauthausen where I worked for a time wasn't reserved for Jews. People were brought from several countries for various crimes. Political prisoners, intellectuals, and many from higher social classes ended up there, as did ruffians of all sorts. Perhaps they chose to transfer me there because, before the war, I was a professor of history at Charles University in Prague. You see, I had talents other than being a good cook, but as an intellectual, I was viewed as a threat – a likely Soviet sympathizer or an all-out communist. At any rate, as I said, many prisoners were worked to death. One man, an intellectual from the upper class, realizing his end was near, cried to me one day, saying this was all so unfair. He didn't deserve to die since he wasn't a Jew. As if the Jews deserved to die. There, in one of the biggest cesspools on earth, such feelings toward us came to the surface, even from those who should have known better."

"Yet you survived. How did that come about?"

"I suppose they had considered killing me, but as I said earlier, since I was a good cook, they thought they would keep me around a bit longer, a week, a month – who knew? As it turned out, the camp commandant kept smelling my cooking and felt I was too talented to be wasted on the camp's inmates, and I was transferred to cook for the officers and himself. Often, I wished I had poison to put in the food, but I didn't know if any items in the kitchen could be used for that. Perhaps if I had a doctorate in chemistry rather than history, I might have been successful. I knew if I made any effort, I would be killed most hideously. Still, I was 27 years old and had lived long enough, and the act would have been worth it."

Hearing that this woman was still relatively young surprised Ari. He thought she was at least in her fifties.

Zosha noticed the surprise on his face.

"Are you surprised I would attempt to poison the officers, or is it you thought I was much older than I am?" she asked. "I'm sure my appearance is less than lovely. I hadn't seen a mirror, at least not a real mirror, for a long time, so I didn't know what I actually looked like. The reflection I could see on the bottom of a pot, or a pail of water certainly didn't offer an accurate portrayal. However, I have since looked into a mirror and I was shocked at the old person looking back at me."

Ari's curiosity was piqued, but he also wanted to change the subject away from her appearance.

"So, how is it you ended up in Poland again?" he asked.

"The few of us who survived were finally liberated by the Americans, and while they could tend to our physical suffering, they could do little to heal the mental wounds. At any rate, they interviewed many of us, perhaps so we could serve as witnesses to the events we had seen. Upon learning I was a historian who spoke multiple languages, they asked me to help document the atrocities in Poland, and I eagerly agreed, especially when I learned that Allies had been planning trials at Nuremberg to prosecute the worst of the Nazis. Along the way, it became clear I was too weak, too tired, and not mentally prepared to deal with such an arduous and psychologically horrific task. They gave me the option of continuing to document atrocities or being taken to Germany from where I could emigrate elsewhere. I chose the latter. And so here I am, along with other camp survivors, all of us heading for the bowels of the horror. Maybe my stop in Germany will be brief, and after that, I will be able to enter America, Canada, or who knows where. Anywhere would be good, just not here, and not in Germany."

She then turned her attention to him, asking about his time in the forest. But before he was even a few words into his tale, she was fast asleep from the fatigue of telling her own story.

Over the next few days, he told her about his experiences, and she was enraptured by their adventures in tricking the enemies. She had said she had no tears, having cried herself out over such a long time. Yet, when she learned of Yankele's death, she did cry, saying, "I had a son his age. He must be dead, too, but I have no idea when or how he would have died. I'm not even certain he really is dead. This uncertainty, this not knowing, this hoping he's alive yet understanding how unlikely this is, eats my *nefesh* [soul.]"

Hearing this, a man who had introduced himself as Motti but said very little before now, whispered, "Nothing is worse than not knowing. Nothing is worse. Nothing."

Ari appraised him and then cautiously said, "Are you the only survivor of your family?"

In response, Motti said, "I don't know who is or isn't alive. As Zosha said, it's eating me from the inside, and my heart feels as if it's gripped by a strong hand. Am I leaving Poland too soon? Should I be home looking for them? I just don't know what to do. I'm entirely confused."

As they traveled, stopping occasionally to go to the bathroom and eat, they witnessed the destruction left by the war. Cities in ruins, farmlands destroyed, and everywhere beggars with crying children.

"This can never be rebuilt," Ari said.

"Oh, it will be rebuilt, and rebuilt better than before," Zosha said. "People will return, and the next generation will try to erase the memories, and the generation after that will hardly be aware of what occurred here. This is history, something I know about well."

At one of their stops, Motti looked in the direction from which he had come and wistfully said, "The further we move from my old home, the more guilt I feel. My shame is even worse. It's impossible to live with this hanging over me."

He then left the group of survivors and slowly began walking back to the beast that had tormented him.

"I hope he finds what he would like," Zosha said sadly.

Standing nearby were two young women, Nela and Rachel, who had survived work camps and kept to themselves for most of the long drive. Nela turned to Zosha, saying, "It's so very sad. He'll discover what we did. Nobody in his family stayed alive and his feelings of guilt won't diminish. He'll only feel self-reproach for why he couldn't do anything to help them."

After getting back in the truck, Nela and Rachel seated themselves next to Zosha, who asked them how they had survived. Nela and Rachel took turns compressing six years of misery in a work camp in less than an hour. Toward the end of her description, Nela said, "Unlike Ari, I don't think God has a plan for us. I wish he were right, but I doubt he is. God just does what God does and doesn't involve himself in earthly matters. We like to believe we're his Chosen People. What were we chosen for?" Then motioning to the others on the truck, she asked dubiously, "Were we chosen for this?"

Zosha put her arm across Nela's shoulders and quietly said, "It's immaterial whether there is or isn't a God and whether God has a plan for us. In the end, we need to find some meaning in our lives, not just to help us cope, but perhaps to help others."

The truck drove through a series of small towns where the destruction was the same as in larger cities. They stopped at Krakow, then Brno, and along the way, several further brief stops were made where a few more survivors boarded the lorry. Once they were settled on the floor, the lorry moved forward, each time with a jerk followed by grinding gears that desperately needed oiling. At one of these stops, an old man and an equally old woman boarded and sat at the center of the truck floor bed. Ari changed spots with the woman so she could have the comfort of the lorry's side to rest against, while the elderly man and Ari sat back-to-back to support one another.

Speaking to the woman, gray-haired and very thin, all skin and protruding bones, he learned that she, like Zosha, was much younger than she appeared. She informed him she came from Hungary, where conditions for Jews weren't good but, except for several mass arrests and deportations, generally their lives hadn't been at risk. For a time, Hungary had been allied with Germany; however, after Germany was defeated at Stalingrad and elsewhere, where thousands of Hungarian soldiers were lost, the government of Hungary wanted to abandon the alliance. In response, Germany invaded Hungary, and with this came the roundup of Jews, forcing them into ghettos, and subsequent deportation to Auschwitz.

"I had a husband and two children when we were taken to one of the camps," the woman said. "When we arrived, we stood in a long line, and an officer at the head of this line directed me one way to the main camp, whereas my husband and children were sent in the other direction. I hadn't realized the separation would be permanent, but maybe we'll be reunited in Gan Eden [the Garden of Eden], where the good ones are all present."

He had surreptitiously looked at the numbers tattooed on her arm. Catching his quick gaze, she said, "Soon after I arrived at the camp, they gave me a filthy uniform that had been used by an earlier victim. A few days later, for reasons I don't know – perhaps it was because I told them I was a seamstress and so could be useful – I was sent to camp two, which I learned was Auschwitz-Birkenau. There they used a device that sent needles into my arm, after which this blue ink was poured over the piercings, which sunk deep into them, creating my new identification. So I became 37175, and Leah Belzer no longer existed."

"What was the purpose of the number?" Ari asked.

"Who knows what fantasies consumed the minds of these butchers? Some of the other prisoners said it was to keep track of us, and using numbers was easier than names. I suppose this might have been accurate, as the numbers were given in sequence, so knowing my number allowed the camp leaders – the Hauptscharführe or his Oberscharführer – to know instantly the numbers of the next prisoners. But so many died or were murdered that the sequence did not follow a steady progression. My own belief is the Nazis despised Jews so immensely that they wished to make us less than humans. Branding us like cattle made us this in their eyes."

Ari commiserated with her for some time about her life in the camps, understanding the Nazis were practical in their selections of who was allowed to live, at least for a time. Zosha survived because she was a cook, and Leah because she was a seamstress.

"Leah," he said, "the numbers on your arm will be a horrible reminder of what you've gone through. Perhaps the American doctors will be able to remove it."

"You think without these numbers I would ever forget the camps?" she responded. "If I still had my children, and they had children, even they wouldn't forget the camps."

"Of course, you're right," Ari said. "Memories can't be erased like ink."

"There were so many shocking incidents, it would take years to recount them all," she said despondently. "I wonder who was better off – those who died during the first days of the war, those who lived for years in the camps only to die just before the liberation, or the survivors like me who will carry the baggage of memories for as long as we live?"

"Maybe those who died quickly were better off," he said. "A bullet in the heart and buried there and then might have been better than dying after a pointless struggle."

"This is very true, but not every death was fast and painless," she said. "In a small town Jedwabne, which was only 30 kilometers from where my sister lived, the Jews were rounded up and killed. About 300 were shot, but more were herded into a barn, which was then lit on fire while the Nazis and their collaborators stood around talking and smoking cigarettes and listening to the screams coming from within the flames. What could have motivated such cruelty? Were these normal people? Nothing and nobody could ever explain such things."

"I know, Leah, these things can't be explained even if we tried until the Messiah comes," Ari said.

In a breaking voice, Zosha interjected, "Ari, the criminals who engaged in such behaviors weren't outliers. They were seen as heroes by the town's people who helped themselves to what the Jews had left behind. The massacre in Jedwabne wasn't an isolated event. Mass graves of Jews are strewn across the country, many from the massacres carried out by the Einsatzgruppen, the mobile killing squads whose job was to find clusters of Jews and then dispatch them. Their killings weren't done in the dead of night without witnesses present. While I was interviewing survivors, I discovered that in country after country, the Nazis and their followers relished the killings. The town's people didn't hide in their homes to avoid seeing the destruction of the Jews. Instead, they came out to the killing sites and behaved as if it were a party. Subsequently, some of these people contributed to filling in the trenches in which Jews were thrown."

Zosha then turned to Leah, adding, "As Ari said earlier, there may be another reason God allowed us to survive. Our stories need to be kept alive to pass on so history won't forget this event."

"That's true, Zosha," Ari said. "We can't undo the past, and we can't forget it. Nor should we forget it. What we can do is tell the world what happened, ask why it happened, and importantly, why so many stood by and let it happen."

"You think that's why we survived?" Leah said. "I had stopped pondering this question, instead asking why I was unlucky enough to survive. What crime did I commit that made God make me live and carry this burden? But if I could find something meaningful through all of this, that would save my soul."

For the rest of the day and the next, both Leah and Zosha sunk into a deep silence. Not so much a despondent silence but one that was accompanied by thoughts and planning. In the quiet, Nela whispered to Rachel, "God doesn't have a plan for me or anybody else. As far as I can see, what we experience is like a play where we are the actors and God is the audience that watches from the distance intrigued by what will come next."

"Maybe so, which is all the more reason we can't sit back and let life happen," Rachel responded. "I don't want to be an actor in the play, I'd rather be the director who determines our fate."

Ari told Asher and Shimon that once the truck reached Frankfurt, they were let off at a camp that offered people a place to stay.

"Getting off the truck, the driver spoke to us smiling broadly. Of course, none of us understood what he said but knew he was being nice. We lined up to embrace and thank him for his kindness. We were then escorted by American officials to a common area where we were told through translators we could stay in a displaced person's camp or choose to find a way to a new life on our own. Some like Leah, who had nowhere to go, chose to remain in the camp. Others like Zosha wavered and chose to stay in the camp until she could find her bearings. A few of us opted to venture out without assistance rather than being restricted to a camp, even if it was very different from the concentration camps some of them had managed to survive."

It took Ari only a few hours to learn of a makeshift synagogue in Frankfurt. However, before he could head off in search of it, he ran into Zosha, who had decided to leave the camp after all, saying it brought back too many cruel memories. When she learned he was heading to Munich, she indicated he would be going in the wrong direction, as it was taking him deeper into Europe rather than to a port that could take him off the continent.

"I can assure you Germany and most of Europe will be a mess for years to come," she said. "Somehow, I'm going to get enough money to find a way out of Europe. Anywhere other than the country that murdered our people, or those that barred us from entering."

"I had similar thoughts," he responded, "but I'm intent on getting to Eretz Yisrael."

"That's good, too. But I'd rather go to the land of milk and honey, which now is America, although, in biblical times, Eretz Yisrael fit that description."

Ari thought for a moment before saying, "Will it be okay if I follow you? You're more knowledgeable than I am. So, even if we have different final destinations, we probably have common traveling ahead of us."

Through an organization that helped displaced persons, they were able to get a ride on a British lorry headed for Bremen, which was near Bremerhaven, where they hoped to get a ship that would take them to their desired destinations. When they reached the city, they searched out the Jewish Agency. Through the agency, they obtained temporary housing and were directed to another group that might be able to help them find employment while they waited for papers to allow them to emigrate, which they were warned could take considerable time.

As Zosha had an advanced degree in history, as well as a sponsor in the United States, she was able to obtain immigration papers relatively quickly, but even with her connection to the US efforts related to the Nuremberg trials, it might not occur for another year or more. Ari likewise discovered his plan of immigrating to Israel would be far more difficult than hers, and certainly more complex than he had expected. The British government had restricted immigrants to Israel to a paltry 18,000 people, essentially preventing most Jews from reaching their homeland.

Desperately, he pleaded with members of the Jewish Agency, imploring them to put him on a ship to the Holy Land. They would have happily done so, but there were few ships and many people ahead of him. With nothing else to do, he volunteered to work for the agency, at least until a spot on a ship came along. When not volunteering, he found odd jobs so he could purchase food and pay for his accommodations. He had been hoping something would materialize soon, but the longer he waited, the more desperate he became.

"Just as I was at the end of my tether, I was approached by a young man who greeted me with the word "*Shalom,*" to which I responded, "*Aleichem shalom* [Peace be upon you]."

The young man said, "I hear you wish to find your way to Eretz Yisrael."

Before Ari could reply, the young man said, "My name is Isaac, and I'm with Beriha. Follow behind me; stay back 20 meters." The man then abruptly walked away.

Ari had no idea what Beriha was but felt something good could emerge from this meeting, so he followed. After a few blocks, the young man entered what seemed like a grocery, and Ari did so a minute later. When Ari entered, Isaac was nowhere in sight. The middle-aged man behind the counter looked at a door at the end of the shop, and with the slightest nod, directed Ari toward it. He moved to the low door and pushed it open. Waiting for him inside the room were Isaac and two others. "*Shalom chaver* [hello, friend]," they said, and he smiled broadly at them.

The two men, both strong and agile, looked poised to react to anything unexpected. The taller of the two said, 'A mutual friend in the Jewish Agency whispered to us you wished to emigrate to Eretz Yisrael."

"Yes, very much," he replied. "Can you help me?"

"Absolutely, but I can't tell you when that will happen. It depends on which ships will be available and when. It could be this evening. It could be next month. You simply need to be ready to go without notice. If that's agreeable, we'll put you on the list."

"That's excellent. But given how many people want to go, why are you helping me? You can't possibly know anything about me."

"We know more than you think, believe me," the smaller man responded. "We've been expecting you. Some of your friends came through here some time ago. We sent them off to Greece and from there to Eretz Yisrael. They told us they believed you would be coming this way soon."

He wondered who could have transmitted this information. Was it possible Yehuda, Kali, or Dov, who had left him and Yankele months earlier, were the sources of the information?

No sooner had the thought entered Ari's head that the shorter man said, "I see it has dawned on you where we obtained our information. They, too, had been heading to Eretz Yisrael, but their ship was waylaid by the British navy, and the boys are presently being kept in Cyprus, although I'm certain we'll eventually have them reach their intended destination. Many organizations are doing what we are, but we've been relatively adept at not being caught. More importantly, for now, Eretz Yisrael needs the most talented people, and you certainly qualify."

The other man then interjected, "We should go now. We've been overly long already. The British are always on alert for potential attempts to enter Eretz Yisrael. You will likely not see us again in the coming days. Isaac will be your contact. He will bring you instructions when the time comes. Leave now the same way you came but stop at the counter on the way out."

Following these instructions, he was handed a cloth bag by the grocer, which turned out to contain a change of clothing and a few food items, which struck him as odd as he didn't need the small amount of food. Later that day, while emptying the bag, he discovered papers had already been created that would allow him to emigrate. The grocer whispered, "If you need to pass information to them and Isaac isn't around," motioning toward the back of the shop, "drop by here."

Three weeks to the day, Isaac came rushing into the Jewish Agency to tell Ari if he could be ready to leave immediately, there was a spot for him on a ship, working as one of the crew members. Without a second thought, he grabbed his prepared kit with clothing in it, hurried to the port, and boarded the ship, where he would serve as a dishwasher, waiter, and short-order cook as well as the kitchen janitorial staff. While not the most desired position, it would get him where he wanted.

Having this job meant he had ample food, and he could never get enough potatoes and bread, especially warm bread directly from the oven. The ship, which carried various types of produce, was manned by 22 men, plus two others who were being smuggled to the Holy Land. None of the three knew of the others, at least at first, but after only a few days, they were easy to identify as they were alone struggling with seasickness. After a voyage of several weeks, prolonged by having to take a roundabout route to avoid interception by British ships and multiple stops to drop off or take on cargo, they were transferred to a small fishing boat that took Ari and his two immigrant friends ashore at a tiny landing near the city of Haifa.

Copy of letter sent by Chana (Henia) and her sister Esther to Yad Vashem to nominate Franek Wincewich as a Righteous Gentile. They had previously supported Tekla and Michael (Michel) Stronsky. Franek and the Stronsky family had hidden Henia and her children in cellars through large parts of the war. The families remained close for years and Tekla's daughter stayed with Chana in Montreal for several months in 1967.

After the war and the death of her husband and children, Chana met and married Shimon. They had a son in 1948 whom they named Chaim, commemorating life. This picture was taken when Chaim was about six months of age, almost a year and a half before the family was able to emigrate to Canada.

Extended Stronsky family at a wedding in 1948. Chana and her two sons had stayed with Franek and Rozina Wincewich for 10 months early in the war. When neighbors became suspicious, Chana and the boys were moved to the home of Michael and Tekla Stronsky and their daughter Rozia. The boys, however, chose to live in the forest in the vicinity, while Chana stayed with the Stronksy's for most of the war. They stayed in touch for many years after Chana reached Canada, and nominated for recognition of the "Righteous among the Nations."

Rozia, the daughter of Michael and Tekla Stronsky, together with her husband and two children, still live in Poland, and are proud of the help they offered to Jews during the Holocaust.

Two generations of survivors celebrate the wedding of Chana's niece.

3
IS THIS THE PROMISED LAND?

War does not determine who is right — only who is left.
– Bertrand Russell

The land had been promised to the children of Abraham, Isaac, and Jacob, and the promise was reaffirmed when Moses led the tribes out of Egypt followed by 40 years of wandering before reaching their destination. Now, more than 30 centuries later, their descendants inhabited the tiniest sliver of their ancient homeland. But even with this smidgen of salvation, their destinies were controlled by the colonialist British, whom Asher viewed as the modern-day legions of Pharaoh. He could have lived with their presence, at least for the moment, awaiting the time that Israel would emerge as an independent country. However, it was infuriating that British interest in Arab oil led them to accommodate the demands of Arab states that were raising havoc to stop the immigration of Ashkenazi Jews from Europe.

The slow motion of the Allied governments in Europe resulted in 250,000 Jews remaining in displaced person camps, many of whom would have readily emigrated as Ari had. Still, attempts to smuggle Jews into the country continued – a perpetual cat-and-mouse game between the British soldiers and those facilitating the entry of Jews to the Promised Land. The British were successful in intercepting most ships carrying Jews to Eretz Yisrael, which only fomented greater resentment. Many organizations, such as the Irgun, Lehi, and the Stern Gang, which had formed years earlier, became formidable paramilitary groups intent on facilitating the entry of Jews to the region and, if necessary, using armed resistance.

The British were widely disliked by most Jews in Palestine. The British suspended normal legal procedures and instituted brutish measures for various infractions. Military courts took it upon themselves to hand down the death penalty simply for carrying weapons or being part of an organization that was deemed dangerous. Attacks undertaken by the Irgun on some occasions resulted in their fighters being captured and sentenced to death. When it became apparent clemency would not be obtained, the Irgun kidnapped British soldiers and threatened to hang them if the death penalty was not commuted. In the end, the fighters weren't executed and instead were given lengthy prison sentences.

Not every skirmish ended well. In response to the flogging of Irgun members, which was seen as degrading and humiliating, British soldiers were kidnapped and flogged. One evening, several Irgun members were arrested and executed. Two other fighters who had been scheduled for execution for other crimes successfully detonated a grenade smuggled to them just a few hours before they were to die by hanging. Enraged at the executions, Irgun members sought retribution, but British soldiers had wisely disappeared from the streets.

The situation deteriorated further when Irgun fighters engineered the escape of 28 Jews from the Acre Prison; during the panic instigated by the detonation of explosive devices, almost 200 Arab prisoners also escaped. Several Irgun fighters were killed, and those wounded were deprived of medical attention and subsequently died. Irgun members who had been captured were sentenced to death by the British military court. In response, Irgun fighters again kidnapped British soldiers, and once the captured Irgun fighters were executed, two British sergeants were hung and their bodies booby-trapped. Incensed, British soldiers and police rampaged through Tel Aviv, killing five and wounding several others.

Asher and Ari were among the many young men angry and frustrated with the British occupiers. They didn't want violence but, as Asher said, "I agree with much of what Irgun is saying and doing. The arrest of more than 3,000 Jews reminds me of SS tactics, which can't be left unanswered. This has been our land for millennia, and now our people are prevented from coming here and imprisoned when we defend ourselves."

"Very true, and since Irgun, Lehi, and Haganah have allied with one another, they may be well equipped to make strides forward," Ari said. "Our job, for now, is to protect the kibbutz; however, when the appropriate time comes, we can do more to help get rid of the British."

Asher and Ari, like several others on the kibbutz, were members of Palmach, a division within Haganah. The Palmach, established in 1942, was an elite fighting force, with members on kibbutzim across the region. The members received training each month, and in addition to their usual duties, served as guardians of the settlements. The Palmach was well respected given their earlier resistance to colonial British rule, which included freeing more than 200 Jewish prisoners from a prison in Atlit, the sinking of British patrol boats, and the sabotage of bridges and culverts needed by the British for rail traffic. Palmach also engaged in retaliatory raids against Arab groups that had killed Jews. Importantly, in preparation for broad Arab attacks, Palmach members received experience with numerous types of weapons, and there was considerable focus on training smart field commanders, which suited Ari well.

"Through the constant harassment, the British may become sufficiently miserable for them to pack and leave," Asher said hopefully.

"I don't see that happening soon; they've invested too heavily to do that," replied Ari. "Destroying a few bridges and railways might make us feel better, but it will be ineffective in making the British leave. It must be done in craftier ways than those that have been conducted. The British won't be convinced by us. They'll leave when the rest of the world turns against them."

"Yeah, but in the meantime, I'm intent on becoming more active in the Palmach efforts. I'm fed up just protecting our kibbutz. It's time we took firm action. My attitude has fallen more in line with the views of Avraham Stern [who led Lehi until his murder by the British]. He maintained the British should never be trusted, and I believe he was right."

"I don't disagree. But as I said, we need to operate strategically, not reflexively."

Asher knew Ari was right, but his discontent grew over the ensuing weeks. His intentions to become more actively involved in the struggle were cut short when the Irgun retaliated against the British arrests of Zionist leaders by bombing the King David Hotel, killing 91 British soldiers and wounding 46 others.

"Now that they know they can't get away with mass arrests, the British tune will change," Asher said.

"They may finally be weary of their losses, both in soldiers and treasure, but the British are stubborn and they're fighters, so leaving would be a loss of face. They'll continue to say they're trying to stop violence, not create it. As I've said before, they will ultimately leave, but only when the politics are right."

And they did. The issue was placed in the hands of the new United Nations, which voted in favor of creating independent states for the Arabs and the Jews, effective upon British withdrawal. Generally, the Jews supported the proposal, although it would leave them with a patchwork of areas making up the country. Still, it would allow them to control immigration. However, the surrounding Arab countries rejected the UN resolution and the Arab League proposed military action. Predictably, the conflict between Arabs and Jews escalated. The Haganah, supported by Irgun and Lehi, would be faced with the much larger Arab Liberation Army.

Shimon, Asher, and Ari sat quietly gazing at their campfire. After some time, Asher said, "Abba, I guess there will be a war soon. Are we doomed to a repeat of the war in Europe, only this time being targeted by several Arab armies, or can this be averted?"

His father put his weathered hand on Asher's knee and said, "There is already a war. It isn't a declared war, but that's what it is, and when the British leave and we exert our independence, the situation will become worse. It doesn't take a cipher to understand what ought to be obvious to anybody who looked. The Arab countries assume we're weak and can defeat us in war. I hope we will come through this with a homeland. As you know, there is rarely a good war, and I don't doubt there will be losses, many losses."

Reaching over and taking his tea, he continued, "At the moment there are so many things we don't know and hardly understand. The Arabs will certainly attack. What I'm unsure about is everything else. There are many Arab states in the region, but we don't know how they will behave. We need to take the view the worst-case scenario will confront us, and we must be ready. What we have learned from recent history – something our children and their children must always remember – is when your enemy promises to destroy you, to push you into the sea, take them at their word. We've learned sometimes people don't do the right things, simply because it's easier to do nothing than to do something. Now we must take the time available to prepare militarily. That means being able to obtain support from other countries. By this, I don't mean hollow support cheering us on from the sidelines but tangible support in the form of munitions."

"I suppose we won't get much help from the Americans, and if anything, the British will side against us and will provide the Arab armies with a large amount of equipment and munitions," Asher said. "The Soviets have claimed to support us, but only with words, although there are signs Czechoslovakia might be helpful. How can we possibly mount a defense against so many well-equipped Arab armies?"

"They have many armies, but the essential question is whether they're coordinated," Ari interjected, jabbing at the table with his forefinger. "Can they fight as a unified force? I sense they can't, especially as their leaders may well focus on their own interests. They not only distrust one another, but they also distrust the leaders of the Arab groups within this region. Some Arab leaders, such as King Abdullah of Transjordan, who controls the Arab legion, appear reluctant to enter a war with Israel, but I suspect in the end he will be coerced into doing so. With such disunion, they might be unable to establish an effective force. We can only hope my analysis is correct. That said, our leaders also seem to be continuously at odds with one another, although with so much at stake, their common cause might hold them together, at least until this is over."

Shimon was impressed by Ari's analysis. His time in the Polish forests had taught him well. Nothing went by him, and he understood that strategy, more than arms alone, would be a deciding factor in many battles.

On May 14, 1948, the day before the end of the British mandate in the region, Israel declared its independence. As predicted, the following day, the combined armies of Egypt, Syria, and Transjordan, along with forces from Iraq, Saudi Arabia, Sudan, Yemen, and Morocco, attacked Israel. The British sided with Arab countries and in some cases gave blatant support. In contrast, France, Czechoslovakia, and a few other countries provided munitions to the Israelis, but for the most part, the Israeli forces were on their own.

The sides initially had even numbers committed to battle, but the Arab states had greater reserves and far more munitions. There were half as many weapons as Israeli soldiers to carry them. Nonetheless, the Jews of Israel were determined to hold their ground at all costs.

Having learned not to rely on others for their defense, the Israelis had developed an arms manufacturing process, even salvaging parts of abandoned British tanks to create workable models. Through previously embedded agents in Europe, the Israeli forces were soon able to double and triple their cache of arms, including half-tracks, light tanks, mountain guns, and mortars. With assistance from France and especially Czechoslovakia, the semblance of an air force was formed. With the help of foreign volunteers, some of whom had experience from World War II, the nascent Israeli air force destroyed numerous planes flown by Arab forces, ultimately dominating the skies.

Initially, the situation in Galilee and the Negev was grim. The resistance by the Israelis in this region – which included Ari, Asher, and his father – was dogged, and the Syrians eventually captured some areas. Perhaps their early victories reinforced the Syrians' belief the Israelis did not have the temerity to fight. Thus, when they eventually encountered strong resistance, the Syrians simply chose to hunker down and rarely made further forward forays. When Israeli reinforcements and munitions arrived, the Syrian army was soundly defeated.

In other parts of Israel, the situation was far direr. Jerusalem was cut off entirely, with many Israeli casualties amid efforts to thwart the blockade. The Transjordanian forces captured Latrun, from which they could fire at Israeli units trying to travel to Jerusalem. After five failed attempts to capture Latrun, Palmach soldiers found a route to Jerusalem, creating an exceptionally treacherous road that allowed convoys to relieve the besieged city.

With perseverance, the Israeli soldiers were able to recapture a portion of Jerusalem, although the battle for the Old City as well as several villages previously occupied by Jews had to be abandoned. Jerusalem became a divided city, with Arabs living in the eastern portion and Jews in the west. The failure to take the Old City was a thorn that would fester until years later when Jews could again enter and pray at their holiest site, the Western Wall, which stood adjacent to the Dome of the Rock – built about 700 years later and among the holiest places of the Muslim religion. The Dome of the Rock was also considered a holy site for Jews as it was purportedly the place where Abraham was prepared to sacrifice his son Isaac to God.

In small increments, the newly minted old country, possibly the oldest remaining on Earth, was able to push the Arab invaders back. After ten months of fighting and the loss of 4,000 soldiers and half as many civilians, plus 5,000 wounded, the Israelis were victorious. Almost 700,000 Arab residents evacuated the area or were pushed out, although a substantial number remained. Over the ensuing years, 850,000 Jews were expelled from Arab countries and Iran, many of whom found their way to Israel. The displaced Palestinians were not so lucky. Arab nations were not keen to absorb them and instead kept them within refugee camps as political pawns, a practice that continued for several generations.

With the end of the War of Independence, Israel was able to focus on agriculture, education, and innovation as well as settling the many Jews who continued to stream into the country. The vibrancy was palpable everywhere, but few deluded themselves that this part of the world was a friendly one. The Israeli Defense Force (IDF) was established, and both Asher and Ari were among those groomed to become officers. Ari felt he was meant for it, whereas Asher had other aspirations. There were so many topics he yearned to explore, and the best way was through a university education. Nonetheless, he followed Ari's lead and continued in the military to train a new generation of soldiers who might be needed to protect the country. He reasoned once the country's needs were met, he would have the opportunity to pursue his passions.

Since the country was small, with only a few million people, the decision was made in 1949 that all Jews over the age of 18 would serve in the IDF. Males were required to serve for three years and females for two. The Druze population within Israel often served in the IDF as well, and Israeli Arabs could join if so inclined, although for a time they were assigned to separate units with lower security clearance. The ultraorthodox were reluctant to serve, maintaining their prayers were saving Israel. Even early in Israel's history, this thorny issue wasn't easily resolved.

With the formation of the defense forces, Asher thought the time was ripe to take his leave and obtain a medical education. He enrolled as a student at the Hebrew University, which had initially been built on Mount Scopus in 1925. But after the War of Independence, it was cut off from West Jerusalem. Temporary alternative sites were established in different parts of the city. It was less than ideal, but in a country where everything was a gift, students had no sense of entitlement.

Asher began medical training in makeshift lecture halls in the so-called Russian compound, and laboratory training was conducted in temporary quarters close to the Jordanian border. Having witnessed the psychological residue that afflicted so many survivors of the Holocaust as well as the War of Independence, he decided to specialize in psychiatry. At that time, effective treatment of psychiatric disorders was still far off, and the psychoanalytic school of thought predominated, reinforced by Sigmund Freud's influence.

During his training, Asher was called back into the IDF to serve in a medical capacity when war in the Sinai erupted in 1956. While working at the rear lines, he met Deborah, a medical student training in neurology. It wasn't long before they were together almost all the time, and they married in 1960. Their first child, Gabriella, was born in 1962, with a second, Zipporah, arriving three years later. Following a parallel course, Ari met Shoshana while she was serving her two-year stint in the army. They, too, were married, and over five years, they had three children. Both families moved to Kiryat Hayovel, a settlement in southwestern Jerusalem. Predictably, they lived next door to one another. Ari continued as a career soldier, whereas Asher completed his residency in psychiatry and obtained a position at a hospital in Jerusalem.

For several years, Israel seemed to be at peace with the Arab countries, although the region was often simmering over some event. Western countries and Russia were both intent on having the Middle East within their sphere of influence, especially considering the rich oil revenues that could be generated through several Arab countries. Occasional rumblings were heard, but it wasn't a daily occurrence. Thus, both Asher and Ari were able to live in peace and their families thrived.

Over the years, the situation within the region began to heat up, repeatedly threatening to boil over. In 1967, aggressive rumblings were again coming from Egypt, Syria, and Jordan, spurred by the vitriol of Egyptian President Gamal Abdel Nasser. Based on intelligence of a potential attack by combined Arab forces, the Israeli government and military decided not to wait to be attacked as they had in 1948. Instead, a preemptive strike was mounted that successfully eliminated almost the entire Egyptian air force. At the same time, tank forces defeated the Egyptians in the Sinai Desert, and within a few days, Israeli forces reached the Suez Canal, capturing Sharm El Sheikh at the southernmost point of the Sinai Peninsula. Ari was stationed behind with Major General Israel Tal, who commanded the operation. Ari did what was necessary, although he felt diminished by not being at the front with his boys, stomping about like an angry lion with a thorn in his paw. "What kind of officer leads from behind?" he asked anyone who would listen. "I need to be at the front to see what's happening there at any moment, not make decisions based on stale information."

Being deceived into thinking Egypt had beaten the Israeli air force, Syria and Jordan initiated an attack on Israel. Israeli jets quickly destroyed most of the Syrian air force, and within a few days captured the Golan Heights, which had been used to fire down at the Israelis below. When Jordan's King Hussein ordered his forces to retreat across the Jordan River, the Israelis captured the entire West Bank without opposition. In contrast, the battle for Jerusalem and the surrounding areas was bitter and intense. Eventually, they obtained the great prize, taking all of Jerusalem, including the Old City in which the Kotel – the Western Wall of the Second Temple – was situated, fulfilling the centuries-old dream of Jews worldwide.

Throughout the fighting, Asher was stationed at the hospital to treat large numbers of soldiers who experienced severe, incapacitating trauma-related psychological symptoms that constituted a syndrome then known as shellshock or battle fatigue. At one time, these symptoms were taken to reflect weakness or cowardice, but Asher strongly believed they were likely due to some sort of brain dysfunction. It would be a few years before the term posttraumatic stress disorder (PTSD) would commonly be used and more effective treatments sought. Given his belief that research could help in understanding and treating this devastating reaction to trauma, Asher was scrupulous in documenting his observations, anticipating one day they might be useful in predicting who might be prone so only particular soldiers would be assigned to certain jobs.

In working with these soldiers, Asher came to realize those who were most vulnerable had also experienced earlier trauma, especially if it occurred during childhood. It was as if the multiple traumas had cumulative or synergistic effects, putting them at elevated risk. That, of course, included children of Shoah survivors. In a manner he couldn't identify, in a subset of individuals, the trauma of parents was transmitted to their children. Would his children, as witnesses of gruesome wars, be among those most vulnerable to pathological outcomes? He wondered whether second-hand accounts of traumatic experiences, such as those recounted to offspring by trauma survivors, could somehow affect the predilection towards psychological disturbances. As interesting as the notion was, having so many patients occupying him made it impossible to pursue his research ideas.

He kept detailed records of which symptoms presented at different times and even took blood samples in hopes of being able to establish biological profiles that might provide clues about the effectiveness of different therapeutic strategies. Ironically, this would later, much later, be the approach used to determine treatment options, but Asher's notions predated the neurobiological revolution that would develop more than 30 years afterward. When pointed out to him in his retirement, he would say it was easy to do "because I wasn't hampered by having too much interfering knowledge."

Asher was convinced that, much like the soldiers with shellshock, his mother suffered from her time in Austria and their run to safety. The many stories she continued to hear from Holocaust survivors who came through their kibbutz may have reinforced her trauma, triggering flashbacks, anxiety, and reactivity to certain sounds and sights. His father confirmed none of the symptoms existed before they escaped from Austria, only emerging while they were in France.

Several days after the 1967 war, Ari appeared in Asher's ward to visit and comfort wounded soldiers, many of whom were from his battalion. Ari's unit had been in peril as they moved forward through the Sinai and he felt great responsibility for his soldiers.

As soon as he could, Ari joined Asher, who had been watching him move through the ward. "It's very busy here and you look exhausted," Ari said.

"I am. So many were injured, and all need to be treated immediately. I've been here all day, every day. It didn't help that the hospital came under fire from Jordanian mortar."

"Well, hopefully, the worst is over," Ari said.

"Not necessarily. I believe over the next few months, we'll start to see the psychological toll of the fighting, and many more soldiers will be coming in."

"I hope that won't happen. The psychological scars are often much more debilitating than the physical injuries," Ari said.

"I've already treated a few of your boys," Asher said. "They told me the casualties in your unit were heavy. I'll keep an eye on them."

"It's been hard," Ari said with a nod. "I'm answerable to the parents of those wounded or killed. I'll visit the parents, but it will be difficult – it's against logic or biology for parents to outlive their children."

"From what I've heard, our victory was decisive, but bittersweet given the cost has been terrifying," Asher said.

Resignedly, Ari said, "I'm sure you've heard all the hoo-ha from the media everywhere. They're kvelling over the speed with which we defeated the combined Arab forces. They make it sound as if it was a walk in the park. They're indicating we just rolled across the Sinai and the Egyptians ran, leaving their rifles and tanks and even their boots behind. There is some truth to that, but many Egyptian units fought very hard and in many places the resistance was fierce. There were many casualties on both sides. The battle for the Golan was also costly, and the fighting for Jerusalem was dear. We don't yet know the full toll. On both sides, the passion for revenge will brew and brew until another war breaks out."

"Ari, you're usually accurate in these matters. This time I hope you're wrong."

"I'm not. I'm definitely not," Ari said. "The Arab armies have been badly humiliated, which will only make matters worse. While many of us hope this will be the last war, it isn't likely. We'll keep fighting war after war, and each time the cost will be far too high. Today we're the darlings of the Western countries, but one day they'll turn on us. They like us well enough when we're down, the underdogs, but how dare we exert our strength. While our goal is to protect ourselves, eventually we'll be perceived as the bully on the block."

In considering events in the political arena, Ari was persistently pessimistic about the future. Whenever Asher pointed it out, Ari's response was, "I'm not a pessimist, I'm a realist."

"Ha!" Asher scoffed. "For you, reality is pessimism, or pessimism is your reality."

"So, after all the training you received in medical school and psychiatry, this is what you can conclude – that there's confusion as to whether I'm a pessimist or a realist. Is this written on my forehead, or can you peer into my brain to discern what my personality is like?"

"The alternative to you being a pessimist is I'm an optimist looking at the world through rose-tinted glasses," Asher said. "That said, it may be wishful thinking, but I hope some sort of agreement can be brokered between us and our Arab neighbors so this war will be the last."

Echoing Ari's opinion, Shimon forewarned him, "Taking East Jerusalem, including the Old City and the West Bank from Jordan, the Golan Heights from Syria, and the Sinai Desert from Egypt will serve as a festering wound for these countries. The humiliation they experienced was magnified tenfold by the speed and decisiveness of the Israeli victory. The Arabs are a proud people, and this will be a bone stuck in their collective throats. As much as I'm not keen to say this, don't count on a lasting peace. There is a possibility that at some time, however remote, good relations will develop among countries within the region, provided it's in our mutual interests."

Although overtures were made to establish better relations with the Arab countries, including some deep behind-the-scenes maneuvering, the primary players within the Arab union refused to take part. Their resolve was subsequently described as the three nos

– no peace, no recognition, and no negotiation with Israel. Thus, despite US efforts to have Israel return the Sinai to Egypt and the Golan Heights to Syria, Israel refused.

The cold war between Israel and its Arab neighbors went on for several years, with threats and counterthreats becoming the norm. With so much bluster and so many maneuvers by Arab forces near Israeli borders, the common view became that the behavior was primarily for show. Among those with better appraisals of the situation, there was no mistaking the intentions of the Arab countries. It wasn't a matter of whether another war would occur, but when. The Israeli military and government had received information weeks earlier that an attack was likely but didn't act on it. As a result, they were less prepared than they should have been.

When subsequent reliable information indicated an attack was imminent, several generals argued for preemptive strikes against Syria and Egypt, but the decision was against it. Such a tactic would have precluded Israel from obtaining munitions from the US, which was made clear by President Richard Nixon and Secretary of State Henry Kissinger. As Ari later said, "Politicians from outside of Israel, not tacticians within, called the shots, and we paid the price."

At 2:00 pm on October 6, 1973, taking advantage of Yom Kippur, the holiest day for Jews, the armies of Egypt and Syria attacked Israel, having been well supplied by the Soviet Union. The attacks were abetted by soldiers, munitions, and weaponry contributed by several other countries. Libya and Algeria provided jet fighters, Tunisia sent soldiers, Morocco contributed an infantry brigade, and Saudi Arabia provided soldiers as well as a light-armored battalion. Several other countries outside of the Arab sphere likewise involved themselves in the war. East Germany sent fighter jets, tanks, and assorted munitions, Pakistani pilots flew combat missions using Syrian planes, while North Korean pilots flew on behalf of Egypt.

The situation on the Syrian front had been perilous. The surface-to-air (SAM) missiles supplied by the Soviets were initially effective in shooting down Israeli planes, and it was only after considerable losses that the Israeli air force was able to adapt and find ways to evade them. Difficulties experienced by Israeli soldiers on the ground were even greater. Israeli forces had one-eighth as many tanks as the Syrians, and despite fighting ferociously, they were initially pushed back in several regions of the Golan, suffering severe losses. Many soldiers died in battle, and those captured were tortured and executed with their hands tied behind them. Once reserve forces arrived, the situation changed dramatically, especially when the air force entered the fray. The experienced and well-equipped Israeli pilots destroyed numerous Syrian jets in dogfights, and they successfully decimated tank battalions, as well as critical power plants, petroleum supplies, bridges, and main thoroughfares needed to maintain Soviet resupplies. Facing diminishing resistance, the IDF eventually came within 40 kilometers of Damascus before peace was brokered.

The concurrent assault by Egyptian forces was as frightening as that mustered by Syria. Unlike his predecessor, Nasser, who was full of bluster and not an effective strategist, Anwar Sadat was far cleverer in his preparations for the war. The initial attack was immensely successful – so much so that during the early days of the war, the odds of Israel's survival appeared slim and war leaders were in a panic. Within hours, Egyptian forces had overrun the chain of fortifications constructed on the eastern bank of the Suez Canal and made significant inroads into the Sinai Peninsula. Making the situation more dismal was Nixon's slowness in delivering weaponry to Israel, likely owing to concerns about a direct confrontation with the Soviet Union.

Despite the initial setbacks and Egyptian protection against the Israeli air force with SAMs, the Israelis were eventually able to dominate the air war. Using its impeccable training, the Israeli military was able to mobilize its army within a few days, and once munitions arrived from the US, the immediate threat to Israel's survival diminished, even though massive ammunition supplies continued from the Soviet Union to Egypt.

Despite the mounting losses, the IDF continued to push toward the Suez Canal. Having detected a gap between the Egyptian Second and Third Armies, and through deft military maneuvers, the Israeli army in the Sinai pushed back with tremendous force, creating a bridgehead that would facilitate the crossing of the canal.

Almost at every turn, the Egyptian high command was outsmarted and outplayed, even failing to grasp the enormity of the threat posed by the Israeli infiltration across the canal. When the situation became clearer, the Egyptian forces mounted counterattacks that were overcome, costing their armies many soldiers, tanks, and aircraft. Israeli tank divisions crossing into Egypt eliminated important segments of the opposing ground forces, while the air force destroyed SAM sites, convoys, and airfields with relative impunity. The effectiveness of the air force was enhanced by planes redeployed from the Syrian front. At the same time, the small Israeli navy soundly defeated the Arab navies despite the Arabs' larger ships, allowing for attacks on radar stations, a few SAM batteries, and oil facilities badly needed by the Egyptian forces.

Ferocious battles continued for days, with Egyptian soldiers often exhibiting courage and resolve, likely unaware of the widespread collapse of their front. Slowly at first, and then with mounting speed, the Egyptian Second and Third Armies were encircled. Fearing the armies' annihilation, which could increase the risk of an American and Soviet confrontation, the UN imposed a ceasefire, although skirmishes continued for weeks, causing severe losses on both sides.

Ari snorted derisively when he heard the statement that a peace agreement had been brokered. "Ridiculous!" he said. "A peace wasn't brokered. It was forced on us. I'm doubtful this peace would have come about if the Syrian and Egyptian armies were heading for Tel Aviv. Even in peacetime, they're closer to Tel Aviv and Jerusalem than we were in moving toward Damascus."

The 1973 war should have been a warning that the hostile attitudes toward Israel weren't likely to cease, but it provided momentum for a cold peace with Egypt and Jordan. Later, Israel would sign a peace agreement with Egypt and return the Sinai, although they were unsuccessful in creating a full framework for peace that included the West Bank and Gaza. As Ari predicted, Sadat paid for his initiative in making peace with Israel. Egypt was expelled from the Arab League, and the Egyptian Islamic Jihad, a group within his army, subsequently assassinated the courageous leader.

The Israeli celebration of victory over Egypt and Syria was subdued as the loss of life was too great to allow feelings of joy; relief was probably a better description of what Israelis felt. Technically, Israel won the war, but it came at a high price, including about 2,500 Israeli dead and three times as many wounded. They could take solace in what the cost of defeat would have been.

At the time, the memory of the Holocaust was still relatively fresh in the minds of Israelis. Just 28 years had passed since the end of the Second World War, and only 12 years since the public trial of Adolf Eichmann, who orchestrated much of the Final Solution to eliminate Jews, served as a stark reminder of the Nazi horrors. For many Israeli soldiers, the knowledge of these events, even if they hadn't directly experienced them, was sufficient to motivate them to protect their homeland. The stories of the Holocaust from parents, grandparents, or family friends were sufficient to create a form of memory, like horrid photographs embedded within brain circuits. For some, these reactions were strong enough to create considerable distress and might have served like earlier trauma that could dispose them to psychological disturbances. Asher described the reactions succinctly, saying, "As a group, the knowledge we share has produced a collective memory that has made us more vulnerable to some health disturbances. Yet this collective memory has reinforced the view that only we can protect one another. If we don't count on other nations, then we won't be disappointed by their failure to support us."

His older daughter, Gabriella, had been too young to serve during the Yom Kippur War, which he believed was a blessing. As she told him, "I was relieved by our victory, but I won't fool myself into thinking this will be a permanent peace. As my friends say, no matter how many wars we win, if we lose only once, it will mean the end of the Jewish homeland."

Asher repeatedly heard this statement from Ari. Was it a common theme among Israelis? He received a very telling response when he asked Gabriella.

"Abba, for young people like me, witnessing a war that led to so many deaths, including friends, our fear of a repeat of it has become second nature," she said. "Likewise, we understand terrorist attacks can happen anywhere – schools, buses, and restaurants. Because of our desire to live normal lives, our anxieties meld into the background. In some odd sort of way, we are aware, but not aware, of the uncertainties of our condition. I don't need to tell you walking on eggshells isn't a good way to live. So we do what we need to do."

Like other young women, when Gabi, as she was typically called, completed high school, she entered the IDF. Although many women received standard military training, there was no intention of having them serve within the front lines unless absolutely necessary. This wasn't a matter of sex bias, as women had previously served in combat roles. However, there was concern a woman captured by the enemy would be miserably mistreated. In line with this thinking, Gabi was assigned to a nascent computer division aligned with the IDF. She received extensive training in computer programming and obtained experience with standard large IBM computers as well as the new personal computers that evolved for home use. Through a highly sophisticated intelligence unit, her training extended into code-breaking, for which she seemed to have exceptional talent.

Gabi's career within the military flourished and she intended to take up medical epidemiology when her IDF service ended, but life got in the way in the form of a medical student, Gilad Elon. She met him during her second month at the university, and they would have been inseparable if not for the classes she took and his heavy load as a medical student. As it was, they rarely had the opportunity to spend time together. So they chose to marry, and not long afterward, Gabi gave birth to a healthy dark-haired son, whom they named Jacob but was usually called Jake. Like most parents, Gabi and Gilad were overjoyed, even if it meant a hiatus as far as Gabi's career was concerned, and Asher and Deborah took to grandparenting at every opportunity. Jake's comfort became the essence of Deborah's day-to-day functioning. She insisted on being called Bubbie, and Asher was called Zaide, which he didn't much like because it made him feel ancient.

For his part, although he was no longer an ardent Freudian, Asher maintained the view that the early years were particularly influential in casting the mold that would drive behavior and personality throughout life. Thus, he was intent on assuring Jake would gain maximal benefit from having his Bubbie and Zaide close by. Based on his clinical experience and emerging data from various laboratories, he was convinced that negative experiences, and possibly those that were positive, could in some manner be transmitted to their children and grandchildren. Assuring Jake's well-being could have beneficial intergenerational consequences that would be Asher's legacy.

As Jake reached kindergarten age, he continued to spend a great amount of time with his Bubbie and Zaide. Thus, Asher had the opportunity to provide his grandson with the lessons he had acquired and those he had learned from his father. He was an adept storyteller. Some stories dealt with history and its intersection with the wonders of science: the detective work that went into uncovering the sources of diseases and the development of various medicines. By converting the history of science into more palatable mystery stories, he was able to explain that scientific study was a difficult job, requiring systematic analyses and considerable perseverance, yet maintaining the excitement of discovery.

Jake took to these stories, but certain themes were his favorites, and Asher was repeatedly coerced into focusing on them. Any medical mystery story from Zaide would be fine, but those about unexpected cures for illnesses were the ones he liked most. He never tired of them and delighted in the element of surprise, not to mention that "any old scientist" could come out as the hero in a science tale. Regardless of the topic, Asher thought, everyone sides with the underdog.

One story Asher told him was about the accidental discovery of chlorpromazine by Laborit and Huguenard to treat schizophrenia. Jake had likewise been enthralled hearing about the first treatments of depression that came about through the observations of Selikoff and Robitzek, who had been treating tuberculosis but couldn't help but notice that administration of iproniazid resulted in the understandably dreary wards changing dramatically. Instead of the patients being sad and lethargic, their moods often improved. Stories focused on mental health disturbances interested Jake, but those about infectious diseases were his favorites.

"Jake, do you remember when we talked about medicines that are used to treat all sorts of infections caused by germs?" Asher asked.

When Jake nodded his head, Asher continued. "Well, I've heard a powerful drug that kills germs was discovered by accident," he said. "It seems a scientist named Alexander Fleming had failed to clean up properly before leaving the lab for a while. When he got back a few days later, he discovered lots of bacteria had grown within the lab dishes. That's what bacteria do when left alone – they multiply and form a group, a colony, which can be dangerous when it occurs inside people. He noticed, however, that in one of the dishes, the bacteria were contaminated by a fungus. The fascinating part was that the bacteria close to the fungus died, but bacteria further away did not. This observation puzzled him at first, but with some clever sleuthing, he was able to identify a substance secreted by the mold. It seems this so-called 'mold juice' didn't much like bacteria and destroyed those nearby. By isolating the mold juice, he and others were able to demonstrate that it could destroy many types of bacteria. Today, this substance is known as penicillin and is one of several agents known as antibiotics, which have saved millions of lives."

Jake seemed to tune out the last part of the story and instead said, "Zaide, do Abba and Eema know about Mr. Fleming's discovery?"

"Of course, they do. Why do you ask?" Asher said. He could see Jake's mind working out the permutations and he waited patiently for Jake to get to his point.

"I suppose it's because they always talk about cleanliness and stuff like that, but if Mr. Fleming had been less messy, then maybe that penicillin stuff would never have been discovered. Tell them that, Zaide."

Laughing at the evident ulterior motive, Asher replied, "Jake, that analysis you came up with might be correct, but even if Alexander Fleming hadn't been on the scene, penicillin or other antibiotics probably would eventually have been discovered. Although Fleming is usually credited for discovering antibiotics that came from mold, it would probably be more appropriate to say he rediscovered this. The treatment is in many ways a very old one. Infections had been treated using a mold for about 2,000 years, but nobody knew why or how it worked."

"That seems sort of weird, Zaide. If they knew about mold back then, how come it took so long before they discovered the reason for it to work?"

"That's an excellent question. I'd guess that at the time they didn't have ways of determining why mold had any beneficial effects. Besides, fighting diseases is rarely a one-person effort but reflects years of research by many scientists. For that matter, even though Fleming made his discovery back in the late 1920s, he could only take his work so far, and others had to step in to help. It wasn't until 22 years later, following intensive research by several scientists, that the drug was used in a human. Many more years passed before penicillin would be produced in sufficient quantities to treat bacterial infections that affected people everywhere."

"Zaide, if sick people feel better after they get the drug, I guess it doesn't matter how these drugs were discovered."

"That's true. But not all people who get a particular drug get better. This is one of the thorniest problems scientists face. By figuring out how illnesses develop, it may be possible to help more people."

"How come some drugs work in one person, but not in another?" Jake asked. "I bet you know how to get the drugs to work for everybody, don't you?"

"I have no idea why there are such differences between people. I suppose they differ in so many other ways, so why not in this regard as well? In my work, I have seen when bad things happen to people, many may become very sad. Most often they recover, especially when they have many good supportive friends. Some people, however, seem to be especially affected by bad events and have a very hard time recovering, and even when they begin to feel better, they often fall back and again feel very unhappy."

"Sometimes bad things happen that make me sad," Jake said. "When our cat Kayla died, I was very sad, and when I think about her it still makes me sad. Next to you and Bubbie, Kayla was my best friend and I miss her. Eema wanted to get me another cat to make me feel better. You know what, Zaide? I didn't miss having a cat. I missed having Kayla."

Putting his arms around Jake, whom he had put onto his lap, and feeling his sensitive grandson needed comfort, Asher said, "I wish I could help every sad person, and I wish I could determine in advance who will be helped by a particular therapy and who won't be. Right now, we just don't have ways of knowing this, but methods will be developed so we can eliminate problems in most people."

"It sounds like it will be hard to make sad people happy because doctors and scientists haven't figured out lots of things about the brain," Jake said bluntly.

"I agree, Jake," Asher said. "It's also true of other diseases you've heard of, such as cancer and heart disease. I think cures for most illnesses will eventually be found. Some will come about through breakthroughs in technology, like those your Eema is working on, while others will come from being lucky."

"I like these stories about drugs being invented by fluke. When I was visiting Abba at the hospital, I saw lots and lots of bottles of different drugs. I don't think all of them were invented by fluke. So, if some were invented in a not-by-fluke way, how did that happen?"

"That's an excellent question, Jake. As I've told you before, this is usually a lengthy process. First, scientists try to determine why certain illnesses occur. For example, is there a part of the brain that is messed up, or is the ability of the body to fight infections not working as it should? Once they think they know the answer, then drugs or other treatments are developed that fix the messed-up part of the body or brain."

"But Zadie," Jake interjected, "if they don't know for sure what's wrong with the person, couldn't the new drug cause bad things to happen?"

"That's true, and that's why doctors and scientists first try a drug in animals, like mice, and if it doesn't cause problems, then experiments are conducted in humans. Since it's never certain how people will react to the drug, only a few people are tested, and then if it isn't harmful, more patients are tested until the answers concerning safety and the drug's positive effects are clear."

"I get it, Zadie. But I don't like the part about using mice to test the drugs. I once found a mouse and her babies. They were very cute, and I wouldn't want them used for testing drugs."

"I know, Jake. I don't like it either. Right now, however, there aren't other ways of testing drugs. Maybe better methods will be available someday, but until then, that's all we have. Some people object to the use of animals for research, but we can discuss this further when you're a bit older."

He felt discomfort about putting Jake off. The question was fundamental to scientific inquiry, but Jake simply wasn't ready for such a complex discussion.

As Asher was thinking over the quandary, Jake asked a different question. "What about the people who are the first to get the drugs to see if they cause problems?" he asked. "Are they like mice that don't have a choice?"

This question hit Asher in the pit of his stomach, stirring memories of the horrendous experiments conducted by Nazis in the concentration camps. He struggled with how to respond.

"Well, Jake, often the people being tested are very sick, and the drugs are given in very small amounts to see if their health improves," Asher said. "It is risky, as the drug can have effects that cause people to become even sicker. In other cases, drug evaluation is undertaken on people who are paid to be tested. There are questions about whether this is the right thing to do, as these people may be desperate for money so they can feed themselves and others who are dependent on them, so it might not be right for scientists to use them in this way."

"That doesn't sound so good, I think," Jake said. "But, at least, nobody is forced to take the drugs. That's true, right, Zaide?"

Again struggling with how to respond, Asher finally answered, "Mostly that's true, although not always. Some very bad people have tested people without their permission or understanding."

When Jake, curious as ever, asked about it, Asher backed off, thinking the issue should wait until his grandson was older. Ruffling Jake's hair, Asher said, "If one day you become a scientist, Jake, I hope you'll be the one to discover new treatments, and you'll do this in ways that don't harm anyone."

Jake took such comments to heart, especially as his Bubbie repeatedly delivered the same message. Her focus was on the notion of the Jewish concept of *tikkun olam* – repairing the world. As she told Jake, "Tikkun olam is a very ancient concept, dating back to medieval times, and probably before that. It's a way of honoring God by taking action to improve society. Whether one believes in God is immaterial. The important point is people ought to behave kindly to one another. One simple act that saves a life, no matter how it comes about, could allow the birth of children and many grandchildren, and one of them might be instrumental in curing some forms of cancer, heart disease, diabetes, or those psychiatric diseases your Zaide has told you about. So, in a sense, this explains the Talmudic expression that 'in saving one life, it is as if that person has saved the whole world.'"

Jake's early life was, fortunately, free of existential wars for Israel. There were several substantial conflicts with Lebanon and perpetual clashes with Palestinians, but no wars threatening the country's existence. Still, the prevalent cautious optimism was always tempered by fear of what might occur, especially with constant, growing threats from Iran.

Upon completing high school, it was his time to enter the IDF, and like many others, he did it with the thought he might be called upon to defend Israel in the future. As Ari expected, Jake didn't intend to make the IDF his career – Asher's influence was just too strong. While still a high school student, Jake's interest in scientific discovery grew exponentially, but it was during his time in the IDF that it became a passion. In his spare time, he read voraciously on various topics related to medicine and was particularly taken by research concerning newly emerging diseases, many of which originated in parts of Africa and Asia.

Like many young Israelis, upon completing his army tour, he enjoyed a gap year before entering college. Some of his friends sought out Asian or South American destinations; others chose rugged adventures or relaxing holiday spots. Jake and two close friends, Toby and Shira, chose to go to Africa, each for different reasons. Jake wanted to explore emerging diseases and find out more about tropical ones and what factors were responsible for their emergence and persistence. Toby and Shira, who planned on studying archeology and genealogy, wanted to find out more about the fate of their ancestors by examining the migration of Jews across the world. While the early evolution of humans likely involved migration out of Africa, much later, Jews might have migrated into Africa.

Although Jake had a bit of training in biblical studies, it was through Shira he learned about a broader history of the Jews.

"As you're likely aware, Jews had been quarrelsome for millennia, and continue so today," Shira said. "At the time of their first temple, they were divided into the southern group, made up of the tribes of Judah and Benyamin and who referred to themselves as part of the Kingdom of Judah, and the Northern Kingdom that comprised the remaining tribes. About 700 years before the Common Era, members of the Northern Kingdom were exiled after an Assyrian invasion. Many were enslaved in Assyria, which consisted of what was to become northern Iraq and southeastern Turkey. Over time, the tribes dispersed broadly and their fate was often lost to history, so they frequently were described as the ten lost tribes."

Toby added: "Many Jews from the Kingdom of Judah have also been lost to history, although as a people, we survived. Following the Roman conquest of the Israelites, many Jews were taken to Rome and other European countries. Some assimilated and married into the existent cultures to the extent that their Jewish genes as well as their customs and traditions were diluted. In countries, such as Spain, where the diaspora had been significant, large and influential Jewish cultures took root. For a time, Christian and Muslim rulers of various areas valued the contribution and services of Jewish doctors, scholars, scientists, and traders, and their presence was welcomed. For all that, by the 13th century, the tide went out for these Sephardi Jews, and things became exponentially worse during the latter part of the 14th century due to the Archdeacon of Écija, Ferrand Martinez, who began an antisemitic campaign through his sermons.

"Riots ensued, synagogues were burned, and ultimately some Jews were forced to convert to Christianity. Others sought refuge in other countries. Those who converted were, in a sense, neither Jews nor Catholics, so these so-called Conversos were not fully accepted by either group. As bad as it had been in the preceding decades, things got worse. Queen Isabella and her lackey husband Ferdinand initiated the Spanish Inquisition in 1478. At its peak 14 years later, they ordered the expulsion of all Jews who refused to convert to Catholicism. Most of the remaining Jews and Conversos fled, ending up in Europe and South America. Ironically, by that time, many Converso genes had infiltrated Spanish nobility, and the migration likely led to their genes appearing in Latin American populations.

"So, Jewish genes may have dispersed worldwide, and many people of other groups carry these genes today. For all we know, some of them may even be antisemites."

"That's possibly correct, and more than a little ironic," Shira said, shrugging her shoulders dispiritedly. "Of the Conversos who reached South America, many continued with their original religious practices, often doing so in hiding. Over the generations, assimilation took its toll on their identity and religion. Still, the histories of some families could be traced, often because they maintained surnames, such as Perez, Espinoza, and Enriquez, that had been adopted by their Converso forebears. Some of these people wanted to learn of their roots, and some even wanted to convert to Judaism. Others did not, even changing their names to disidentify from their Jewish heritage."

"You'd be surprised at the wide migration of Jews," Toby added. "A few Jews migrated to China to escape from the pogroms in Russia. With the development of the Trans-Siberian Railroad, some Jews found their way to a small fishing village that later became the city of Harbin, which eventually had an overall population of about ten million. Because of various conflicts, the Jews of Harbin left to find other homes. Shanghai likewise had a sizable Jewish presence, amounting to about 20,000 people. Unlike other countries, China didn't block the immigration of Jews. Unfortunately, during the Second World War, the Japanese imprisoned Jews in a ghetto, and later the civil war in China and the 1949 Communist Revolution caused Jews to leave to find safer places."

Jake was astounded by this history. "I never even thought of Jews living in China," he said. "I suppose I shouldn't be surprised given we've migrated to so many other places."

"I presume you're unaware a modest number of people, fewer than 9,000, also immigrated to India," Toby said. "The Mizo, Kuki, and Chin peoples believed they were descendants of the tribe of Menashe and came to be referred to as Bnei Menashe, the children of Menashe. They shared customs with other Jews, including celebrating several festivals, and their birth and marriage ceremonies were likewise similar. Although DNA analyses didn't reveal Middle Eastern descent, there were indications of such roots among females diluted by centuries of intermarriage. Following some debate, the Bnei Menashe were accepted into the fold of the Jewish faith and a good number immigrated to Israel."

"If Jews could travel to distant places in Asia and Europe," Jake said, "then it's likely they also migrated to regions of Africa that were much closer. I don't mean just the Mizrachi Jews, who had been plentiful in Iraq, Syria, Yemen, and Iran, or those who lived in North African countries, including Egypt, Tunisia, Algeria, Morocco, and Libya. I'd surmise Jews might have migrated to more southern regions of Africa."

"That's well documented in some respects," Toby said. "The thousands of Ethiopians endangered due to political turmoil and were airlifted to Israel had identified as part of Beta Israel, who originated from the tribe of Dan. Genealogical and DNA analysis similarly revealed that members of the Yibir tribe that lived in Ethiopia, Somalia, Djibouti, and parts of Kenya might also have had Jewish roots. Moreover, many Bantu-speaking people – the Lemba – in the southern part of Africa maintained several Jewish customs and rituals. Among a fair number of men, DNA sequences on the male Y chromosome were similar to those found among Jews who were *kohens* – priests – who descended from Aaron, the brother of Moses."

The group didn't have a fixed itinerary, so they went along with Toby's wish to visit the Igbo people in Nigeria. The detour required many days of cramped, slow travel on old, patched-together buses that traveled through villages lacking most necessities. They found the recorded history of the Igbo people to be limited, although it was clear they had a rough go of it for a long time. A civil war in 1960 that began because the Igbo wanted independence from Nigeria resulted in the deaths of over a million people. Further persecution of the Igbos through 1966 left many more dead. There was the belief among a great number of the Igbo that they descended from Jews, and in recent decades, several thousand left Christianity and took on Jewish traditions. Many identified strongly with Judaism, and some even considered the 1960 civil war as their own Holocaust.

According to elders they met, the Igbo had links to ancient Israel. Gad, the seventh son of Jacob, had three sons, Eri, Arodi, and Areli, who migrated and settled in what is Nigeria. These prolific sons were said to be the fathers of clans that were instrumental in the formation of towns, some of which still exist, such as Owerri, Umuleri, Arochukwu, and Aguleri. Curiously, the religious authorities within Israel didn't accept the Igbo claim to Judaism despite the fervent desires of some members of the group.

Toby shared the perspective voiced by Jake and Shira. "I think it hadn't been possible to know whether there was any validity to their claim of Jewish heritage, and genetic data haven't supported their contention," Toby said. "It's been a perplexing issue that produced considerable debate, and even the genetic data have been questioned."

"That makes sense, yet this still puzzles me," Jake said. "I would have thought the identity they adopted, rather than their genes, should have been sufficient for the religious authorities. After all, people of other religions frequently convert to Judaism, so why exclude the Igbo?"

"As I indicated, for centuries we've been a querulous group," Shira responded. "We still are, especially between the religious authorities and the rest of us. It doesn't help when outsiders, such as the Messianic Jews, who hold Jesus as their savior, have inserted themselves into the debate to reject Igbo claims. Look who has the belief it's appropriate to decide which groups are Jews and which aren't! Go figure."

They had planned to travel to other countries, but their time was running short. Besides, the more they learned about some areas, the less inclined they were to visit. They were appalled by the brutal slavery and genocide that King Leopold II of Belgium unleashed within the Congo in the late 19th century. He was obsessed with obtaining the region's natural resources, to the extent whole villages were decimated if they didn't meet their rubber quota. The estimated deaths owing to vicious King Leopold's policies varied widely, but it was certain that millions had been killed.

"The atrocities that accompanied control over the Congo weren't unique occurrences," Jake said. "They were common among the darkened hearts of several colonial powers within Africa. I interviewed several elderly individuals whose families had emigrated from Namibia. The detailed descriptions they provided concerning their family's gruesome experiences were reminiscent of those encountered by Jews at the hands of the Nazis.

"At the turn of the 20th century, the region was a colony of Germany, and the indigenous Herero and Nama people encountered wholesale slaughter by German forces throughout a three-year period beginning in 1904. More than half the members of these groups were killed as part of the final solution aimed at them. Following a battle against the Indigenous warriors, thousands upon thousands of people who were not directly involved in the fighting were forced into the Omaheke Desert, where they died of starvation or thirst. Others were placed in *Konzentrationslager* [concentration camps] or taken away and placed in cages on the beach of Shark Island, where they experienced starvation and rape and were subjected to medical experiments. I later learned the head of the German colony, Heinrich Göring, was the father of Hermann Göring, who subsequently became one of the leaders of the Nazi movement. Moreover, the experiments conducted using Namibian people were conducted by Dr. Eugen Fischer, a professor who trained the infamous Josef Mengele, who took his studies seriously."

Toby, who had previously heard of these occurrences, said, "It strikes me these events seemed to be a training exercise for what was to come more than three decades later. The Germans colonizers saw Indigenous people as barbaric who neither cultivated nor built upon the land, and they were thus deserving of extermination. While the Namibians were being exterminated, the world stood by idly allowing this genocide to occur, much as they did when the Nazis did their best to eliminate Jews."

"Our experiences here have been surrealistic in so many ways," Jake said. "Not to diminish the impact of the brutal occupations and civil wars, diseases have taken a still greater toll. Before our trip, I knew that within Africa the greatest causes of death were HIV/AIDS, diarrheal diseases, and malaria. Influenza has also been deadlier in Africa than in the West, particularly among the elderly, and respiratory illnesses have been among the greatest causes of infant death. Being here, I've seen for myself many other preventable and treatable diseases have been endemic to various African countries. Several of these conditions, which come from various worms or other small creatures, have wreaked havoc. They cause schistosomiasis, African trypanosomiasis, leishmaniasis, hookworm, lymphatic filariasis, ascariasis, or onchocerciasis, as well as about a dozen other tropical diseases that affect more than a billion people every year. It's appalling that almost half the school-aged children in sub-Saharan Africa were infected in some way."

Agonized by this revelation, Shira said, "I can see why you feel as strongly as you do. Can these conditions be treated?"

"Some certainly can, often with minimal expense – nickels and dimes – but they're largely ignored. I suspect to a considerable extent, since this has been happening within the poorest parts of the poorest continent of the world, it's not a major concern for those in Western countries."

"It's probably naive on my part, but do you see things changing any time soon?" she asked.

"I suppose these and other emerging illnesses and new viruses and bacteria may only receive sufficient attention when they become a threat to Western countries. Zoonotic diseases – those transmitted from animals to humans – can mutate so they can be passed between humans. It's well known some viruses make this sort of jump, and experts in the field have been adamant some of the viruses can and will migrate to Western countries. Unfortunately, the generally lackadaisical attitude in the West has left governments woefully unprepared for a pandemic. Scientists who understand the dangers faced have repeatedly warned governments of the risks, but I get the impression they've been screaming into the ether. Government officials don't pay attention to such things, foolishly believing the West is insulated from far-off threats."

Resignedly, Toby said, "Viruses and bacteria aren't concerned about borders, are they?"

"And why hasn't the United Nations been more involved in dealing with these diseases?" Shira asked.

Jake replied, "They've made efforts, largely focusing on acute respiratory infections, HIV/AIDS, diarrhea, malaria, and tuberculosis, which are the greatest killers. However, they've been only moderately successful, and other diseases haven't received adequate attention. Poverty in some countries has been devastating, and in remote rural communities, access to the most basic health services as well as safe drinking water have been inaccessible. The UN and the World Health Organization need a better strategy to deal with these diseases."

Jake returned to Jerusalem disheartened by the problems he witnessed but excited at the prospect of entering the Hebrew University. Like others who had gone through IDF training, he entered college with considerable maturity and seriousness. The university, which was now at its original campus on Mount Scopus, had facilities for first-class research training on the development and treatment of diseases. Beyond these attractions, he simply liked the idea of health-related research. His passion was to reveal the secrets that nature seemed intent to keep hidden by conniving multiple ruses and feints to keep scientists dancing around the edges of discovery.

His trip to Africa ignited his interest in newly emerging illnesses, particularly zoonotic diseases. In addition to his courses in immunology, microbiology, parasitology, and virology, he focused on others related to global health since they would be relevant to the worldwide spread of viral and bacterial illnesses. His introduction to the topic of population health was interesting, especially as he had already witnessed some of the devastating outcomes that could emerge in the absence of effective policies. The misuse of nonrenewable resources, climate change, deforestation, and air and water pollution – it just didn't matter which factor was considered, it typically boiled down to the same thing. Abject poverty and overpopulation, so often accompanied by inadequate sanitation, poor nutrition, and a lack of health care, were at the root of many diseases. Given the limited resources to deal with many conditions, it was understandable they were referred to as neglected diseases, although he thought the carriers of the diseases, rather than the diseases themselves, were most neglected.

In his most pessimistic moments, Jake would talk to his Zaide. "I think the great equalizer will come in the form of an outside force like a powerful virus that creeps up stealthily and might only become apparent when it is too late for anything to be done," Jake said.

"Your concerns are consistent with the views of most virologists," Zaide replied. "It has often been said the greatest threat to the world's population will arrive in the form of a microbe – a bacteria or a virus humans wouldn't be prepared to handle. Hundreds of millions might die because of the invasion. This wouldn't be a war like your Uncle Ari had fought. The enemy would largely be invisible, massively powerful, cunning, duplicitous, and indiscriminate in its killing, although the most vulnerable, the elderly, the very young, and those with certain preconditions would most readily be victimized."

"It seems nobody is listening to them except for other virologists. People have forgotten the 1918 influenza pandemic and assume smallpox and bubonic plague are ancient diseases that no longer affect us. Today, with air travel being so common, a person carrying a novel virus could infect a planeload of people, many of whom would be traveling to different endpoints, and along the way, they could infect many others. Diseases like HIV/AIDS, as wicked as they might be, wouldn't hold a candle to a new virus that could be transmitted through the air."

His years at the university were gratifying, and based on his grades and varied experiences, he believed he would readily be accepted to one of Israel's medical schools. It certainly would be a safe route to a comfortable life. However, he couldn't see himself assessing patient after patient every day. Instead, to his Bubbie's regret and Zadie's surprise, he chose to enter a graduate program in immunology and virology.

It was largely felt that doing undergraduate and graduate training at a single university would leave an individual myopic. Consequently, he had intended to do his graduate work elsewhere. Yet, the best program on the topics in which he was interested was at Hebrew University, so he decided to stay put. He had the passion for research and the resolve necessary to carry him through the ensuing years, although he harbored uncertainties as to whether he could do anything significant in the field.

His graduate supervisor, Professor Isaac Dov, who had an enormous reputation in the field, sat behind his desk, which partially hid a small paunch.

"So, you're young Jake," he said, reaching out for his coffee with a strong, weathered hand that spoke of a life that hadn't always been behind a desk or in a classroom. "I've heard about you from some of your professors and looked forward to meeting you. Before we talk about what you'd like to do, tell me, how's your grandfather?"

"You know my Zaide?" Jake asked, pleasantly surprised.

"Of course, I know him. We're in Israel. In a small place like this, everybody knows everybody. I first met him during my time working in the Immunology Department at Ein Kerem Hospital. He was considered a wonderful psychiatrist who helped many wounded soldiers in '67 and '73. Tell him I send regards. Maybe we can share a glass of tea soon, and tell him to bring Ari, his 'twin' along."

"I'll do that. I'm sure they would welcome the reunion."

"We'll talk more about such things later. More important for now, Jake, is that you tell me what you want to do in your graduate studies. What's the endpoint you want to reach, and if you get that far, how meaningful do you believe your findings will be?"

Too many serious questions were coming at him too quickly. Nonetheless, Jake gave it a try. "My ideas are still vague, but for the moment my preference is to research emerging diseases," he said. "At the same time, I hope the benefits gained from our research might have translational implications to enhance the well-being of vulnerable populations."

"That's a good perspective, and I wouldn't make any effort to dissuade you, although your intentions may be overly ambitious," Professor Dov said. "My experience has been sometimes we have an enormous appetite, but without the proper utensils, we might never have the opportunity to grow or prepare the food needed to sate our appetites, not even to boil a measly potato. We'll start by training you so you'll have the needed utensils and know how to use them. Of course, there will be the risk that, once you get all the utensils, your great appetite may encourage you to gorge yourself, and aside from getting an upset stomach, you might miss the subtle taste of the food."

"I get it," Jake responded. "For now I'll sate myself with the appetizers rather than sitting down for the main course."

"Excellent. My assistant, Dina, will take you to the lab, and you can set yourself up there, and when you're ready she'll teach you some of the basic procedures. Once you're comfortable, we can meet as often as you like."

Dina, a little over 1.6 meters, with long brown wavy hair and a sprinkling of brown freckles, introduced him to the various techniques he needed to learn. Dina was a good teacher, just as Jake was a good student, and it wasn't long before he could delve into the analysis of viral and bacterial factors relevant to the emergence and spread of diseases. With her help, he came to appreciate the complexity of the challenges in assessing the pathogens with which he would be dealing. He liked the idea of a basic science approach that involved analyses of the characteristics of bacteria and viruses that allowed them to multiply and how they avoided detection.

This game of wits with pathogens was intellectually challenging, With a lot of lucky breaks, which wasn't likely, he might be able to contribute to the development of treatments. The time needed to satisfy these interests, unfortunately, competed with the time he wanted to devote to analyses of newly emergent zoonotic diseases, which would inevitably appear and could have monumental global consequences. Based on Professor Dov's teaching, he believed strategies to deal with illness were consistently based on what was happening currently and not on what might happen in the future. Thus, he attempted to determine whether mutations in viruses occurred on a wholly random basis or were DNA viral sites more prone to mutations that could be relevant to zoonotic diseases, morphing so human-to-human transmission would be more likely to occur.

Within a short time, Jake and Dina became close friends, often sharing their life stories. Her family had come to Eretz Yisrael a decade before Jake's family, having escaped the pogroms in Russia. Her grandfather had been a fighter in the Palmach, although he rarely spoke of those experiences.

"I wanted to write a memoir of his experiences, but he was

resolute in not visiting the past," Dina said. "He would tell me to look to the future and not visit the turbulence of the past. His admonitions did little as my primary focus before working as a technologist was in medical history and anthropology. I hold a master's degree in medical anthropology, and once I have enough money saved, I hope to go back for a Ph.D."

"I know only a bit about medical anthropology," Jake said. "Where do you think your studies will eventually take you?"

"I'm not certain at the moment. However, I suspect it won't be far from your interests concerning the biological, social, and cultural factors that dictate the occurrence of varied illnesses. It's even possible the diversity of approaches to deal with prevention and treatment of illnesses may lead to new, better strategies, to deal with varied diseases."

"How would medical history and anthropology help determine the development of new therapeutic strategies?" Jake asked.

"The anthropology component is fairly obvious," she replied, her enthusiasm apparent through her animated gestures. "Many diseases are shaped by historical and cultural factors, and that includes various lifestyles endorsed. The medical history part is fascinating to study as well. Besides, it could also have implications for current approaches to developing assorted illness remedies.

"That sounds cool. Are there specific aspects of medical history that are especially interesting to you?"

"Mostly, I've been intrigued by the persistence of epidemics and pandemics that were common for millennia and how they came to influence later discoveries to prevent contagious diseases."

"And approaches adopted centuries earlier were relevant to subsequent effective prevention strategies?"

"You bet they were," Dina said. "Did you know, for example, that although Edward Jenner was credited with the development of the vaccine that saved the world from repeated smallpox epidemics, a rudimentary form of vaccination for this disease had been around for hundreds of years before his seminal discovery?"

Recalling that the development of penicillin also had its precursors centuries earlier, Jake said, "Was the treatment in widespread use, or are you referring to something that an isolated philosopher-scientist wrote in an obscure text?"

"Hardly," she replied. "As you're certainly aware, smallpox had been around for thousands of years, probably originating in India before it appeared in China around the sixth century. It didn't take very long for people to realize individuals who had survived a bout of smallpox never developed it a second time, which led people to make efforts to purposefully prevent infection."

"How did they do this without people becoming seriously ill?"

"The procedure likely originated in India or China, and within a few centuries, it was adopted in numerous other countries, including in Europe and subsequently North America, where semiformal studies were conducted by Reverend Cotton Mather and Dr. Zabdiel Boylston. It was done by administering pustular fluid – essentially pus or dried scabs taken from a person with smallpox – to a recipient who developed a mild form of the disease, which protected them from subsequently developing full-blown smallpox.

"This variolation procedure, as it came to be called, occasionally resulted in people dying, but the frequency was much lower than that produced by naturally occurring smallpox. Unfortunately, individuals who had undergone variolation and experienced a mild case of the illness were allowed to wander about within the general population, infecting others willy-nilly. At the time, not enough was understood about the illness and its spread, leading to unexpected negative consequences."

"So, the accumulated knowledge set the stage for Jenner to develop a smallpox vaccine!" Jake said.

"That, together with an understanding of the relationship between cowpox and smallpox. Like other people, Jenner became aware milkmaids who had been exposed to cowpox, a disease like smallpox that developed in cows, didn't develop smallpox itself. In essence, being exposed to cowpox acted as a vaccine against smallpox. Jenner put the pieces together and, instead of using variolation that involved smallpox administration, he administered cowpox to immunize a child against subsequently administered smallpox. It was much later, almost a century, before Louis Pasteur began using vaccines to prevent illnesses more broadly."

"It's remarkable Jenner and others tested the efficacy of cowpox by exposing kids to potentially lethal smallpox. That would never get by an ethics review board today."

"Oh, don't be naive," Dina chided. "The use of drugs on people to determine their efficacy and side effects is still being done, often in developing nations, including some in Africa. In some cases, appropriate consent wasn't received from participants, and it's known in several cases these agents caused deaths that were not reported. Think of this, Jake, when you're informed about the side effects of drugs, you can be fairly certain some of them were first noted in test subjects in these countries. There's more I should mention that is still more outrageous. When a drug trial ends, the pharmaceutical firm packs and leaves. The participants who had benefited from the therapy are left without anything since the drugs often need to be taken for their lifetime."

"Some time ago, my Zadie intimated such things had occurred," Jake said. "I would have thought that other than the Nazis, nobody would have done so in modern times. No doubt, the greatest beneficiaries of these questionable experiments are patients in Western countries, while those within developing countries may or may not gain."

"That's about the size of it," Dina said. "Oh, Jake. I can see your mind churning. You think you can do something to remedy this, don't you?" She didn't wait for an answer. "I don't mean to be a Debbie Downer, but I can't say I share this optimism. The problems are too great, and it will take large organizations, like the UN or the World Health Organization, to make concerted efforts for meaningful changes to occur. It doesn't seem to be high on their list of priorities."

As Jake's work progressed, he became increasingly excited by an area of study that seemed to be evolving concerning the role of microbiota, the trillions of bacteria that reside in the gut and other parts of the body, in working against or in favor of certain illnesses. Some bacteria could be harmful, but many others lived in harmony with their human hosts. Essential to well-being was the existence of a sufficiently diverse population of bacteria, in great abundance, and with an appropriate balance between good and potentially harmful types. The foods people ate, the medicines they consumed, or the stresses they experienced could affect gut bacteria that affect immune functioning, thus having profound effects on health. Increasingly, data had emerged that changes in beneficial bacteria could have lifelong repercussions, including vulnerability to psychological and physical diseases. These data led him to consider whether microbiota alterations might have a particularly significant bearing on the health of disadvantaged populations and could perhaps diminish the high incidence of infant mortality within Africa.

The decision to pursue this topic proved wise, and it wasn't long before he was conducting research showing, as others had before him, that while some bacterial colonies in the gut had negative effects, many others had positive ones. Moreover, his research pointed to the possibility that microbial changes in the gut, including those brought about by stressful experiences, could affect immune-related disorders. This finding was a necessary first step in the development of suitable targets and treatments that could attenuate or even reverse some disease processes.

"It's odd how things work out," he told Dina. "While thinking about the work I've recently been conducting, I found my thinking coming full circle to my experiences in Africa. If chronic stressful experiences and certain nutrients could affect gut bacteria and, hence, later well-being in rodents, similarly profound effects might occur in humans."

"That sounds reasonable, Jake, but I have the sense you're thinking a couple of steps beyond this."

"You're right. I've been thinking that stressful experiences or malnutrition that occurred in one generation could somehow be transmitted to the next and the next. A hot new research idea in recent years is transmission could occur through changes in gene function without actual changes in the genome. If such so-called epigenetic changes can be transmitted from parent to child, and then on to their children, vulnerability to illnesses might similarly stem from events experienced by our recent ancestors."

"Including the experiences of your parents and grandparents, as well as mine," Dina said.

During his last year in the doctoral program, Asher received a visit from Toby and Shira, who would occasionally drop by. They were more animated than usual, apparently excited by an unexpected turn in their research. He was happy to celebrate with them, accompanied by Dina, whom they had met during earlier visits.

"Okay, share your exciting news!" Asher said.

"This goes back to our visit to Africa years ago when we first considered the migration of Israelites to various parts of the world," Toby said.

"After we returned home," Shira said, "I began to look into archeological findings relevant to the early migration of Jews to Europe and other Western countries. I was especially focused on pinpointing when today's Ashkenazi Jews first settled in Europe. At the same time, Toby was hunting for DNA evidence that could shed light on this."

"On our own, we wouldn't have been able to get very far," Toby said. "Fortunately, we were able to join up with others who had been on a similar hunt. Archeological evidence had already indicated that during the fourth century CE, a Jewish community had existed in a region of Germany, that of present-day Cologne. Similar findings indicated that by the tenth century, Ashkenazi culture had also flourished in pockets within Germany, namely Worms, Mainz, and Speyer. Curiously, the history of the Jews in the region between those periods has been unclear."

Shira then took over the story. "We're still minor contributors to this, but it's exciting," she said. "It turns out that during the last days of the medieval period, Jews prospered in the nearby town of Erfurt. Unfortunately for them, in 1349, townspeople who owed the Jews money instigated a pogrom so they could escape their debts. The culprits were severely punished, which eventually led to Jews returning to the region, where they again prospered. Then, the situation again became perilous for the Jewish population of Erfurt. Precisely 100 years after the pogrom, the Jews were kicked out of the town. Jewish sites were destroyed and a granary was constructed over the cemetery where Jews had previously been buried. Even the burial stones were taken for the construction of walls."

"The same practice the Nazis used in constructing roads," Dina noted.

"Indeed," Shira said. "But a few years back, archaeologists began digging at the site of the granary and found 60 skeletons, and when possible, DNA analyses were performed using teeth that had been dislodged from the bodies. They found that sections of the genome, including the presence of many mutations, closely mapped onto those of Ashkenazi Jews who are currently alive and living throughout Europe and North America."

Surprised, Dina asked, "Are you saying today's Ashkenazi Jews, perhaps worldwide, can be traced back to the people of Erfurt? My family who escaped the pogroms in Russia decades ago, and Asher's family who escaped Austria before the Holocaust, both came from the same small gene pool dating back to the 1400s?"

"Perhaps not all Ashkenazi Jews, but it is estimated two-thirds of the millions of Ashkenazi Jews alive today are descendants of that small number of Erfurt Jews," Shira said.

"I know it sounds unrealistic," Toby said. "Yet that's where the evidence points. A couple of hundred Erfurt people who survived blatant antisemitic attacks by townspeople were the first of what is referred to as a bottleneck that occurred six centuries ago. The ongoing pogroms may have reduced the size of the population so the assortment of genes present was drastically reduced, thereby limiting further diversity. With continued breeding, these particular genes may have remained within the gene pool irrespective of where Jews emigrated over successive generations."

"A bottleneck!" an intrigued Asher said. "That just doesn't mesh with the science. The limited genetic diversity stemming from the bottleneck ought to have resulted in their offspring being less able to deal with challenges. That would have undermined the population's well-being."

"Perhaps it could have such an effect – unless, of course, the initial core group, those 200 individuals who survived the pogrom, were especially resilient and carried just the right mix of genes so their offspring inherited ideal characteristics to enhance survival," Shira replied.

"At the same time, they might have inherited several mutations that made them vulnerable to specific diseases, such as some forms of breast cancer, Tay-Sachs disease, celiac disease, and Crohn's disease, which are relatively frequent among Ashkenazi Jews," Dina added.

"And who was the group of 200 that formed the basis for future generations?" Asher asked.

"That's hard to know, but there is reason to suspect most descended from a small number of women who had been in the region 500 to 1000 years earlier, essentially around the fourth century, which jibes with archeological data," Shira said. "Of course, some of the core population might also have come from other parts of Europe, perhaps a small family or group that had migrated to the area sometime after the first group arrived."

Seeing Dina had become pensive, Shira turned to her. "What's up, Dina? We've been discussing a topic that's right in your field of interest, and then you suddenly become very quiet and thoughtful."

"Yeah, the discussion has made me realize how much I miss doing my own research. Professor Dov has been encouraging me to go back to graduate school. Maybe it's time. By next year Asher will be done, and that would be a good time for me to move on as well."

"Terrific," replied Shira smiling broadly, "there will be a spot waiting for you in our group."

As satisfying as his research had been, with his desire to pursue ideas about intergenerational effects of stressful experiences having grown,

Jake had come to the end of his doctoral research. His thoughts turned to the uncertainties about his future. His training was suitable for employment within the pharmaceutical industry, but he wasn't interested in pursuing that path. He wanted a position at a university, conducting the research on which he wished to focus. To attain this goal, he needed to conduct postdoctoral research that could provide him with broader research experiences, preferably in the lab of a notable scientist who was conducting cutting-edge research.

There were many excellent scientists in Israel with whom he could conduct postdoctoral work, but one researcher outside of Israel could offer him what he needed most. Through Professor Dov, he managed to land a postdoc position in the prestigious lab of Professor Max Sokolov in Montreal.

Jake told Dina he was sad leaving Israel, especially as his family was there, as was his heart.

She replied, with a tinge of sadness at his departure, "You'll end up doing great things. Even if you don't save the world, I'm confident you'll help lots of people, which would make your Bubbie happy. So, go and make us all proud."

4

ZOSHA: THE RECKONING

> ... Tyranny does not result from blind conformity to rules and roles, it is a creative act of followership that flows from identification with authorities who represent vicious acts as virtuous. ... Just following orders... may have been the defense they relied upon when seeking to minimize their culpability, but evidence suggests functionaries like Eichmann had a very good understanding of what they were doing and took pride in the energy and application they brought to their work.
>
> – Alex Haslam and Steve Reicher, 2012

She had received preferential treatment because of her background as a historian who worked briefly with the Americans. She had believed that perhaps she was simply a lucky person who, by the dint of circumstances, received a visa to immigrate to the US much sooner than most others, although being incarcerated in concentration camps for years certainly wasn't the hallmark of a lucky person.

Like so many immigrants, she arrived at Ellis Island in 1946 carrying a single valise and few plans for what she would do with herself. Being in New York was a startling change from what she had experienced in Germany. Instead of destroyed buildings, she saw remarkably large and artfully designed ones. Shops were filled with assorted items and food products unlike those she had seen in Europe. She rarely saw people with shattered lives. Instead, the streets were filled with seemingly happy people. The postwar period was filled with enthusiasm, hope, and celebration. The US had become the premier nation of the world and New York was its epicenter.

Awed by her surroundings and the din around her, Zosha wandered about, hardly aware of the time passing, and ignored her growing fatigue. Fortunately, she was able to find a room in a small hotel at a price she assumed was reasonable. After a night of sleep, she was ready to embark on a new life, determined to overcome any challenges she might encounter. Following the pattern that was effective when she first reached Germany, she went to a nearby synagogue and, after the morning services, she approached the rabbi, hoping he could help her in some way.

They went to his office and, speaking in Czech, the language of his parents, he phoned several people. Finally, he turned to say, "I have found an inexpensive room for you in the home of one of our congregants. We also have a fund meant for Jews who are destitute, and I can arrange for funds to be transferred to you."

"That's very kind, Rabbi, but I have savings from my position as an interpreter in Bremen," Zosha said. "The money saved by the synagogue ought to be provided to a person in greater need."

"You were an interpreter?" the rabbi asked. "How did you acquire these skills?"

"Mostly, it came from being involved with people from diverse countries and cultures, and as a history professor, I needed the ability to examine historical tracts that appeared in various languages."

Her response resulted in the rabbi becoming more animated. He quickly phoned a friend at Yeshiva University in New York. He arranged an appointment for Zosha to meet with Rabbi Noah Davidson, a lecturer who also served as chief administrator as well as liaison to the broader community.

Zosha met Rabbi Davidson at his office, where she introduced herself in Polish, which was the primary language she had spoken in the camps during the past years.

The rabbi was able to recognize what language she spoke, but that was it. He pursed his lips, shook his head, and said, "No *Polski*. Do you speak English?"

She shrugged her shoulders and said, "*Ukrayins'ka, Russki, Deutsch, Československý, français.*"

Smiling, he again shook his head and with a questioning look asked, "Yiddish?"

She laughed and said, "*Zicher* [of course]." Then, using their common language, she said, "Over the past year I've earned a living as a multilingual translator, so I fell into the habit of using the most common European language in whatever place I had been. I should have known better as Yiddish is the common language of the Jewish diaspora."

They sat comfortably in his office for about 20 minutes while she briefly described her recent history, to which he listened attentively without interruption. When she seemed to have completed her story, he stood and began to pace. After a few moments, he apologized profusely, saying, "I need to do something very important. Be comfortable here, and I'll be back very soon. Ten or fifteen minutes."

To pass the time in his absence, she began looking through the new and very old books that were neatly arranged on shelves on two walls of the office. There were different prayer books, a complete set of the many volumes that comprised the Talmud, as well as Talmudic commentaries. There was also an assortment of other books in English, Yiddish, Hebrew, and Aramaic covering diverse topics such as mathematics, history, and ethics. As she leafed through one book after another, she came across a few with which she was familiar. They brought back memories of her life before the war. Speaking to the books, she said, "Oh my dear friends, how I've missed you." Her eyes misted over as she clutched one to her chest. "I never dreamed I would hold such beautiful books ever again."

As she said these words, Rabbi Davidson reappeared, followed by two elderly, bearded men, who half-nodded, half-bowed in her direction, expressing their pleasure in meeting her. At Rabbi Davidson's invitation, they seated themselves while he approached Zosha. Gently putting his hand on her shoulder, he said, "I see how precious these books are to you. Please keep this book and any others you feel passionate about."

Once she recovered her composure over his generosity, he continued, "I very briefly told my friends, who are learned rabbis and scholars, about our earlier discussion, and they wished to meet you and pay their respects. If you feel up to it – and please forgive me if it's an imposition – would you be willing to share your story with them?"

She nodded. "Most certainly, but you know my history is not unique. You've probably already heard many stories of anguish and pain from survivors."

Rabbi Davidson said, "This is true. Your history isn't altogether unique, but you are."

"You're so kind. Thank you," Zosha replied, embarrassed by his praise. She then turned to the rabbis and began her story:

"I was born in Czechoslovakia before it declared its independence from the Austro-Hungarian Empire toward the end of the First World War. Jewish inhabitants of the region could be traced back about 1,000 years, and while antisemitism reared up occasionally, as it did throughout Europe, over many centuries Jews were fully emancipated, being allowed to own businesses and land. After Czechoslovakia gained its independence, Jews became more influential, even holding seats in parliament. Like so many other Jews who had lived in the countryside or small villages, my family moved to Prague. By the late 1930s, about 35,000 Jews lived there and prospered in peace and relative security. Together with other Jews my age, I attended university, where I focused on history, eventually obtaining a doctorate, specializing in the lives of Jews who existed in different regions of the country during the golden period of the 16th century. My work was well received, and I was fortunate in obtaining a position at Charles University, but this was only for a short time owing to the increasing influence of the German National Socialist Party."

After a brief pause to collect her thoughts, she continued. "Antisemitism had increased over the preceding few years, encouraged by the populist Slovak People's Party, which was led by a priest, Jozef Tiso. With the tacit approval of the United Kingdom and France in their futile attempts to appease Hitler, Germany occupied the Sudetenland, the border region of Czechoslovakia. One can't appease the wild beast with morsels; having had a taste, it comes back to eat the whole carcass.

"As the Nazi influence gained a stronger foothold, and parts of the country became a client state of the Nazi party in Germany, the persecution of the Jews became more intense. It didn't take very long before the Nazis began rounding up Jews with the help of their local collaborators. Along with other Jews, I was sent to the Theresienstadt concentration camp, which was used as a decoy, a stage, to convince international authorities, including the Red Cross, that Jews were being treated humanely. The camp was populated by talented Jews, musicians, writers, artists, and scholars. It was relatively civilized as far as prisons go, and I was able to engage in discussions with excellent scholars on a variety of topics, including whether bad people could be good at their craft, even if it seemed counterintuitive."

"I'm sorry to interrupt," Rabbi Davidson said. "This is a topic that has interested me for some time. Did the collective wisdom of your colleagues lead to any conclusions?"

"There were as many conclusions as there were participants in the discussion," she laughed. "I still ask myself how was it possible that literary figures such as T.S. Eliot, who wrote the most compelling poetry, Richard Wagner, who composed numerous remarkable pieces of music, or Edgar Degas, who painted so beautifully, could be ardent antisemites? Poets like Ezra Pound could perhaps be tolerated for their antisemitic views given he was likely insane, but the others seemed to be clinically unimpaired. Perhaps their early upbringing caused their hatred, perhaps it came from jealousies, or they may have been following the zeitgeist or the norms endemic to the countries in which they lived. They were all antisemites, and each had a different reason for being so. For us, it made no difference. In our eyes, all vultures looked alike.

"It might seem incongruous that under the conditions we were kept," she continued, "I had the opportunity to practice the culinary skills that I had abandoned for years. My cooking was broadly appreciated, and I frequently prepared meals for groups of people on Friday evenings to celebrate the incoming Shabbos, which lifted our spirits. But just as I had begun adapting to the camp, I was transferred to Sobibor, and later still to one of the Mauthausen subcamps, which was known to be the final stop before heaven. To my astonishment, not long afterward, I was transferred to yet a different camp even though few Jews ever left that hellhole. It seems my ability as a chef was appreciated, so I was in high demand by officers with influence. At the time, I lamented being taken from Theresienstadt, where life was kinder. It was only after the war I learned that of the 140,000 people that had been kept at Theresienstadt at some time, very few survived. Most of the Jews there were eventually transferred to extermination camps, such as Mauthausen and Auschwitz, and many died at Theresienstadt as conditions there deteriorated."

She glimpsed one of the elder rabbis shaking his head in utter despair as he spoke in a whisper, "Such a loss, such a terrible loss. The beauty of their art and the beauty of their minds can never be recovered. Never."

His comment triggered despair in Zosha. Needing to regroup her emotions, Zosha asked if they could take a few minutes to have something to drink. Rabbi Davidson quickly went out and returned with coffee, sugar, and cream.

As she heaped several spoons of sugar into the coffee, she said, "After so many years of not having tasted sugar, I can't get enough of it. It has become an addiction, I'm afraid."

When she resumed, her sadness was apparent from the tone of her voice and posture. "As bad as the situation was in the various camps to which I was assigned, this was made worse by not knowing what had become of my handsome and talented husband or my young son, Moshe. I continue to pray that Hashem helped them survive, although I know this is unlikely. My devotion to Hashem has never wavered, although I confess I've questioned why our God allowed this to happen to his Chosen People. My brain would scream 'We're the Chosen People. Is this what we were chosen for?' At other times my grief made me delusional, and I would fantasize my husband and child would somehow reappear at any moment. As you are aware, in the 16th century, Rabbi Judah Loew ben Bezalel, the Maharal, who lived in Prague, is said to have created a clay Golem and brought it to life to protect Jews from pogroms. Although I took this to be a myth, despite the legend of the body of the Golem lying in the attic of the Old New Synagogue, in my delusions I believed somehow the Golem would return and bring my husband and son with him. Yes, those were foolish thoughts, delusions. But in desperation, I hung on to any shred of hope."

While stroking his long gray beard, the elder of the rabbis who sat across from Zosha, Rebbe Vichnin, said somberly, "There is nothing foolish about hope. Jews live in hope every day. We hope and pray we will have healthy long lives, we hope our children will give us pride and pleasure, we hope we can return to the Promised Land in peace, and we hope Moshiach, the Messiah, will come to us, riding on a white donkey and blowing a shofar. I've hoped and prayed for many things over the years and, thank God, some of my hopes have been realized. It may be foolishness on my part, but I believe that when Moshiach finally does come, you'll meet your husband and son again."

The second rabbi, introduced as Rebbe Kramer, said, "I tell my rabbinical students our time in this world is exceptionally brief. When we live through horror, it seems never-ending, but in the greater scheme, our being is equivalent to that of a single letter of a word inscribed in the entire Torah. I, too, believe Moshiach will come, and our souls will live on forever, but when he comes is beyond us to know and understand."

Rabbi Davidson then spoke up. "My colleagues and I share our hopes and dreams of the future, but for the moment we need to deal with the present," he said. "That said, please, would you let my learned friends know what you experienced after the war that led you to be here."

Turning to them, she said, "Thank you very much for your thoughtful comments and your sincere beliefs concerning my hopes."

She then continued her postwar history: "The last camp in which I was placed was Buchenwald. I had only been there for a few weeks when the German guards began evacuating the camp. Many prisoners were forced to march further into Germany, but the Nazis hadn't been able to mobilize fully as American forces were quickly approaching the camp. Once it was clear the Nazis were abandoning the camp, prisoners seized control, and I was among those liberated by the Americans.

"Often, the healthier prisoners among us were interviewed by special teams within the American units. When they realized I spoke several languages fluently, they asked me to join a detail within Poland where I would serve as a translator to record the histories of other survivors. Of course, I immediately agreed to do this, and soon afterward I was transported back to Poland, where I worked in collaboration with other translators, including several who had been camp inmates. After about a month, I was offered the opportunity to work with other historians and lawyers who were preparing for the Nuremberg trials that would imminently begin. Unfortunately, by then, it had become apparent my mental condition was fragile and repeatedly hearing the experiences of other survivors was incomprehensibly distressing. The horrid memories of what I had previously encountered were repeatedly triggered by the appalling and tragic experiences of some of the women and men whom I interviewed. As unfathomable as it was, their captors found increasingly horrendous ways of murdering Jews, including subjecting them to hideous experiments conducted by Nazi doctors."

Taking a few moments to wipe away tears, she said, "I'm ashamed to say I simply wasn't fit for the work, as much as it was important for me to find meaning in my survival. Indeed, I believed my inclusion might have hindered the investigation of the beastly crimes that had been committed."

During the latter part of her story, she had been looking downward to avoid eye contact. When she finally lifted her head, she saw Rabbi Davidson and the others looking downward, too, as they didn't want the others to see their moist eyes.

Finally, Rebbe Vichnin said, "There is no shame in having a soul and being able to feel the pain of others. In the absence of these characteristics, we aren't human."

Nodding in gratitude again, Zosha sighed heavily and continued. "The Americans were disappointed but sympathetic to my distress," she said. "They provided me with some money and transport on a lorry that would take me to Germany, which I hoped would allow me to get to America. Along the way, the lorry stopped repeatedly to pick up survivors on the roadside, and we came to share the history of the abuse we suffered, the hope we would find family members still alive, and our partially formed plans for what we would do once we reached Germany. I don't know what became of most of the people on the lorry. Some intended to go to countries where they had relatives or friends, and one young man, Pinye, he was named, was intent on reaching the Promised Land. He hadn't been impressed by stories of streets paved with gold in America and indicated he would be happier to simply taste pomegranates, dates, and olives.

"To our collective dismay, we discovered that despite the horrors we experienced, the doors of most European countries weren't open to Jewish survivors. Likewise, countries such as Canada, Australia, and the United States, which hadn't readily accepted Jews before the war, were hesitant to accept any afterward. Years would pass before survivors could reach other countries. It would be comical if it weren't so sad, but elements of the US government engaged in a secret program, Operation Paperclip it was called, in which German scientists who had worked with the Nazis were brought to America to create new weapons. Indeed, the Americans competed with the Russians to obtain these scientists. That these scientists had not only helped the Nazis but also used concentration camp prisoners as slave laborers to create weaponry was of little consequence. Of course, I didn't fall into the select group taken to America soon after the war, so my entry to this country took longer. Still, as I had helped the Americans, however briefly, and because of my academic background, I was permitted early entry."

When Zosha completed her history, the two rabbis went to Zosha and expressed their sympathy and sorrow. Then, turning to Rabbi Davidson, they almost imperceptibly nodded their heads.

Rabbi Davidson drew his chair closer to Zosha so their knees nearly touched. "Zosha, Yeshiva University is still a relatively young institution, and it was only granted a charter in 1945," he said. "We intend to make the university a premier center of knowledge in the arts, humanities, social sciences, and life sciences. We will have a first-rate law school and a medical school that will be the envy of all others. For our hopes to come to fruition, we need the best and most dedicated scholars. All that said, we would like to offer you a position in the History Department here at Yeshiva. You have so much to offer, and if you're amenable, then we can negotiate terms when you feel up to it."

Overwhelmed, she covered her face with both her hands for a full minute. "You are all so wonderful and kind, and I would be honored and delighted to work here," she said. "It isn't necessary to negotiate. I'll be content with whatever you think is reasonable."

The excitement of her new position was all-encompassing. She couldn't stay away from her office, arriving before 5:00 every morning to begin her research. With freshly brewed coffee on her desk, she pored over the transcripts of the Nuremberg trials that began in 1945 and lasted four years. She also received unofficial reports from social scientists who attended the trials as well as translators and interpreters whom she had befriended. In addition, she obtained information from journalists who had often consulted her because of the high profile she built from amassing such large amounts of information.

In public forums, she would say the decisions of the court and the sentences delivered were appropriate. What she believed and said in private was very different.

"To be brutally frank, I'm appalled at all I've heard," Zosha said. "The United States alone had collected thousands of files, as did the British, French, and Russians, but only a small number of perpetrators were tried. Of the 22 top leaders of this heinous regime, only 12 of the butchers received death sentences, and seven were committed to Spandau prison to serve sentences. It's stunning the judges couldn't agree on several decisions, so three defendants went free. I don't want revenge, but I do want justice – there must be a reckoning. By no means did the decisions made reflect this."

When she found later decisions still more appalling, she made her views widely known. "How is it possible that of millions of Nazi soldiers, SS members, SD security agents, Gestapo, and cruel prison guards, only 100,000 or so were arrested?" she asked. "Remarkably, just 2,500 were considered war criminals of the highest order, and a mere 177 were tried, of which just 142 were convicted and only 25 were given death sentences."

Her greatest ire was reserved for the Doctors Trial, which involved the prosecution of physicians who engaged in experimentation using humans. She talked about it with Rabbi Davidson, who periodically dropped by to chat.

"Nazi doctors were the worst barbarians of the lot, many of whom began their debauchery within Germany well before 1939, eliminating those considered to be 'feeble-minded,'" she told him. "It's incomprehensible that children – young children – were killed for the crime of lacking intellectual abilities.

"Despite the many doctors who committed these atrocities, just 23 were brought to trial, of which 16 were found to be guilty. Seven were sentenced to death, and the remainder were given sentences that ranged from ten years to life, but the length of the terms was often reduced on a later appeal. It's profane that in the face of massive evidence, seven of those tried were acquitted."

"Zosha, your interest in the Nuremberg trials is contagious," Rabbi Davidson said, pointing to her thick file of information. "The extent of the depravity exposed by the trials has been mind-numbing, which paradoxically has me reading more rather than avoiding the horror and reading less. The newspaper articles I've read concerning the Nuremberg trials have pointed to the involvement of major industries in supporting the Reich, which was essential for the war machine."

"That's a certainty, Rabbi. Every war brings out the profiteers; some make their money in anticipation of the war or during the conflict itself, and after the war come the carpetbaggers who engage in lucrative reparation businesses."

"And which companies were the greediest and made the most of the situation?" he asked.

"The vast industrial complex played a role in supporting the military and frequently colluded with the generals. Frankly, this wasn't unique to Germany, as this sort of collaboration was the norm in most countries. The military often relies on industry to provide everything from airplanes, ships, ground vehicles, bombs, bullets, and anything else you can think of that can be used in a war. Within Germany, a great number of companies did precisely this, but unlike other countries, they often used slave labor and looted the property of Jews to fund their goals.

"I suppose financial institutions likewise gained from the war?" Rabbi Davidson asked rhetorically.

"They were very big profiteers," Zosha said. "They included many within Germany and many outside. Switzerland was the fence-sitter that portrayed itself as a neutral country despite government officials having filthy hands. Many high-ranking Nazi officers hid their wealth in Swiss banks, which operated as intermediaries to assure Nazi Germany had adequate credit to purchase what it needed.

"Before the full scope of Nazi intentions became apparent, some Jews kept their money in Swiss accounts hoping to reclaim their wealth later. As whole Jewish families perished, Swiss bankers kept the unclaimed funds. Likewise, insurance companies such as Allianz cooperated with the Nazi regime and all too frequently didn't pay out life insurance benefits. I have heard reports numerous banks among the Allied countries behaved similarly. Several French banks, as well as Barclays Bank, which is British, colluded to take Jewish money on deposit. It has been said that Chase Bank, especially its branch in Paris, and J.P. Morgan also didn't return monies owed to survivors or their families. "

"Is this widely known?" Rabbi Davidson asked.

"Some of it is, especially as some cases were part of the Nuremberg trials, but there is more that remains unknown to the public. The US government has been reluctant to release the information as it might turn the German people against us, which could undermine their efforts in competing with the Soviets. Many Germans who previously indicated the trials were appropriate now believe the trials led by America were unfair and feel especially aggrieved by the collective guilt being imposed on all Germans. They have been petitioning for sentences at the Nuremberg trials to be commuted. I have no idea why we care what the German people think. They supported Hitler, may his name be erased from history. They idolized him and followed his orders – and now *we* need to be careful not to insult their sensibilities. How absurd, how Kafkaesque."

"I agree," Rabbi Davidson replied. "Evidently, the politicians have a different script they read from. Do you have any plans to expose the military-industrial collusion that was critical to the Nazi war machine?"

"Not really," Zosha said. "There's no need since many citizens of Europe know what occurred, and they are angry and loud. Numerous journalists and newspaper editorials have likewise been expressing negative opinions concerning the limited actions taken at the Nuremberg trials."

"Although the Nuremberg trials weren't as effective as hoped, if nothing else, they have brought needed attention to vital issues," said Rabbi Davidson. "Also, through the hard work of Raphael Lemkin, a consensus has been reached in the definition of genocide as 'behaviors directed against a national group, and against individuals, not in their individual capacity, but as members of the national group.' Lemkin was outraged that there were no specific laws against targeting large segments of society, so the killing of a million or more people was, in a sense, a less serious crime than killing a single individual. Now, genocide is viewed as an international crime, and specific actions that constitute genocide and crimes against humanity are well defined."

"Oh, dear Rabbi Davidson," Zosha said, "do you really believe having these statutes in place will prevent further atrocities? I can assure you that in the coming decades, we'll see genocidal behaviors play out worldwide. I'm reminded of a fable I heard in Theresienstadt."

Sitting back, after sipping her coffee, she continued: "A large aggressive wolf had decided to make his home at the side of a stream. Some distance downstream there was a family of rabbits living happily, finding the food they needed and enjoying the peacefulness. Having badly soiled his den, the wolf began relieving himself in the stream, which affected the rabbits that lived downstream. Cautiously and with great reverence, the rabbit family approached the wolf and, in the most diplomatic way, explained that his urinating and defecating in the stream was making them ill, and would he consider finding an alternative place to do his business. Well, the wolf sat back on his haunches and thought about this for a moment and then viciously killed and ate the rabbits."

"So, might makes right," Rabbi Davidson said.

"Exactly," replied Zosha, "and in coming years the bullies of the world will dominate and act in the most egregious ways whenever they're inclined to do so."

"I have become increasingly obsessed about the many high-ranking Nazis who escaped and found refuge in various South American countries and how they were able to achieve this," Zosha said. "Was there a network that facilitated their escape, or were random individuals duplicitous in helping these Nazis either because of their devotion to the cause or because they were paid for their efforts?"

"I had wondered about that," Rabbi Davidson said. "Have you reached any conclusions, and would you be willing to share these with me?"

"I'll give you much more information once I've done my due diligence. I don't want to be premature. For what it's worth, clearly hundreds, perhaps thousands, of war criminals were able to obtain refuge in Argentina, Brazil, and Chile, which would have required considerable help."

Clasping his hands together as he often did when distressed,

Rabbi Davidson asked, "Can they be deported to the US or to some other place where they can be tried?"

Zosha laughed mirthlessly. "Let's be realistic," she said. "The Nuremberg trials, which had the benefit of help from thousands of personnel and vast amounts of money and connections, were not overly effective in bringing justice for the crimes against humanity. There frankly isn't the capacity, or probably the will, to venture into South America to bring out these criminals. Maybe back in 1945 when it was still fresh, but not anymore. Appealing to these countries won't get very far since they appreciate the money brought by the Nazis, and they often gained from technical and military skills they possessed."

"Are there specific Nazis who are of particular interest?" Rabbi Davidson asked.

"There are many, but getting to them is very difficult," Zosha said, "as they seem to have obtained safe haven in South American countries, such as Argentina. It's already well established that President Juan Perón welcomed Nazis into Argentina. He was involved in the establishment of escape routes, so-called 'rat lines,' to smuggle former SS officers and Nazi party members out of Europe. The Perón government, through their emissary, Cardinal Antonio Caggiano, sent the message the country was prepared to welcome Nazi collaborators from France who faced potential war crimes prosecution. I heard just a few days ago that with the help of a Franciscan monk, Eichmann, who was key in establishing the "Final Solution", was able to reach Buenos Aires using a false passport in the name of Ricardo Klement. Likewise, after hiding in Germany for several years, Mengele, the Angel of Death, was able to recruit the assistance of Catholic clergy to reach Argentina. Similarly, Walter Rauff, who was responsible for the creation of trucks modified to gas prisoners, evaded arrest by hiding in an Italian convent and then found his way to Chile."

"It seems the common denominator for their successful escape was the intervention of the Church," Rabbi Davidson said. "This fits with the seeming friendly relations maintained between the Nazis and Pope Pius XII, Hitler's Pope."

"Yes, indeed, other clergy may have followed the lead of the soulless Pope in facilitating the escape of Nazi perpetrators," Zosha said. "One, in particular, Bishop Alois Hudal, was complicit in the escape of Erich Priebke as well as Franz Stangl, who was known as the 'White Death.' When I was in Sobibor, I would see Stangl walking about dressed in a white riding uniform, always carrying a whip to increase his ferocious appearance. He had a long history of murder, having been involved in the euthanasia of individuals with mental or physical disorders before moving on to become commandant of Sobibor and Treblinka, where one million combined were killed. He had no conscience and no sense of morality. When I cooked for him, how I wished I could do away with this pompous ass."

"Do you believe Pope Pius XII was antisemitic and thus did nothing to interfere with Hitler's Final Solution?" asked Rabbi Davidson.

"I generally avoid attempting to look into what was in the head of the many people who had directly or indirectly engaged in murderous behavior. If one cared to be generous, it might be concluded Pope Pius XII was attempting to appease Hitler to protect the Church."

"But, surely, as the leader of the Catholic Church, Pope Pius shouldn't have been indifferent to the fate of Jews," Rabbi Davidson said.

"There is no question about that," Zosha said. "The politicians within the Vatican are already maintaining Pope Pius was unaware of what was happening to the Jews. There is, however, incontrovertible evidence he knew, especially as he had received eyewitness testimony about the butchery and received reports to this effect from various bishops. I don't doubt the debate regarding what he knew or didn't know will continue for decades. Unfortunately, the Vatican is influential, and I'm afraid they'll be able to bury the evidence, however impressive it might be."

Holocaust deniers became more prominent, spewing revisions of what happened to the Jews in Europe during the Shoah. In some cases, their ranks included well-educated academics and people in high positions who typically fell back on the same script: The Holocaust hadn't occurred and was in reality a well-planned hoax conducted by the Allies and the Soviet Union, likely fomented by Jews. Moreover, the purported number of Jews who died during the war was far lower than the six million bandied about and certainly didn't exceed a million. Furthermore, the aim of the Reich was not to exterminate Jews but to deport them. In fact, the concentration camps, gas chambers, and crematoria never existed and were made up from whole cloth.

Zosha believed these deniers were adopting the playbook used by propaganda minister Josef Goebbels and Hitler. If they repeated the "Big Lies" often enough, they would eventually be believed. Certainly not by everybody, but the fiction would be accepted by those with a proclivity to accept an antisemitic version of events.

The campaign of the deniers began soon after the war. One of the earliest and most influential of the group was French journalist Maurice Bardèche, who published a book in 1948 attracting many supporters. He said, "Only lice were killed in Auschwitz." Despite the evidence to the contrary, with time and changing world views, the deniers gained supporters, and Zosha predicted eventually sympathy for the Jews would be replaced by antipathy.

On the surface, Zosha appeared driven, and her work provided satisfaction. Below the surface, however, she suffered mightily. She continuously revisited the past, her heart shattering with every memory – memories of her husband, son, parents, and her two brothers and sister who hadn't survived the Shoah. She didn't know the dates of their deaths, so she selected ones that seemed about right, and on these days she would recite the Kaddish. Invariably, on certain High Holy days she would attend synagogue services where she would join with others to recite Yizkor, the pryer of remembrance of those who had passed.

Like so many others, she would repeatedly ask: "Why did I survive when so many others didn't?" which only served to foment survivor guilt. As Ari implored while on the transport from Poland, she had followed the plea of Simon Dubnow, the great scholar murdered by the Nazis in the 1941 Rumbula massacre. He had encouraged Jews to write it down, record it all. It was after she read the work of Viktor Frankl, which was based on his three years in concentration camps and the loss of his wife, parents, and brother in camps, that she found relief from her vivid ruminations. His dictum that happiness can't be pursued but instead occurs as a side benefit of dedication to a cause greater than oneself moved her from feeling like a victim to someone who could champion a cause for Jews.

With Rabbi Davidson's encouragement, she began touring parts of the United States, visiting synagogues where she would deliver powerful speeches about the Shoah, focusing on young people who were most impressionable and could be fooled by revisionist history. On one occasion, when she returned to Yeshiva University feeling dissatisfied with her efforts, Rebbe Vichnen said, "It's a mitzvah, a good deed, what you're doing. I sometimes give lectures to young students at Hebrew high schools, and while I'm gratified to be able to encourage their religious views, I occasionally come back feeling like I haven't created anything that wasn't already there. Maybe it is the same for you. In my case, it's more gratifying to be able to reach people who have lost a bit of their faith or who are aimless in their life trajectory as Jews."

This perspective resonated deeply with Zosha – Rebbe Vichnen had precisely described her feelings. She continued to lecture at synagogues, but in every city she visited, she would also give speeches at community centers where she addressed people of various religious beliefs, including many who knew little about the Holocaust. She also made a point of providing lectures to students in high schools and universities.

She was certain an account of the millions that died couldn't be properly absorbed. In contrast, the experiences of a single person with whom the audience could identify would have a much greater impact. Thus, at the start of each lecture, she would describe the attitudes of the National Socialist party, their policies toward Jews, Roma, and political rivals, and conditions in the forced labor and concentration camps. Then she would talk about the policies of Western countries that allowed Hitler to pursue his murderous aims.

Once she completed her account, a survivor, often an elderly person, would describe what they endured. Some recounted the sense of unreality upon first being arrested and placed in a camp. Or they might describe their initial feeling that this couldn't be happening, only to find it was their new reality – living with little food, hard labor, and frequent beatings. All the survivors invariably described the fear, helplessness, and horror they felt, and some told of the deep, relentless depression that overcame them as their children or grandchildren were taken to gas chambers and their bodies burned in the crematoria. One survivor described the horror of seeing her grandchild, a girl of six months, being grabbed by the legs and swung so her head shattered against a wall. A set of elderly twins who managed to survive Mengele's debauchery described their terror at being subjected to poisonous gases and the trepidation of receiving chemical treatments that might attenuate the actions of the gases. Even though they told these stories frequently, they were never able to suppress their deep emotions with the telling. The reconstruction of the events by the survivors was met with a heavy silence, penetrated only by muffled sobs that were accompanied by wet eyes and tear-streaked cheeks.

Occasionally, students would ask about postwar experiences, even hesitantly raising the views of the Holocaust deniers. Zosha would say the facts are undeniable, but if one were inclined to twist them, then alternate conclusions could be derived. Pointing at the bright lights in the room, she would say, "I can proclaim this room is dark, but that doesn't make it so. One could argue a dog has four legs and that a table has four legs, and thus a dog is a table. But this, too, is a nonsensical break with logic.

"Let me tell you a little story. A man appeared before a magistrate to obtain compensation for a valuable, pristine book he loaned his former friend who had returned the book in tatters. In response to the accusation, the defendant said, 'Your honor, first, my friend never loaned me a book. Second, when I obtained the book from him, it was already in terrible condition – pages were torn from the binding and had been immersed in water. Finally, and most importantly, when I returned the book, it was in mint condition.' This parallels the fantasies created by the deniers. What they argue is illogical, based on lies, and is abject idiocy."

Zosha's reputation spread widely, and she was frequently asked to give university lectures as well as be invited to be a keynote speaker at national and international conferences. These invitations often came with modest remunerations, which she redirected to local charitable causes.

She had made it her job of countering the loud voices of the Holocaust deniers. To her pleasant surprise, laws were passed making hate speech a criminal offense. Yet she was nobody's fool and believed the hiatus in beating up on Jews would be brief. She was fond of saying, "Today, people greet me and others like me as if we were golden salmon, but with time we'll be viewed as smelly old herring."

Her experiences as a historian had informed her of the unpredictability, arbitrariness, and capriciousness of history. She was enamored of the opportunities and the good life America offered. At the same time, she was affected by the history of antisemitism in the US. The bond many Jews felt toward the US was unwavering, even if it wasn't always reciprocated. She found it curious those enamored of the US seemed to have a selective historical memory. With their greater presence and prominence had come increased antisemitism. Even in the absence of frank antisemitism, they had been treated as outsiders. For ages, they were excluded from the social, political, and economic life of the country. It was exceedingly difficult for Jewish students to enter medical schools, and it was rare for Jews to attain professional positions and white-collar jobs, including at universities, hospitals, or legal firms.

"Rabbi Davidson, you would know better than I that people in the US were readily swayed to adopt antisemitic attitudes," Zosha said. "During the 1930s, well-known antisemites, such as the radio preacher Father Charles Coughlin, railed against the Jews and favored the views of the Nazis. They accused Jews of being responsible for the Great Depression, being communists, or being capitalists intent on gaining economic control of the country. Whether through these vile influences or prejudices already present, most Americans held a low view of Jews, labeling them with racist stereotypes, and considered them a threat to the welfare of the country. As a result, for decades the US was reluctant to accept Jews to its shores, not wanting to inherit a European problem. Even during the worst of the Shoah, ships carrying Jews were refused entry into the US, just as they were denied entry to other countries, leaving them to meet their miserable fate. Similarly, many Jews could have been rescued by paying the Reich a relatively modest sum, but it wasn't done, leaving the Jews to certain death."

"That's true enough," he replied. "My sense, however, is that attitudes toward Jews are becoming more positive."

"Maybe less negative, but not more positive," she said. "To a degree, the attitudes of Americans toward Jews changed in the years after the war, but hate crimes continue to occur, and some antisemites organized efforts to disturb the well-being of American Jews as well as the safety of Israel. Most US Jews have maintained an unwavering allegiance to the US, reinforced by the view that antisemitism is on the run. They believe the 1950s are the 'golden age' for Jews, reflected by the attainment of greater social acceptance and enhanced political and economic security."

The extent of the misconceptions held by Jews was brought home to Zosha when she met with Nela, whom she had first encountered while on her journey to Germany after the war. Nela had contacted Zosha after seeing an article about her work in a newspaper. In their meeting, Nela described a series of tragedies she encountered in America, including unfair treatment at the hands of US government officials. Still, she unreservedly adored the country. When Zosha mentioned the earlier antisemitism, Nela responded, "That was then, and this is now."

Zosha chastised her, saying, "You should know better. When they come for the Jews again, and eventually it will happen, the capitalists, the communists, doctors, lawyers, and merchants, the men, women, and children, will all be lined up together in front of the same wall."

Nela simply responded, "It's true that in many ways, I've had a terrible time. Yet look at me now. I walk the streets freely, I don't have to look over my shoulder every ten steps, and I'm not in a camp taking orders from tyrants. Tell me, is there a better place to live? This is the *Goldeneh Medina* [the golden country] largely because we're free of the discrimination faced in Europe."

Always the historian, Zosha replied, "When I was doing my research before the war, I focused on 16th century Czechoslovakia and a similar period in Spain in the 13th and 14th centuries. They were often viewed as the golden age for Jews, just as you think of our experiences in America today. Unfortunately, in each instance, and many others, these periods were inevitably followed by intense antisemitism, and the Jewish communities turned into a wasteland. For that matter, the Jews in Germany had to a considerable extent become assimilated, and they, too, seemed not to comprehend their golden period had reached its end, and even seemed in denial when they initially faced the Nazi threat. Believe me, Nela, there is always the risk the pendulum will swing in the opposite direction and this Goldeneh Medina, this golden country, may become a hellscape."

Zosha was taken aback one day when she received an overseas phone call from a man who introduced himself as Ari, adding, "You know me better as Pinye."

Upon recovering from the shock, Zosha said, "Oy, Pinye, my dear, dear, Pinye. I think of you so often. At one time I tried tracking you down, but nobody had heard of a Pinye that fit the description I provided. Pinye, what have you been doing with yourself? Tell me everything."

He laughed. "I can't do it all in one phone call. I live in Israel, and when I came here, I changed my name to Ari, and Pinye disappeared. I'll tell you everything in person if you'll allow me to meet with you."

"Are you here in New York?!" she exclaimed.

"No, I'm in Jerusalem, but I can come to New York whenever you're free," he replied.

"Better still, I'll come to you. I'm not the young woman you knew so many years ago, and I've longed to be in Israel. I'll rearrange my schedule and will be there as soon as possible."

Having obtained her itinerary, Ari met her at Ben Gurion Airport in Tel Aviv. Despite the crowd in the arrivals area, she immediately picked him out just as he spotted her. They rushed toward one another and hugged for what seemed an eternity.

After retrieving her single suitcase, they drove to Jerusalem. On the way, he explained that he lived with his family in Jerusalem, although he frequently returned to the kibbutz where he had spent many years.

Asher had been waiting for them, and after greeting Zosha, he rushed about getting her coffee, biscuits, and a large Jaffa orange, which he explained couldn't readily be obtained elsewhere. As she drank the coffee approvingly, she leaned over and stroked Ari's cheek, saying, "You've changed so much Pinye. You're not the emaciated young boy I had known. Where did those muscles of yours come from?"

Chuckling, Asher said, "Pinye! I haven't heard anyone call him that in years. Now he's Ari, the brave lion. In the months after I first brought him to our kibbutz, this little rabbit hid in his hole. As much as we tried to get him out, the rabbit would tell us he was safe in the hole and wouldn't come out to face dangers. But when he fully emerged, he had changed to the lion you see now."

"I knew him as Pinye, and in my mind, he will always be Pinye," she said, laughing at her own humor. "But I'm not too old to change. What do you think, Pinye?"

Asher had made a reservation at a nearby restaurant. While indulging in a traditional Israeli meal, they traded historics that followed their separation in Bremen. Afterward, they returned to the apartment and made themselves comfortable. When they were settled, Zosha turned serious and said, "Ari, this has been a wonderful reunion. But you still haven't told me why you wanted to see me after so many years and why it was so urgent."

"I'm aware of that but wanted you to feel comfortable before we delved into those issues," he said. "As I've told you, I'm a colonel in the IDF, and in a discussion with my general, the topic of Holocaust deniers came up and he mentioned your fine work. It was a topic I hadn't followed, having been so immersed in training new recruits. So I was utterly surprised to learn what you've been up to. At any rate, when I told him about our experiences together, he became very excited, and we immediately returned to his office. He showed me a file about your work, which surprised me still more as he had so scrupulously been following your efforts."

"That's gratifying to hear, but it still doesn't explain why I'm here – not that I object," she said.

"Well, a few days after I met with him, I was invited to his office again, where I was introduced to two members of the Mossad. In short, a unit has been established to find Nazi officers who committed the greatest offenses and bring them to trial here in Israel."

"That's excellent. I assumed such a unit existed. It's unfortunate extradition from other countries, especially those in South America where so many are located, has been difficult."

"You're likely right, but Mossad doesn't involve themselves in extraditions they know won't be productive. They'll determine the measures needed to achieve their goals."

"And they would somehow like me to help them, but I don't have any abilities that can be of value," replied Zosha.

"I'm frankly uncertain specifically what they have in mind. I'd guess they're likely interested in your knowledge and the information you've gathered. So, with your permission, they would like to meet with you."

"Certainly. Where are they now?"

"Nearby I suppose, given they indicated they would arrive soon after I phoned them," Ari replied.

With her agreement, he phoned the number he was given, and shortly thereafter two men arrived at Ari's apartment. Neither stood out in any notable way. They seemed like average men, dressed modestly, and wouldn't stand out in any group.

Once the agents were seated, they thanked her profusely for agreeing to meet with them, indicating they were fully aware of her many skills and the work she had done in recent years to bring attention to the shortcomings of the Nuremberg trials and her efforts to persuade people to reject the irrational preaching of Holocaust deniers.

"Thank you for these kind words, Zosha said. "Yet, I'm puzzled how I could be of help."

"It's not particularly complicated," one of the agents said. "You have a trove of information, including who is connected to whom, that may help us find top Nazis who escaped Europe and are now comfortably established in other countries. Of course, we have numerous sources that can assist us, but you can be especially helpful since you've developed a worldwide web of relations among journalists, academics, Shoah scholars, and progressive politicians who could be instrumental in helping our cause."

What the Mossad men asked of her coincided directly with her desire to bring the escaped Nazis to justice and concurrently expose the behind-the-scenes dealings that enabled the Reich to corrupt the minds of so many millions. The high-ranking military and political figures, industrialists, perverse doctors, faux scholars who abetted the abhorrent philosophy perpetuated by Hitler, and enablers within the Catholic Church were all on her list of those she was determined to expose.

After living in Israel for only a few months, Zosha was approached by a woman who appeared about 35 years old. She introduced herself as Chaviva and came straight to the point. "I'm a Shoah survivor and I'd like to help in the work you're doing," she said. "I'm presently tracing the lives of survivors, with a focus on their postwar lives, and through my searches, I came across what you've been working on. As I frequently have some time on my hands, I'd be honored to help however I can."

After chatting for a while, it was clear to Zosha that while Chaviva was open to any discussions of the Shoah and what others had encountered, she avoided speaking of her own experiences. She was part of a broad conspiracy of silence Zosha had frequently seen among Shoah survivors. Zosha most often observed it among survivors who wouldn't speak of it with their children, perhaps in a vain effort to protect them from the horror. Although it was unusual for survivors without children to adopt this attitude, she didn't question Chaviva about it and was delighted to welcome her to the project, saying, "My experience and your drive will make for a perfect team."

Zosha was initially occupied reaching out to her many contacts and reestablished connections with those she hadn't heard from recently. Through this network and with the help of Chaviva and her Mossad associates, she confirmed her earlier belief that before the Nazi defeat, an organized plan was established to smuggle war criminals out of Europe.

"Some Nazi hunters, such as Simon Wiesenthal, asserted the human smuggling was conducted through a well-organized group, ODESSA, but I believe it was more likely several independent organizations had been established, although they may have coordinated with one another," Chaviva said. "The complexity of setting up escape lines was considerable, especially as conditions were confusing and disorganized. Regardless of whether ODESSA existed, it was certain that organized groups, including rich bankers and industrialists, were complicit in helping the sadistic murderers escape. My information from South American contacts was that many of them hoped the Nazis who escaped would eventually be able to establish a Fourth Reich."

Zosha replied that those were very much her feelings. "It wasn't difficult for Mossad operatives to discover the whereabouts of many war criminals," Zosha said. "Indeed, a large number within South America made little effort to hide their identities, even gathering for social events. Some engaged in the publication of magazines and newspapers with the intent of establishing enough adherents to regain political influence within Germany. Finding others was far more difficult. Many of the former Nazi officers had changed their names and no longer held high positions of any sort, and some passed their days in common jobs without underlings and sycophants who would obey their every command."

"Coming down from their vaulted positions within the National

Socialist party and having to work in menial jobs must have made them bitter and resentful," Chaviva said with a smirk. "I wonder whether there have been efforts to use these miscreants to determine the whereabouts of higher-level Nazi leaders."

"Perhaps Mossad agents have attempted to do so even though it would be difficult to accomplish," Zosha said. "If it can be done, they'll find a way."

As expected, it wasn't necessary to coax Ari to become engaged in determining how Nazis had escaped and what became of them. Once he had sufficient reliable information, he informed Zosha what he had unearthed.

"Several of the former Nazi officials who had been caught and managed to escape died in mysterious circumstances," Ari said. "Otto Wächter, who was largely responsible for the establishment of the Krakow ghetto and the subsequent death of more than 130,000 people, hid in the Austrian Alps and managed to escape to Rome, where he was well treated despite the full knowledge of his war crimes by his host, the Austrian bishop Alois Hudal. Wächter died in 1949, allegedly of kidney disease, but my sources indicated our people, directly or indirectly, played a part in his death. I've also learned that when the Mossad abandoned the idea of negotiating with South American governments, a few of those who escaped were assassinated. The 'Butcher of Latvia,' SS General Herbert Cukurs, was lured to Uruguay, where he was killed. Likewise, Eichmann's right-hand man, Alois Brunner, who had been living in Syria under a false name, was severely injured by a letter bomb."

Zosha discovered that others who were thought to have escaped had died toward the end of the war or shortly afterward, making her load lighter. Martin Bormann, who established the slave labor program, hadn't escaped as initially believed, having committed suicide during the last days of the war.

"The Gestapo chief Heinrich Müller had also died in 1945, but his death was only discovered when his grave was found," Zosha said. "It would have disturbed him immensely that he had been buried in a Jewish cemetery – but it would have been more disturbing to the souls of Jews who had this monster buried among them. Many other

Nazis who disappeared were captured by the Soviets. Some may have been dispatched unceremoniously, whereas others were publicly tried. Franz Murer, the 'Butcher of Vilnius,' had been recognized by a camp survivor and was captured by the British. They passed him to the Soviets, who sentenced him to 25 years of hard labor, but because of political niceties, he was released after only five, allowing him to return to Austria.

"Israel was not shy about using former Nazis to protect the country, however, just as other countries had done," Ari said. "Former SS Lieutenant Colonel Otto Skorzeny was successfully recruited by the Mossad to eliminate Heinz Krug, a former rocket scientist who worked with the Nazis and subsequently provided his skills to Egypt's rocket program," he said. "Likewise, Walter Rauf, who had escaped Germany, was said to be a paid informant who reported on events in Syria that might have been a threat to Israel." These were not-very-kosher collusions that Zosha and Ari kept to themselves.

"With all the successes, the most repugnant of the vicious brutes, the "Angel of Death" Josef Mengele, who experimented on so many Jews, was never captured," Ari said bitterly.

"Of course, I'm aware of that," Zosha said. "He reached Argentina in 1949 through the help of former SS members. He initially lived in the area around Buenos Aires before moving to Paraguay and then to Brazil ten years later. Despite being hunted by West German operatives, the Mossad, and Nazi hunters, he eluded capture."

It wasn't until 1979 that Zosha received unofficial word he had drowned after experiencing a stroke. She didn't celebrate his long overdue death but took it as symbolic that drowning was the cause of Mengele's death.

"I don't know how well-acquainted you are with elements of the Bible," she said to Ari and Chaviva. "When the Red Sea parted and Pharaoh's chariots attempted to race through, they drowned when the sea closed upon them. The least bad among them died quickly, those who were worse died more slowly, and the worst of the lot died the slowest after struggling uselessly for many hours. I expect Mengele struggled much longer than the worst of Pharoah's soldiers."

Well after Zosha and Ari had ceased their search for escaped

Nazis, several more were found. Among the most despicable escaped Nazis was Klaus Barbie, who headed the Gestapo in Lyon, where he was known as the "Butcher of Lyon" based on the immense pleasure he seemed to take from causing maximum pain to Jews and resistance fighters. Owing to his strong anti-communist activities, US intelligence services helped him escape to Bolivia, where he was active in advising on torture methods to suppress opposition and may even have played a role in a coup led by General Luis García Meza in 1980. When the brutal regime of García Meza ended after only a year, Barbie fell out of political favor and was extradited to France. He was sentenced to life in prison in 1983 and died of leukemia in 1991. The government of Bolivia wouldn't allow his burial there, and the French government fittingly had him cremated, not disclosing the site of his ashes.

Zosha frequently told visitors that the longest hatred, that of antisemitism, had existed for centuries throughout Europe and continued to be present. What Hitler had done was foster the open expression of the venom already existing within Germany and Austria, allowing the haters to come together and create a common social identity.

Leaning back in her chair, Zosha said, "With some exceptions, the followers of National Socialism weren't innocents who simply found themselves swept up in the fervor of the day. They weren't forced to shower Hitler with adoration, they weren't seduced into their actions, and they weren't neutral individuals who simply went along with the perfidious acts of the fascists. Contrary to their assertions that they were also victims of the National Socialist movement, the German people had already been primed and were ready to accept and act on their latent hatreds and were frequently active and willing participants. Unlike sociologists and psychologists who seem intent on exposing the root causes for Hitler's rise, I'd rather bring the Nazis and their collaborators to justice."

In later years, she became especially vocal about Hannah

Arendt's view that even the common person could readily be turned into an ardent supporter of an extreme position.

"Hannah Arendt has maintained that evildoers such as Eichmann performed their acts without any motives other than their desire for advancement and were unable to perceive the impact of their actions on others," Zosha said. "Her views sparked a decade of scientific research to support the notion that the average person, unthinkingly, would simply follow orders from authority figures and commit grievous harm to others. As a result, those who had committed or abetted horrors could claim their innocence – 'I was only doing what I was told to do,' 'I was only following orders' – as though anyone in their position would have committed the same atrocities. It was only many years later these views were questioned and shown to be fundamentally flawed and misguided. But by then, they had found their way into scientific and popular lore through the training of generations of students. The insidious and long-lasting damage was done. Rather than adopting Arendt's view of the 'banality of evil,' it's more appropriate to think of the 'evil of banality' in which people ought to have called out the immoral behaviors they had witnessed."

It subsequently became apparent that people do not engage in barbaric acts because of a lack of insight regarding their bad behaviors. On the contrary, several scientists argued, they "conform slavishly to the will of authority." When individuals want to belong to a valued group or society and want to be perceived as model citizens, they show a zeal to outdo one another. The escalation of evil actions can be encouraged and their enactment fervently embraced.

After being immersed in her research for more than a year and finding comfort in living in a Jewish homeland, she made the difficult decision not to return to New York. Hesitantly, she phoned Rabbi Davidson with the news. He wasn't at all surprised.

"I expected as much," he said. "In the event this might occur, I have arranged an emeritus position for you at Yeshiva University so you would remain part of the family."

"Oh, Rabbi Davidson, that's immensely meaningful to me," she said. "Thank you, thank you for your thoughtfulness and understanding. What I've been doing here has been rewarding, but I will miss the university, and I will miss you terribly."

"What, you think you can get rid of me with a phone call?" he said. "I had toyed with the idea for several years and finally decided I, too, would make *Aliyah* so I can spend the rest of my life in Israel. In a few weeks, we'll see one another again."

True to his word, he appeared in her office in Jerusalem 15 days later, where he was greeted warmly.

"I had arranged for a furnished apartment before I arrived, so I'm ready to begin working with you," he said.

Zosha was caught by surprise. "You must have great confidence in what I can achieve, but before we speak of this, what is the news from home?" she asked. "What has been happening at the university?"

"I was reluctant to bring this up so soon. The only news I have is sad."

Reaching into the inner pocket of his jacket and holding an envelope, he said, "I'm afraid Rebbe Vichnin, may his memory be for a blessing, passed away ten days ago. He felt it was imminent and asked me to pass a letter to you."

Zosha read through the letter quickly and then reread it more slowly.

Looking at Rabbi Davidson, she asked, "Do you know the contents of the letter?"

"No, it wasn't my place to ask him."

Her eyes moistened as she said, "Rebbe Vichnin asked me to bear the honor of saying Kaddish and recite *Yizkor* for him. He had no children to do so and indicated he viewed me like a daughter. Touchingly, he indicated that through my work I might be close to God, who would be receptive to my prayers on his behalf."

Leaning forward, his hands resting on his knees, Rabbi Davidson replied, "I knew how Rebbe Vichnin felt since he mentioned it often in recent days; he was very proud of you and believed God's purpose was for your blessed work to continue."

"Perhaps he was right. Many of the survivors of the camps with whom I've worked have repeatedly asked why they survived, whereas others perished. What did God have in mind for them? I've frequently had these very same thoughts and then concluded God doesn't have specific plans for any of us. Instead, we have the opportunity to make choices.

"In our life journey, we reach choice points again and again, and we can choose whether to go this way or that. Sometimes we choose what appears to be the long but safe path, whereas at other times we select the route that is short but covered in brambles. Only in retrospect can we conclude whether we made the right choice. I don't yet know whether my decisions have been the best, but I'm gratified Rebbe Vichnin, who had foresight better than mine, believed I did."

"Our religion, as you are aware, is in many ways a mystical one," Rabbi Davidson said. "Hundreds of years ago, the notion abounded that in every generation the world rests on the shoulders of *Tzadikim Nistarim*, hidden righteous people. They are often referred to as *Lamed-Vav Tzaddikin*, which is taken to mean there are 36 of these holy people. They are thought to be humble, good people who are unaware that they are among this select group and thus remain concealed. But when our people are threatened with annihilation, their combined mystical powers somehow prevent this from occurring."

"And you believe Rebbe Vichnin was among the 36?" Zosha replied.

"I would like to think he was. Then again, how could I possibly know, given they're hidden? In the end, does it matter what I believe? Frankly, I'm very taken by mystical texts, such as those related to Kabbalah that first emerged in the Middle Ages. Brilliant scholars had promoted Kabbalah, which refers to 'received tradition,' and I often find value in Kabbalistic thoughts, but I'm not a strict adherent of it. What I do believe is that monsters exist that are exceptionally powerful, so much so that just 36 kind souls weren't enough to save six million."

Over the ensuing years, Zosha and Rabbi Davidson diligently tracked the monsters who facilitated the Nazi efforts, especially individuals and major corporations that seemed to have flown beneath the radar and not been implicated at the Nuremberg trials. Funding from donors and government agencies allowed them to hire experienced investigators to supplement information flowing through Zosha's network. In addition, through his university connections, Rabbi Davidson was able to enlist a rotating cadre of students who were devoted to the cause of uncovering the perfidious actions of Nazi collaborators.

Among their targets were companies that colluded with the Nazis, including several major American corporations that were instrumental in allowing Hitler's war machine to flourish. Zosha and Rabbi Davidson didn't have the resources to investigate all these companies and chose to focus on those that used slave labor to achieve their goals as well as those that had been engaged in creating concentration camps, facilitating ways of murdering people, and incinerating their bodies.

"More than 90 major German companies engaged in the Nazi war effort in one way or another, and dozens used slave labor to achieve their goals," she told her student volunteers. "These weren't minor players who disappeared after the war ended but major corporations that would stay in business long afterward. Bayer, Audi, BMW, Mercedes-Benz, Porsche, Zeiss, the Volkswagen Group, Telefunken, Siemens, and the German-American Petroleum Company all participated in the odious use of slave labor. Yet, of the many companies, only a few, such as IG Farben, Krupp, and Flick, were indicted in such crimes at the Nuremberg trials. Numerous other companies should have been tried, but they were left untouched.

"Large companies such as Siemens were involved in constructing the electrical infrastructure of concentration camps, Bosch performed the plumbing, and Topf & Sons had the job of creating gas chambers to kill Jews and crematoria to burn the bodies. Following the war, they mounted impressive campaigns aimed at describing their corporate behaviors as reasonable and that they weren't involved in 'the Jewish question,' ironically using the language of the Nazis with whom they collaborated."

Nodding vigorously, Rabbi Davidson added: "Several American companies also benefited from collaborations with the Nazis. Through its subsidiaries, the Ford Motor Company, headed by Henry Ford, a great admirer of Hitler, worked with the Nazis using slave labor. Ford had been a rabid antisemite well before Hitler's ascent. Indeed, he owned a newspaper, *The Dearborn Independent*, which he used to spew his venom. General Motors likewise had a stake in continued collaboration with the Nazi regime, as did many other American companies, such as Dow Chemical, Alcoa, IBM, Standard Oil, and General Electric, to name several. Since exposing these companies might have had serious economic repercussions, as well as undermining the faith of American citizens in private sector business, the US government applied sufficient pressure and delay tactics so the scope of the Nuremberg trials was severely narrowed. We don't yet know how extensively American companies worked with the Reich, but in coming years, much more information will be released."

Zosha's team wasn't so naive as to believe these companies could be brought to trial, but it was possible to expose the role of these companies and allow an informed public to make choices about the products they purchase.

As much as exposing corporate entities was important, especially given her particular animus toward Henry Ford, she turned her attention to other war criminals. She, Ari, and Chaviva had been resolute in digging more deeply into how these war criminals were able to gain access to various countries, how they hid so effectively, and why it was so difficult to prosecute them. Now, her attention was on the role of Catholic clergy in facilitating the escape of Nazis. Too often, beneath their stiff white clerical collars, lay the unmistakable parallel lightning bolts of the SS.

Addressing her student volunteers, she said, "As Chaviva has discovered, with the assistance of Catholic clergy, rat lines had been established to take thousands of former Nazi officers to safe havens, often within South America. Some were harbored in monasteries in the South Tyrol region of northern Italy until arrangements and finances became available for their travel. As an alternative to the more common term of 'rat lines,' they came to be called the 'monastery route,' although there wasn't a single route out of Europe; instead, there were multiple routes that frequently intersected. Of course, there were other ways Nazis escaped, including through disorganization within the Red Cross that issued exit permits to a great number of war criminals. Britain and Canada alone received more than 8,000 former Nazis, most of whom were never arrested."

Her students repeatedly asked whether the involvement of Catholic clergy to safeguard the Nazis reflected isolated events or whether there was an organized effort, originating in Rome.

"The available information makes it clear that collusion existed between some members of the Catholic Church and high-level Nazis to facilitate their escape," she said in one of these instances. "The efforts of Bishop Alois Hudal, as well as the Archbishop of Genoa, Giuseppe Siri, and Cardinal Antonio Caggiano in Argentina, is well documented. Likewise, a Croatian priest, Krunoslav Dragonovic, was instrumental in facilitating the escape of Croatian fascists through Rome, and the Pope was aware of it. If those high in the Catholic hierarchy were involved in the smuggling of Nazis to other countries, many others likely were also involved, too, and ought to be exposed. Even with a limited investigation, we became aware that false identification was provided to war criminals by other Catholic priests. This may not have been an institutional policy, but through individual Catholic clergy, former Nazis regularly received *Persilschein*, a 'soap certificate,' to eliminate the Nazi taint."

"It sounds as if many clergy members were involved in helping Nazis escape," one of the students said. "I'm curious to what extent the Church was covering up the misdeeds of its priests and whether Pope Pius XII colluded with Hitler."

"As I've mentioned frequently, there is no longer any question whether Pope Pius XII cooperated with Hitler and may have even given him the legitimacy he needed," she replied. "What motivated the Pope to behave as he did is another matter entirely. His predecessor, Pope Pius XI, had objected to the extreme attitudes and behaviors adopted by the Nazi regime. This elicited Hitler's ire, so he responded by placing many priests in concentration camps, where a large number died. It has been maintained the behavior of Pope Pius XII toward Hitler may have been motivated by his desire to protect the Church. It is equally possible Pius XII might have been more intimidated by the influence of communists than the Nazis, and he consequently acceded to virtually all of Hitler's demands. These political considerations might also be relevant to his never uttering a word to defend the Jews, although he was fully aware of what was happening as early as 1942. The Jews simply didn't register as being of any consequence. Given the Pope's apathy – and perhaps even antipathy – toward the Jews, I suspect many other Catholic clerics followed his lead. It is said a fish rots from the head down, but in this case, the rot may have progressed simultaneously in both directions."

While attention had been devoted to exposing the antisemitism within the Catholic Church, much less attention was dedicated to the Jew-hatred that had long been endemic among Protestants. Zosha was determined to look into their involvement as well.

"Martin Luther, a key leader of the Protestant Reformation, was an ardent antisemite who agitated against Jews and offered specific remedies to eliminate them from Germany," she told her students. "His callous speeches and writings fomented antisemitism in Germany in the 16th century and created the subsequent foundation for the Nazi views of Jews. At the time of the rise of the National Socialist movement, Germany's 45 million Protestants were divided into separate denominations that differed in their political stances. Factions within the Protestant church struggled to preserve their independence from politics and government, whereas many within the clergy supported Nazism, referring to themselves as 'stormtroopers of Jesus Christ.'

"Through political manipulations, Ludwig Müller, a well-known pastor and Nazi Party member, gained the support of two-thirds of Protestants, becoming head of the Reich's bishops. He was intent on nazifying Christianity by banning the Old Testament and revising hymns and liturgies. Several Protestant leaders went so far as to assert Germans were God's 'Chosen People' and even maintained

Jesus was an Aryan who typified the beliefs and ideals of Nazi Germany. In their eyes, Judaism was not a benign noninfluence and was instead a danger to Christianity. Many Protestant leaders who opposed the Nazi approach to Jews felt the wrath of the government, being placed in concentration camps or assassinated, thereby muting the voices that might otherwise have emerged."

"After an extensive investigation," Chaviva told the students, "as much as Protestant clergy supported the National Socialist aspirations, we haven't uncovered evidence supporting our suspicions Protestant clergy facilitated the escape of Nazis. That said, they were certainly instrumental in helping Nazis and their sympathizers in other ways. Among other things, they actively worked to minimize the individual and collective guilt of war criminals and entirely failed to address the prevailing antisemitism. They were attuned to the well-being of Nazi internees and prisoners of war, and except for those who had engaged in the most hideous acts, they characterized Nazis as 'men of our people.' A sense of national solidarity promoted by clergy largely ignored criminality and culpability among most Nazis. Likewise, the wrongdoing that so often was readily apparent, including among pastors who promoted the Nazi regime and engaged in overt antisemitism, was not widely addressed. Few of these clerics were dismissed from their posts."

Zosha added: "I can recall that after 1945, churches of all denominations spoke of their remorse for the fate of the Jews, even if they didn't acknowledge their culpability in fostering the Nazi domination. It's no surprise the initial sympathy toward the Jewish ordeal waned and was eventually replaced by hostility driven by the guilt imposed on them. It was perfectly predictable. My concern now is how far antisemitic feelings will spread in the rest of Europe and elsewhere, and what excuses will be used to promote this attitude."

As Rabbi Davidson knew, Zosha had an especially profound enmity toward the doctors who engaged in experiments on concentration camp prisoners. The passage of time did not diminish these feelings, and the longer these doctors were free, the more intense her disgust and contempt became.

She discussed this with her students frequently, often repeating herself.

"The Nuremberg Doctors Trial was a sham from the outset, given only 23 individuals were put on trial," she told them once. "Hundreds of doctors cooperated with the Nazi regime in conducting the most monstrous experiments imaginable. At least 15,754 prisoners in several camps served as guinea pigs, but the number could be higher despite the meticulous notes they kept. Experiments with children and adults were conducted to examine survival in freezing water or at high altitudes, people were subjected to mustard gas and various poisons, or they were infected with diseases, including malaria, hepatitis, typhus, tuberculosis, yellow fever, and spotted fever to examine the effects of antidotes. To evaluate the effectiveness of balms for wounds stemming from incendiary bombs, concentration camp inmates were severely burned using white phosphorous. Still, other physicians conducted studies evaluating bone transplantation and bone, muscle, and nerve regeneration in healthy individuals. When confronted at trial regarding experiments to evaluate how long it would take certain treatments to cause death, in his defense a physician claimed that although he was a doctor, he was a 'legally appointed executioner.' These physicians, these purported healers, conducted studies more gruesome than anything imaginable."

Rabbi Davidson had worked with Zosha long enough to sense when she became overly worked up and knew when to interject a few comments.

"As you're well aware, the greatest horrors were committed by Josef Mengele, the Angel of Death, may he burn in hell for eternity," the rabbi said. "His sadism included analyses of twins in whom he studied limb amputation, viral and bacterial infections, and the injection of dyes into the eyes to change their color. In these so-called medical experiments, one child would be treated and compared to the untreated twin. If the treatment caused the death of one twin, the other was killed so the bodies could be dissected and examined at precisely the same age. He also surgically joined twins so he could evaluate whether a treatment in one would affect the conjoined twin. What sort of malignant mind could devise such cruelty?"

Zosha chose her words carefully. "By trying so few doctors at the Nuremberg trials, other guilty doctors were essentially absolved from crimes against humanity," she said. "The reality is it wasn't simply the behavior of individual doctors that was so egregious; the behavior of leaders of the medical community and their organizations led to the broad acceptance of many horrendous practices. These doctors weren't coerced into their repugnant practices. Their heinous acts predated Hitler's ascent and may even have influenced the policies adopted by the Third Reich.

"These medical organizations initiated a euthanasia program within Germany that led to the deaths of more than 200,000 disabled and mentally ill people whose lives were deemed not worthy of living. Many more people who were said to have hereditary illnesses were sterilized without their consent. In 1920, Dr. Alfred Hoche, a psychiatrist at the University of Freiberg and a coauthor of a work entitled 'The Permission to Destroy Life Unworthy of Life,' argued that the adoption of euthanasia was both compassionate and consistent with medical ethics. He viewed those with psychiatric disturbances, brain damage, and retardation as already being mentally dead, comprising 'empty shells of human beings' and that promoting their death should be allowable and even useful."

In describing her feelings to Chaviva, she went even further. "The view promulgated by these doctors took hold and ultimately became a component of the Nazi vision of racial purification," Zosha said. "A distorted logic was adopted to rationalize killing Jews within the concentration camps and then cremating them. An SS doctor at Auschwitz, Fritz Klein, explained, 'Out of respect for human life, I would remove a gangrenous appendix from a diseased body. The Jew is the gangrenous appendix in the body of mankind.' This twisted logic was baffling, but it had the desired effect."

As they dove deeper into the actions of doctors, Zosha and Rabbi Davidson found more than half the doctors in Germany had become members of the Nazi Party and benefited financially by obtaining patients that Jewish doctors were no longer allowed to treat. During the war, not every physician had horrible intentions, and many medical students attempted to create a resistance movement to counter the abuse by doctors. Unfortunately, these students were captured and summarily executed, which aligned with how Nazis dealt with political threats.

In her meetings with those who held public office or could influence public opinion, Zosha said: "Shockingly, many physicians who had been tied to the Nazi regime continued in their medical profession after the war, and even doctors who had been in the SS and SD came to be leaders of medical associations. Physicians who attempted to expose the crimes of their brethren were frequently ostracized or sued for their efforts. The medical establishment created a wall of intentional ignorance to protect the reputations of National Socialist doctors, thereby allowing them to continue to practice. For decades, some members of the medical profession continued to hide the 'Betrayal of Hippocrates.'"

Realizing the efforts of outsiders to challenge the German and Austrian medical establishments couldn't readily succeed, Zosha and Rabbi Davidson quietly fed their information to influential journalists and more liberal politicians. Perhaps Zosha believed her statement that "We might not have been able to bring the deceitful doctors to justice or to even get them to admit to their moral failings, but if nothing else, our work will broadly expose the role of doctors in the Reich's deplorable behaviors, and others will eventually challenge the Reich's doctors who aligned themselves with warped medical practices."

It was unlike Zosha to engage in negative thoughts. She typically would vigorously move forward in reaching her goals even if the odds were against her. She would frequently brood about one topic, however.

"Of all the perfidious behaviors, none was as disconcerting as that of kapos, the Jewish prisoners whom the SS had assigned to guard other inmates in concentration camps," she said. "Most often, the SS overseers selected members of criminal gangs to serve as kapos and preferred those who appeared to be the most vicious. In return, the kapos received preferential treatment that included better food, civilian clothing, and rooms for themselves. If a kapo failed to impress the SS guards, they would be demoted and become an ordinary prisoner and would be subjected to the cruelty of the new kapo running the barracks. There might have been kapos who engaged in their job reluctantly, but more often they had sold their souls to the devil, identified with their German superiors, and forfeited their Jewish identities. Like their camp superiors, they seemed to delight in their power and were exceptionally brutal, frequently whipping inmates, kicking them in the face, stomach, and genitals, and even beating them to death. This was done with the full assent of their SS masters. For the Nazis, the kapos avoided the cost of having more guards and the kapos could be especially efficient in determining what the prisoners might be up to."

Rabbi Davidson agreed with her entirely and wasn't sympathetic to their postwar fates.

"These traitors were appropriately despised by other prisoners, and when camps were liberated, gangs of inmates would confront the kapos, beating them mercilessly," he said. "Partisan fighters likewise took it upon themselves to eliminate the kapos. Within Jewish communities, even in displaced persons camps, 'honor courts' were established that investigated the behaviors of kapos and then decided their fate. I think they've been dealt with appropriately, and I'm not sure if there's much left for us to do."

"You're probably right," Zosha replied. "Since you didn't witness the behavior of the kapos as I did, you're more likely to see things in an unbiased way, although it may also be a naive, idealistic perspective. A part of me, a small part, says we should show compassion, and another says that is impossible. Here in Israel, there was little sympathy for these degenerates, initially considering them no better than the SS guards, although leniency was shown by not sentencing them to death. With time, the opinions expressed by the courts changed so that kapos were viewed as victims of the SS unless they exhibited especially depraved behaviors. My view is less kind.

The kapos were betrayers of the special relations that ought to have existed between all Jews within the camps."

Having heard her comments concerning the Israelis' forgiving attitudes toward many kapos, one of her students approached Zosha, asking, "Does it make any sense that a kapo who was aware of how horrible they were would come to live in Israel? Perhaps those who came here could be distinguished from those who immigrated elsewhere."

A second student supported this view hesitantly, asking, "Is it even remotely possible some of the kapos may have felt that by taking control they could save Jews from still worse punishment?"

A third chimed in, saying, "I don't agree at all. Many kapos terrorized other Jews even when out of sight of SS guards. They did what they did because they were sociopaths who enjoyed their power and enjoyed harming helpless people."

After listening to the different perspectives, Zosha said, "These are all excellent comments, and given the differences of opinions among us, you can see how difficult it was for judges and prosecutors to deal with the issues, especially as some people were mistakenly accused of being kapos. At the same time, there is no question some of the identified kapos were scum who committed the vilest offenses. Like you, I would have been content to expose these brutal bullies for what they were. As far as I'm concerned, their appropriate place ought to have been in Dante's ninth circle of hell – they would reside there only because Dante hadn't had the foresight to create a tenth level.

"That's how some of us feel," one of the students said, "and we even considered an attempt to track down a few of them. However, the reality is the kapos who escaped are likely spread across so many countries it would be exceptionally difficult to find them."

Seeing their dismay, Zosha added: "Not only that, but I also question what you'd do if you were successful in finding a few kapos. There is no guarantee the governments of their home countries would prosecute them. In the end, will your efforts have been worth the outcome? An alternative might be to use your combined skills in writing about how cruel humans can be and to examine what drove kapos to take the actions they did. This said, no matter how much I've tried to understand their actions, no sane human could ever understand their inhumanity."

"And when we think we have some viable theories about what motivated the kapos, what would we do with the information?" one of the students asked.

"There are several possibilities," she replied. "What you uncover can be instructive for social scientists and lawmakers, or the information can be passed to writers already engaged in similar efforts. Doing this is a big endeavor, but if you're up to it, I would help however I can."

Invigorated by her comments and encouragement, the students began to separate into groups of two or three that would undertake specific tasks. Before they went off to do their research, Zosha said, "While you try to understand the minds of kapos, you might find it worthwhile to investigate the Judenrat, councils that existed in Jewish communities within occupied regions."

Realizing most of them were unaware of what the Judenrat was, she said, "The Nazi regime required Judenrat be created in ghettos and wider Jewish communities, ostensibly to represent the people. The Judenrat typically comprised about a dozen or more council members selected by other Jews and then approved by the Nazis. To be sure, the coerced collaboration was shameful as the Judenrat was forced into an untenable position of protecting their fellow Jews and yet meeting the demands of their Nazi occupiers.

"Among other things, the Nazis required the Judenrat to facilitate the confiscation of homes and valuables that had to be handed over to their oppressors, provide the Nazis with a list of individuals who would be used for forced labor, and eventually they were even tasked with turning over Jews for deportation to camps where they would be killed. In their defense, council members subsequently argued they had hoped through cooperation with their tormentors, even giving up some Jews for deportation, they could protect the rest. Besides, if they hadn't done this ignominious job, then the Nazis would have killed all the inmates in the ghettos. They pointed out that failure to comply with Nazi orders resulted in still more dead Jews without obstructing the Nazis in any significant way. In other instances, resistance was met by the death of the council members, who would then be replaced by others. Worse still, in several ghettos in which the Judenrat resisted, they were replaced by Jewish police, who like the kapos, were as cruel as their Nazi oppressors."

"So, the Judenrat served a valuable function for the Nazis in that the Nazis wouldn't be responsible for the day-to-day administration of matters concerning Jews?" one student asked.

"At the same time, the Judenrat might have provided an essential function for Jews by protecting as many as they could," interjected a second student.

Zosha expressed a degree of ambivalence about the actions of the Judenrat. "The leading members of ghettos might have thought they could save Jews from death," she said. "In retrospect, their best intentions came to little, as they were simply used to facilitate the extermination of the Jews. Furthermore, the presence of the Judenrat caused divisions among the Jews in ghettos, as it was believed members of the Judenrat offered preferential treatment to some people. I don't doubt this might have occurred in some instances. In the greater scheme, the Judenrat members were powerless to prevent the atrocities the Nazis had already planned."

Her student audience waited patiently for her to continue. Finally, one of them said, "I don't know what I would do if I were in the position of having to become a member of the Judenrat. I can see many behaved in the best interest of the community, whereas others may have acted in their self-interests. In retrospect, we may be painting all of them with the same brush."

Zosha replied, "I should clarify I didn't mean to suggest the members of the Judenrat were bad people. They were in an unenviable position, and while they might have exhibited biases, at least concerning helping family members, I don't begrudge them taking this liberty. It would have been better if they hadn't done so, although I can't imagine how they could have faced family members if they hadn't.

"The kapos and the Jewish police in the ghettos are a different story, and I have tried to understand what psychological processes were damaged that could make them so vile. We wouldn't be the first to try to understand the motivation of people under the most miserable, traumatic situations. Great scholars who survived the Shoah, including Primo Levi, Viktor Frankl, Elie Wiesel, and Imre Kertész, couldn't fully come to terms with the behavior of kapos, offering different perspectives and questions. Was the kapo behavior a normal response to an abnormal situation? Was it a reflection of how far people will go to survive? How would any of us behave in similar situations? What could have caused individuals to choose to simultaneously be both a victim and a perpetrator?"

"Could you ever forgive them for their transgressions?" another student asked hesitantly.

"Not ever. No. Absolutely never," Zosha said. "My disdain for the kapos has made me disagree with comments made by our great scholars, and I feel little compassion for our betrayers, as much as I would like to understand them. In my worst moments, I reflect on whether I could have done more for my fellow inmates in the camps. I have even asked what our obligations ought to be. I was recently reminded of the comment made by the writer E.M. Forster, who said, 'If I had to choose between betraying my country and betraying my friend, I hope I should have the guts to betray my country.' That's certainly a noble sentiment. However, it was offered from the vantage of privilege and safety, and one never knows what they would do when actually faced with unappealing choices."

Zosha aged well and maintained her daily routines, even slightly upping her exercise regimen to maintain her health. She cut back on trying to organize large investigative groups and worked only with Rabbi Davidson, Chaviva, and two students who helped her write a book spelling out the intricacies and collusions between countries in the decade following the war. In addition, together with a young man and woman she had met in New York, both of whom originated from Czechoslovakia, she became enmeshed in a project to document the rampant corruption within the United Nations. She believed the UN was morally bankrupt and worsening each year and wasn't shy about saying so. She was incensed at the repeated sanctions of Israel that largely stemmed from political maneuvering and biases. Then again, what could be expected of an organization that inadvertently elected Kurt Waldheim as Secretary-General from 1972 to 1981 and only later discovered he had served with the Abwehr, the German counterintelligence division?

The disclosures about Waldheim bothered her immensely. As she said to Rabbi Davidson, "We didn't do our job properly. Had we been more thorough, we might have uncovered his duplicity before he ever became Secretary-General. I blame myself as I didn't do enough in searching for Nazis who escaped or were hidden in plain sight."

After a long pause and a sip of sugared coffee, she added: "Ah, I'm sounding like a crotchety, bitter old person. It's ridiculous to believe I could have righted every wrong, but this one galls me to no end."

Over the years she had many wins and few losses. She hardly remembered the successes, and when they were mentioned, she would wave them off with a hand gesture, sometimes saying "nah" or "fish wrap – yesterday's news." The failures, however, were never forgotten and seemed to drive her more.

The years in the camps hadn't seemed to have impaired her health and she remained mentally sharp. Perhaps her mission to expose villainy kept her as clever as she was. But time finally began to catch up with her. Her body began to run down – first slowly, then quickly.

She invited Rabbi Davidson, Chaviva, and Ari to join her for Friday supper. When they arrived, she didn't answer her door, and finding the door unlocked, they entered. She was sitting in her sofa chair with her legs on a footstool, eyes closed, and deeply asleep.

As they approached, her eyes opened, and she smiled at them. "You're early," she said. "I haven't had a chance to prepare the Shabbat meal."

"Zosha, we're not early. You must have fallen asleep, and the day went by," Ari said. "Don't be concerned about supper. I'll run over to Shlomo's Deli and pick up a few things we can reheat."

"From Shlomo's Deli? Who can eat what he cooks?"

"Soup, cabbage rolls, chicken, and potatoes or farfel. Like in the shtetl. Even Shlomo can handle that."

Laughing, she replied, "Not a problem. I'll chew some very hot peppers first to numb my taste buds."

When Ari returned shortly afterward, he met Chaviva's worried gaze with a whispered comment: "Zosha is tired and very weak, and I had to help her to the table. I'm not sure she's up for a big meal."

"I may be old, but my hearing is fine," Zosha interrupted in a low voice. "A little fatigue won't keep me from dinner with you, even if it's Shlomo's cooking."

She ate sparingly, and not long afterward they helped her back to her sofa chair, where she seemed more relaxed. Taking the hand of Rabbi Davidson, who stood at her side, while Chaviva and Ari sat at her feet leaning close to hear her weak voice, she said, "I've survived a lot. I'm like the little reed that could bend with the strong winds that could destroy large oak trees."

After another pause to regain her strength, she said, "Ah, even the little reed has its limits and loses parts of itself in the fall and winter, but with the wind and rain, it will already have spread its seeds."

Again, she closed her eyes as if to sleep and continued speaking in a voice as low as a whisper. "It will be peaceful in Gan Eden and I look forward to reuniting with my husband and son," she said. Squeezing Rabbi Davidson's hand and then gently stroking Chaviva's and Ari's nearby faces, she added: "Please say Kaddish for me."

In addition to treating wounded soldiers, Canadian medical personnel helped displaced Jews traveling to Germany so that they could leave Europe. Picture was taken by a Canadian officer in the medical corps in an unidentified town in Germany. In the side mirror a survivor and child approach the medical truck.

5

A DREAM UNFULFILLED IS LIKE A BOOK UNREAD

> What happens to a dream deferred? Does it dry up like a raisin in the sun?... Or does it explode?
> – **Langston Hughes**

For several hundred years, Poland was a country that was not a country. It existed and then didn't, and then it was resurrected with altered borders. For a time, it seemed the country might prosper, and even a degree of political order was created. Jews were present throughout Poland, residing in shtetls and large cities. Warsaw had been established hundreds of years earlier from a cluster of small villages and, despite multiple setbacks, became a center of tolerance, science, and enlightenment. By 1939, its population was 1.3 million, of which more than a third were Jews. Krakow, which was likewise among the oldest cities in Poland, had become an important political center in Poland and was home to economic, academic, cultural, and artistic affairs. Its much smaller population also included many Jews, making up about a quarter of the people. Lodz was formally established later than Warsaw and Krakow. Since its establishment in 1820, Lodz had become a thriving city so by the Second World War, it had grown to 670,000 people, including more than 230,000 Jews. The dominant Christian population seemed to accept the Jews, even though a fair number harbored covert ill feelings.

Once the Wehrmacht invaded Poland, it took little time to subjugate the country. Krakow surrendered without a fight in six days, Lodz was similarly occupied in just a week, and Warsaw fell to the Nazis in less than a month.

The repression of Jews began almost immediately after Poland was invaded. They were prohibited from engaging in trade and prevented from having bank accounts or carrying much money. Then came the humiliation of being required to wear a yellow armband; failure to do so could lead to imprisonment and fines. Not long afterward came another edict that forbade Jews from simple liberties such as having radios, walking on the main street or in parks, and using public transportation. Predictably, synagogues were destroyed, Jewish shops were plundered, and German citizens who had been living in Lodz joined the Nazis in their hooliganism and stole apartments and businesses from Jews.

Nazis, working with the civil police, regularly conducted raids and seized Jews – sometimes off the street – and sent them to slave labor camps. Within weeks of the occupation, Jews were imprisoned in ghettos, where they lived in overcrowded conditions with limited access to the most basic amenities. These prisons, situated in the least desirable parts of cities, were created primarily to create a sense of terror and to separate Jews from the remainder of the population. Typically, there was no running water or sewer system. In some ghettos, Jews would be taken to work camps where they would be used as slave labor. Periodically, they were transferred to concentration camps, where they were murdered. The Lodz ghetto itself became a slave labor camp in which factories were created to produce assorted textiles and Wehrmacht uniforms.

In Lodz, the Nazis required the creation of a Judenrat, which would be required to provide workers for the Nazis. But the numbers they were required to hand over grew progressively greater, making these efforts unsustainable.

While the local Germans and the police in Lodz were ruthlessly doing their job, members of the SD were busy rounding up Jewish intellectuals as well as political and social activists, who were either killed or sent to Radogoszcz concentration camp, and then to Dachau and Mauthausen concentration camps, where they were killed. Even the members of the Jewish Council of Elders were taken and imprisoned in the camp, where most were tortured and then killed.

Of the more than 160,000 Jews in the ghetto, upward of 20 percent died from the harsh conditions, and most of the rest were transported to concentration camps so few remained by 1944. The final group survived because they were needed to clean the ghetto, and very few remained alive by hiding successfully.

Born in Lodz in 1925, Nela was the first of her parents' three children. She was her father's greatest joy, and he catered to her every whim. Reza, the middle child, received equal attention from both parents but often felt like a third wheel. Thus, Nela took it upon herself to be Reza's protective big sister and also look after Moishe, the youngest child.

The family lived on the third floor of a large apartment building that had shops on the main level and apartments above them. The building was owned by Nela's grandfather, and being business-minded, he assigned his son Mordechai Shimon one of the less desirable apartments while leasing the more luxurious suites to paying tenants. This rankled her father, who never ceased complaining about it, but only to his wife and children.

The building was located near the center of Lodz, which had all the amenities of other large European cities. When she wasn't at school or with her many friends, Nela had the opportunity to sample what the city had to offer. She frequently went to the Jewish theater, where she saw a variety of plays and performances by orchestras that traveled from distant cities. She walked through parks and was particularly fond of the arboretum. Life was good – until it wasn't.

The Wehrmacht surrounded the city and the soldiers entered with tanks, half-tracks, and an assortment of trucks that pulled artillery. Officers in black sedans drove through the city as if inspecting their booty. Having been defeated so quickly, the people of Lodz abided by the Nazi dictates, especially as a substantial number of its citizens were of German descent and favored the presence of the Wehrmacht.

On the first day of the Lodz occupation, Nela's mother, Liba, came home in a frantic state. "They have taken your father, but I don't know where," Liba said. "Tuvia Semple said your father had been walking along the street when soldiers grabbed him, along with several others, and put them in a truck.

"What can we do, Mama?" Nela asked in a panic as great as her mother's.

"I have no idea, but I can't just stay here doing nothing. I need to find out what became of him."

She bolted out of the apartment, leaving Nela to care for the younger children.

Liba returned several hours later, distraught, and frantic. After pacing restlessly for several minutes, she fell into a sofa chair and covered her eyes, not wanting the children to see her weeping.

Nela took the children into another room. When she came back in, her mother said, "The police wouldn't speak to me, no matter how much I pleaded. Some of the police officers were obvious Nazi sympathizers and wouldn't pay any attention to me. I went to the Jewish Council and spoke to friends there, but none had anything to offer other than their sympathy."

Kneeling on the floor next to her mother, Nela quietly murmured, "Mama, we can't panic now. Not yet. They may have released him, and he'll be home soon."

"From your lips to God's ears," her mother replied, although she instinctively knew it wouldn't happen.

As feared, Modechai Shimon didn't return in the ensuing days. Other Jews had been taken in similar raids, and rumors abounded they had been taken to labor camps far outside of Lodz.

As distressed as she was, she told Nela, "We have little money, and with your father gone, I'll have to find a way of obtaining food for us. On those days, which will likely be many, it will be up to you to look after your sister and brother. Perhaps you can set up a small school room and you can teach them all you've learned. On no account are any of you to go outside. Stay here, and don't answer any knocks on the door. Not for anybody under any circumstances."

"I won't, Mama. We'll be safe, you needn't worry."

Liba used her winter coat to sell her wares the way peddlers use horse-drawn carts. She could hide items within its inner pockets and along the inner parts of her sleeves without drawing attention to herself. She obtained small items on the black market such as cigarettes, sugar, coffee, and even some drugs for pain relief, and was able to sell them and obtain enough money for food. Unfortunately, the prices of most items almost doubled in a short time, so what she brought home was hardly enough to feed the four of them.

As she walked near the train station, heading home after a tiring day, she saw a Nazi officer watching her, perhaps suspicious of a woman walking alone at dusk. Liba quickly pulled a cigarette from her pocket and brazenly approached the officer smiling at him. She said, "*Guten Abend, haben sie Feuer* [Good evening, do you have a light]?"

He quickly withdrew a lighter and lit it. She cupped her hands around his, inhaled, and then murmured, "*Danke sehr*" while looking at him coquettishly.

In response, he said, "*Bitte, Fraulein*" and watched as she slowly sauntered away.

She was enthralled at having been able to fool the officer so easily and was still feeling relief as she climbed the stairs to their apartment. However, when she opened the door, she stopped abruptly as she faced two uniformed men with SD insignias.

"So, you have finally returned?" the older of the two said. "We have been waiting for you, and your children have been keeping us company. Your daughter was kind enough to serve us tea."

"I wish there was more we could offer you, but our cupboard is bare," she replied, hoping her anxiety wasn't apparent. "Of course, you're welcome to stay as long as you like, especially as it's such a cold evening,"

Waving away her invitation, he sternly stated, "That won't be necessary. We'll all be leaving together, and it's comfortably warm at our headquarters."

Liba and the children were escorted to the street level where a large black car awaited. They were taken to an old three-story building near the center of Lodz and brought inside.

They were forced to stand in a small room for a lengthy time, during which Liba held Moishe in her weary arms. The senior SD man returned and walked directly to Nela and gruffly took her by the arm and said, "*Komm mit mir* [Come with me]."

Frantically, Liba beseeched him to let her stay with them. "Please, don't separate my daughter from us," Liba said. "I'm begging you, please have sympathy."

The SD officer regarded her with disdain, and then he took Moishe from her arms and placed him on the ground saying, "Stand quietly, you little leech."

Smirking, he then grabbed Liba by the scruff of her neck, saying, "That's fine with me. I'm only too happy to comply with the wishes of a Jewess – you can go with her. The leech and the other one will stay here."

Nela and Liba never saw the children again, leaving them to imagine the horrid fate that awaited.

After being kept in a dark room for a day, Nela, her mother, and several other women were loaded onto the back of a windowless army truck and taken to a labor camp. She had no idea where the camp was, but given that several hours passed before the truck stopped, it was obviously far from Lodz.

They were rushed off the truck and divided into three groups, with Nela and her mother separated from one another. Nela was taken to a nearby encampment housing those working in the adjacent labor camp. She assumed her mother was taken to a similar camp.

Upon arrival, Nela had her clothes taken and was provided with old, stained, unwashed putrid clothing. The clothes were several sizes too large, but it was better than several sizes too small.

Turning to another inmate, Lotti, who had been there for some time, Nela asked, "What do we do here? Some of the women have said this is a labor camp, but what sort of labor do we do?"

"Whatever they ask us to do," Lotti responded wearily. "Some days we are tasked with making clothing or required to engage in heavy labor, such as carrying wooden beams for the construction of new buildings. I've heard some of the women are transferred to other camps where specific jobs are assigned, such as the production of armaments or parts of war machines. Many women at these camps die of starvation, disease, or being overworked. Those who don't die but are used up disappear, and I assume they are killed. For what it's worth, my advice is no matter how sick and tired you feel, appear to be healthy. It would be advantageous to have a piece of a beet you can use to brighten your cheeks so you can escape selection and be put to death."

Just as Nela had begun to adapt to her horrid surroundings, she and several other women were transported to another camp. The barracks had a series of floor-to-ceiling bunks, with three or four women occupying each. Beyond the barracks were stark buildings that Nela assumed were the factories.

"Can you sew?" an inmate who introduced herself as Tanya asked.

'Not very well," Nela replied. "I helped my mother a bit, but she did all the sewing that was complicated."

"That's fine, the stitches we use are simple. Tomorrow, stay near me and I'll teach you, and I hope to heaven you're a fast learner."

"What do we sew?" Nela asked.

"Until now it has been uniforms for the Wehrmacht soldiers and officers. We receive different portions and put them together. I've only been here for a few weeks, so we may eventually sew other things. I believe we serve a German company that made a bargain with the Nazis, although I don't know which company, not that it matters. I suppose what we sew will depend on what the company is doing for its Nazi patrons."

"And how many people work in the plant?"

"Many, far too many. There are eight barracks like this one, each with about 100 women. There are also a few men, fewer than 50, I would guess. The men direct the women at the factory, but within the barracks, female guards are in charge. I've heard men are most often placed in other labor camps needing stronger workers."

"I suppose the Nazis have committed their people to fight and need slave labor to provide the basic materials for the war. If the Nazi regime occupies other countries, and if this camp is successful, then labor camps will be established across many other countries," Nela said, thinking this meant she would spend a long time as a slave laborer – unless she died first.

"Perhaps so," Tanya replied. "These are things I don't think about. My thoughts and goals are limited to just surviving one day at a time."

The next morning, before sunrise, the women in her barracks were awoken by the clanging of a wooden baton against a metal pot. The menacing camp guard, a large woman who didn't brook laggards, stomped around wordlessly beating women who weren't moving quickly enough for her liking. She similarly beat women who were too slow using the bathroom. After the women formed a double row between the beds on either side of the barracks, they were marched out and forced to stand in front of a smaller structure. After a lengthy period, they were permitted to enter the building, where each woman was given a hunk of stale black bread and a cup of warm water containing a thin slice of something that appeared to be a lemon.

As Nela walked out into the darkness, holding her sparse breakfast, Tanya whispered, "Save some of the bread for later. We won't receive anything else until the end of the day."

Still holding their scant meal, they joined the line that had formed in front of them. They ate the bread sparingly, savoring each small bit, and after a time, a woman came by carrying a pail into which they placed their tin cups. The pail and its unwashed contents would be used again at their next meal. Following a loud order from the guard, they moved to a building that was used as a factory.

Once more, Tanya directed her: "Stay behind me and follow my lead."

Nela nodded and did as she was told. Throughout the morning, she watched Tanya intently, observing how to sew. The stitch was simple and repetitive, and she was able to mindlessly continue throughout the morning, simultaneously trying to ignore her hunger pangs and growling stomach. Only when the feelings were sufficiently intense did she break off a small piece of bread and surreptitiously place it in her mouth, chewing slowly to absorb the slight relief it provided.

Other than being permitted to use a foul-smelling outhouse behind the building, the women continued their menial tasks until well after sunset, when they again formed a line and marched to obtain their supper, which comprised a piece of dried black bread and thin lukewarm gruel that sometimes contained a few peas or small piece of potato.

As soon as they reached their barracks, the women climbed into their bunks and fell asleep except for Nela. As tired as she was, her thoughts kept her awake; where were her father and mother, and what happened to Reza and Moishe? Finally, overwhelmed by fatigue, Nela fell into a deep sleep, haunted by terrifying dreams.

The routine of the first day was repeated on each ensuing day. The only change occurred some nights when she awoke to hear women being taken out of the barracks by male guards, who returned them a short time afterward. Although Jewish women were viewed as vermin and sex with them was forbidden in Germany, here these inhibitions were absent, and the guards did as they liked.

Nela whispered to Tanya, "Are they doing this to satisfy their sexual needs or is it a way of humiliating us."

Tanya shrugged and whispered, "I don't know how to understand the mind of depraved murderers. I suppose they do what they do because they can."

The guards returned several nights later, intending to take a woman named Rachel in the next bed. Nela feigned a hacking cough and said, "Good, take her and don't bring her back. She might have tuberculosis and she could infect me." The guards moved away as quickly as they could.

Although this ruse was effective, there generally was no such respite from multiple forms of abuse. It was not uncommon for a woman to die overnight from starvation or disease. Some succeeded in hanging themselves under the cover of darkness. They could just as easily have attempted to escape, but if unsuccessful, they would have been severely beaten before being shot. So, dying by suicide was preferable. Two guards would unceremoniously remove the dead bodies, dragging them across the floor and tossing them into the back of a truck, before moving to the next barracks to repeat the chore. Within a day, a new woman replaced the one who had died... the supply was endless.

At one point, Tanya noticed Nela had lost a lot of weight over the past month. "Your ribs are protruding, as are your shoulders bones," Tanya said. "There's nothing you can do to change this, but don't allow your mind to decay. If you lose the will to live, then the predators will sense it and take you away."

"It's too late, Tanya. My mind has already betrayed my will to live. This will never end – I can die slowly and miserably, or I can choose the time I die."

"Please don't speak like that. Hashem, our God, doesn't condone suicide and your soul will forever be in *gehennom* [hell]," Tanya said vehemently.

"I'm sure we're already in *gehennom*," she replied dourly. "So if I die through my choosing, where will I go next?"

"God has a plan for us," Tanya said. "We have to find some meaning to this ordeal. When this all ends, as I believe it will, then..."

Before Tanya could continue, Nela cut her off. "Yes, our merciful God has a plan," Nela said. "This is the plan. We are already in God's plan. This is it."

A month later, the usual routine changed dramatically. At the end of the day, a female guard named Greta approached her bunk and threw a package on it, saying, "The commandant has sent this to you. You must have caught his eye, although I can't imagine why he would be attracted to an emaciated, putrid runt like you."

Several women gathered around her, curious about what the package contained. Nela sat staring at the package and said, "What do you think the commandant wants from me? Greta, that swine, is probably right. He wouldn't be doing this out of kindness."

"Who cares what he wants? Just open the parcel," one of the women implored impatiently, unable to contain her curiosity.

In the package, Nela found a bonanza. "Look. Biscuits, chocolates, dried dates, a small package of sugar, and even a bar of soap."

The women wordlessly looked at Nela. She took a few of the items for herself, handed a similar pile to Tanya and Rachel, and then said, "Please, girls, help yourselves, but be smart and don't stuff yourself. Save some for later."

They continued to stare at Nela, awed by her generosity. They finally took some when she smiled and repeated, "Go on, we all need it."

Three more weeks passed, and another package came, and it happened again after another few weeks. The packages continued for several years, arriving on an unpredictable basis. Time in the camp moved ever so slowly, the grief being eased only by the arrival of a package. To her relief, the commandant made no overtures toward her, which left her wondering who her benefactor was and why she was so blessed.

Unbeknownst to Nela, her father was still alive and in a labor camp not far off. Having learned where his daughter was from an inmate transferred to his section, he devised a way to get her some food.

Hearing Mordechai Shimon, was an excellent chess player, the commandant of his camp had recruited him to play chess as his underlings were no match for his superior skills. Mordechai Shimon, who the commandant had simply called him Shimon, had been a master's level player before the war and playing against the commandant was hardly a challenge. He understood the mind of authoritarians and manipulated games so the commandant savored enough victories to make him happy, yet Shimon won sufficiently often to represent a challenge.

The commandant also invited him to play cards. The commandant viewed himself as an adept card player, but Shimon had the advantage of an excellent memory. It helped that Shimon used his thumbnail to mark the side of cards so he could influence wins and losses, although he preferred chess, where chance played no role in the outcomes.

Through subtle hints, Shimon persuaded the commandant to make wagers to make it more interesting. Shimon suggested that when he won three games, a package would be delivered to Nela. If Shimon lost, there would be no penalty, although he offered to shine the commandant's boots, which was gentlemanly rejected. The commandant felt very good about himself, and he felt gentlemanly in rejecting this offer of subservience from a fellow chess player.

The excitement Nela felt upon receiving a package of food was dwarfed by reports from new inmates that the Allied armies were making progress against the Nazis. The optimism was reinforced by more frequent sightings of planes flying overhead. The sound of heavy artillery could be heard in the distance, raising hope they would soon be liberated.

These hopes were dashed early one morning when their routine was altered. Instead of being taken for breakfast, the women were herded out of the camp, with guards stationed about them. They were given no information other than being told to march behind an armored car at the head of the line. The forced march continued for days, and when women fell to the ground too fatigued to continue, they were left there while the rest moved on. After a minute or two, a shot was heard behind them. On one occasion, when a woman seemed to have lost her mind and began snarling at a guard, he simply shot her in the forehead and kicked her frail body aside.

Nela walked alongside Tanya and they spoke softly. "I don't know where they're taking us, but it won't be good," her friend suggested.

"With the Nazis now losing the war, they may be intent on killing us all so there won't be witnesses to their atrocities," Nela said.

"I don't think that's it at all," Tanya said. "If they intended to kill us, that could have been done in the camp. Perhaps they want to continue using us as laborers, but further from the front lines."

"Or we might be useful as hostages if they are in a precarious position and want to sue for peace so the Nazi regime survives," Nela said.

With their number substantially reduced by deaths along the trek, they reached another camp where they were made to bunk with women already there. They were kept in these dark barracks for four days. A few inmates served a bit of food to the rest. But it was only sufficient for the inmates who had been there earlier, leaving everyone hungrier and more desperate than before.

On the fifth day in the camp, they weren't awoken in the usual harsh manner. Instead, they were nudged awake by those inmates who had gotten up on their own. The deathly quiet outside was both confusing and frightening. Some of the women wanted to go outside and see what was happening. Others cautioned against it, concerned that armed guards awaited.

The debate was cut short by the distant sound of heavy machines approaching the camp. As the sound grew louder, the inmates from several buildings dared to come out, which encouraged the others to do the same. They soon realized the guards were no longer there, having abandoned the camp during the night. With the thought their release was imminent, they ran or hobbled to the camp's perimeter, peering through the barbed-wire fences. Hundreds of people screamed with happiness as they saw tanks and trucks approach from the east and joyously embraced one another's thin frames.

The first Soviet soldiers to arrive stood motionless at the fence, shocked by the scene before them. A few soldiers affected by the gruesome scene bent over and vomited, causing some of the prisoners to turn away to hide their humiliation at appearing disgusting in the eyes beholding them. The soldiers were unable to fully absorb the wrenching scene for some time. Finally, a few had the presence of mind to tear down the fence while others rushed to bring rations for the inmates.

As the Soviet soldiers entered the camp, they were mobbed by prisoners who hugged and kissed them. Others, having encountered horrible treatment at the hands of the Soviets early in the war, were wary and watched from a distance.

Once the celebration dwindled, prisoners gathered in small groups. Some prayed or sang songs of thanks, and a few sang *Hatikvah* [the Hope], which later became the Israeli national anthem. Nela and her group of friends sat on the ground quietly luxuriating in the food they had received. The army rations, as simple as they were, had flavors they hadn't savored in years.

For the longest time, no words were spoken between them. Finally, one of the women who had been with Tanya and Nela from the start, asked, "How long has it been?"

They looked at one another before Tanya said, "I'm not sure. Maybe five years, or perhaps six. I stopped counting long ago. One day blended into the next and one year into another. I simply lived from day to day."

Another woman then said what many others had been thinking: "Now what? What should we do now?"

Not having had the opportunity to make decisions for themselves for so long, and not even knowing where they were, the inmates were lost as to what to do next. Until then their focus had simply been on survival, obtaining scraps of food, and avoiding the attention of the Nazi guards. Now they were confronted with the reality of how to function daily, to simply know whether any of their relatives had survived, and how they could build new lives.

Russian officers gathered large groups around them to explain the soldiers could not remain there any longer as their job was to catch or kill the Nazis, which drew cheers from everyone. Raising his hands to quiet the crowd, an officer informed them they would be left with some food, and those who were too infirm to walk would be rescued by medics that were a few days behind. Those who could walk were told of several towns nearby where they could head.

Together with seven of her friends, Nela set out the next morning. As they entered a town at about midday, the absence of activity was notable. Perhaps aware of the Russian approach, the local people had left or were hiding. Near the edge of town, they found a hotel that had just been abandoned, which they figured was a good place to rest for a while. The hotel rooms had baths and showers and even hot water, and the women took advantage of their good luck to attempt to remove the years of dirt that encased them. Although hotel soap was available, Nela had saved the bar of soap she found in her very first package and used it to scrub herself. They took long baths and showers, coming out only when the water turned cold.

"I feel lighter now that I'm unburdened by so much filth," one woman, Clara, said happily. "I had to empty and refill the bathtub three times as the water had become dark with grime."

The hotel had beautiful curtains in the lobby and each of the rooms, and they set about removing some of them and cutting them up. Using needles and thread from the storage room, they sewed clothes to replace the putrid rags they were wearing. When done, they hardly recognized one another.

The pantry next to the main dining area was filled with a variety of foods, and they would have stayed at the hotel for many more days, but they had other priorities. Each wanted to return to their homes in hopes of finding survivors. After helping themselves to the food they carried in hotel bags, they split into two groups – those heading east and west.

As they were about to separate, one woman said, "I'm hoping to find members of my family, but I'm saddened having to leave this one."

Another replied ominously, "You never know what each of us will find. We may end up in the same place and we'll be sisters again."

Nela and her three companions headed west. Reaching Warsaw, two of the women went in search of their families who had lived there before the war, while she and Rachel continued to Lodz. They walked long stretches and, on occasion, a passing truck or car stopped to give them a ride, usually for a short distance. Upon reaching their destination, they went to Rachel's former home, only to find it occupied by people who had no knowledge of her family. They knocked on doors hoping to find former neighbors who might know the fate of her family. After several failed attempts, an elderly woman whom Rachel knew welcomed her into her home. Panye Bartczak informed Rachel that at the start of the occupation, her parents and sister were taken to the ghetto. Then, taking Rachel's hands, she sympathetically said, "I don't know what became of them, but people say few Jews survived. I'm so sorry." Rachel had braced herself for this news, but it was devastating nonetheless.

They sat with Panye Bartczak for a while, reminiscing about the times before the war. The elderly woman excused herself and returned with a black photo album. Together they looked through the album, which reminded Rachel of the life she might have had if not for the fascist swine. As they turned the pages, they came across two photos – one of Rachel with her smiling mother in a park, and the second of Rachel and her family standing in front of the apartment building in which they had lived. Carefully, Panye Bartczak lifted the pictures that had been lightly glued to the page and handed them to Rachel. Her eyes moist, Rachel held the pictures to her heart.

"This is all I have of them," she said. "The only evidence they ever existed in this miserable, capricious world."

Sympathetically, Panye Bartczak moved to Rachel and gently said, "Dziewczynka, little girl. You are the evidence they existed and I'm certain you will make them proud."

After tucking the pictures in her worn bag, they headed toward Nela's apartment. Upon seeing her, a neighbor came running over. "Nela, how are you still alive?" the neighbor, Pan Kowalczyk, said. "I hadn't recognized you at first, you've become so thin, and your hair is different. I'm so happy you survived."

"I'm glad to be alive, too," Nela said. "We can talk later, but first, tell me whether you've seen or heard anything of my family. I'm fairly certain my mother and both my sister and brother were murdered, but perhaps my father survived."

"I know very little, I'm afraid," he replied. "I was with your grandfather when he died in 1940. Regrettably, I haven't seen or heard anything about your father or the rest of the family. Some of the people who have returned have posted small signs in public places asking for information about their families. They have hope, but it is unlikely it will come to anything. I believe very few Jews survived, and most probably died in the ghetto or were transported to camps."

"I think you're probably right," Nela said, "but I need to find out whether anyone survived. If there is any chance at all, I can't abandon them."

"I understand, Nela. Why don't you come in and rest, and then tomorrow we can look around together? Perhaps a neighbor might know. There are several empty apartments, and you can use anyone you like."

"Can we obtain keys to open the doors?" Nela asked.

"Yes, I have all the keys since I've looked after the building for the past six years. I wish I could tell you rent was collected so I could pass it on to you. However, very little money was obtained during the war, not even enough to pay what bills there were."

"Thank you, Pan Kowalczyk, it was very good of you to look after the building."

"Of course. You needn't thank me. Your grandfather and I were close friends, and he would have been cross if I had let it fall into disrepair, but as you can see, even with my best effort, it isn't in very good condition."

"That's to be expected. What you did do was more than enough."

Her grandfather had been wealthy and a community leader, so she thought they might be able to obtain information about her family. Over the ensuing week, they searched the area for anybody who might have information. As she feared, they learned little.

"Nela," Pan Kowalczyk began awkwardly, "I don't know what your plans are, but if you intend to stay, then I'll help you with the apartments. However, believe me when I say Poland isn't a place you want to remain. Hatred for Jews is rampant. Some say the Nazi destruction of Poland was brought about by the Jews, while others maintain Russia will occupy Poland with the help of Jews. When the

Jews were taken away, some neighbors took their possessions and even moved into their homes. They will certainly be loathe to return them. Pogroms will ensue – it's the fate of Jews."

"Yes, that's been that way for millennia," Nela said. "I can assure you we have no intention of staying where the ground is soaked with Jewish blood."

"I'm relieved," he replied kindly. "I would like to leave, too, but I have nowhere to go. At the risk of sounding greedy, if you plan to leave, then I would like to purchase the building. I can't afford very much, but whatever I pay you will make your journey easier."

After negotiating briefly, they agreed upon a price far lower than the value of the building, but Nela wasn't in a position to obtain more, and Pan Kowalczyk certainly didn't have enough to pay more.

"Nela, where will you go?" he asked. "I don't know whether any country in Europe would be any good. I've been told all of Europe is a shambles, and as pitiful as it is, our priest has said not many countries are taking in Jews from elsewhere."

Both women were astonished by this comment.

"After all this, after all that has happened, we're still unwanted everywhere," Rachel said, shaking her head angrily.

Pan Kowalczyk shook his head in sympathy. "Nela, our priest has also told us the Americans are now in parts of Germany, and many people are heading there to be able to migrate to countries outside of Europe," he said. "Some are intent on reaching America, Canada, or another friendly country that hasn't suffered the destruction that befell European cities. For now, I think you should head for wherever the Americans are – Berlin, Munich, or better yet, a city that has a large port nearby from which people can depart."

They remained in Lodz for several more days in the faint hope they might find news of their families, but they achieved nothing. So, they told Pan Kowalczyk they would be leaving, and using his ancient truck, he took them to the road leading to Germany.

As they were about to get out of the truck, he said to Nela, "Whenever Jews were taken from the apartments, the Polish police and neighbors descended on the apartments and took what they could." Handing her a small tin box, he said, "I managed to take this from your grandfather's apartment before the hordes descended on it. It's all I can offer."

They stood at the side waiting for a kindly driver to take them where they were headed and Nela looked through the box, finding assorted items, including several pictures of her father taken when he was a young man. Turning to Rachel and showing her the photos, she wistfully said, "My father was once a young man. Oddly, I never thought of him that way." Staring at the picture, she said, "It's strange, I can visualize him perfectly, but I can't recall what his voice sounded like."

Within a few minutes, an American soldier driving a truck pulled over, and the driver motioned them to get in the back. Others like them largely filled the space but were able to make spots for them. Nela and Rachel differed from most of the others only insofar as they were newly washed and had proper clothing rather than rags. Embarrassed by their riches, Rachel briefly explained how they obtained the clothes, which brought smiles from the rest. For the most part, they remained quiet and listened to the stories of a woman, Zosha, and of a sad young man, Pinye, whom they recognized as smart and resourceful. Although they had only met these people hours earlier, owing to their shared tribulations, they bonded.

The ride on the lorry might have felt uncomfortable to others, but for Nela and Rachel, it was sublime – they were leaving Poland, which they had come to despise. Soon after arriving in Berlin, using a few zlotys from Pan Kowalczyk, they were able to board a train to Bremen and, with luck, would be able to leave Europe behind.

They were disabused of their dream of reaching America any time soon. "Tens of thousands of people from many countries have the same intentions we do, but the US and Canadian governments haven't yet opened their doors to Jews," Rachel lamented.

They maintained their hope, although they realized leaving wouldn't happen for several years. In the interim, they obtained jobs and shared an apartment to reduce their expenses. With their health returning and their gaunt faces and bodies almost restored to what they had been before their ordeal, the women were attractive and were aware of the stares from men wherever they went.

Months later, while waiting for a tram, a dark-haired, handsome man several years older engaged Nela in a conversation.

"*Czy ty jesteś Polakiem* [Are you Polish?]" he asked.

When she smiled and nodded at him, he extended his hand and introduced himself: "Isaac Rosenzweig, from Warsaw."

"Nice to meet you, Isaac. I'm Nela, from Lodz. So, we're almost neighbors."

They boarded the tram, where they spoke amiably until they reached Nela's destination. As she got off, he said, "I haven't had anybody from home to talk to for a long time, and since my workplace is only a few blocks away, I hope you won't mind if I walk with you."

"Of course, please do," she answered. "Other than my friend Rachel, I've been socially isolated and would welcome talking."

They met frequently going to or coming from work, and they exchanged their stories of the war years.

"I had been a medical student before the Nazi invasion, and through my sister, who has since died, may her name be a blessing, I was able to connect with Polish farmers who hid me throughout the war," he said. "My experiences during that time were miserable, although from what you've told me, yours were far worse. Now, meeting you, I feel my luck has changed."

Every day, he would bring her a small gift, such as delicacies comprising small pieces of milk chocolate or a difficult-to-obtain fruit. One day, he said, "Today, I brought you this small flower. It was growing through a crack in the pavement, which I thought reflected your resilience."

She was taken by the gesture but thought to herself, "That flower worked so hard to grow where it wasn't supposed to, and now that brave little flower will die."

They frequently shared their hopes for the future. "I'm passionate about reaching America to continue my medical studies," he said.

"However, I realize there will be a considerable delay before it becomes possible. Until then, I'm working as an orderly in a small American-run hospital and I'm learning English from the patients and staff." Then with a thick Polish accent, he showed off his new language: "*How do you do, Sergeant Moore? I em Isaac Rosenzweig, and on this very nice day, I will look efter you. If I don't make good job, den you can tell me.*"

"You speak beautifully, Isaac," she laughed. "Then again, I have no idea what you just said or if it really was passable English."

After many such meetings, he asked whether she would honor him by having supper together, and she delightedly agreed. Increasingly, they enjoyed one another's company, and it wasn't long before they had supper together every evening.

Walking along the street with her head in the clouds thinking of Isaac, she was unaware of events going on about her, only snapping back to the present when she heard her name called out. Standing before her was an older man, perhaps 30 years her senior. "Oy, Gott. Nela, is it really you?" the man said.

She couldn't place him initially, then suddenly exclaimed, "Mr. Greenblatt, I hadn't recognized you. I'm so happy to see you."

"I'm not surprised. I've aged badly after spending so long in Bergen-Belsen."

"But you survived. A miracle," she said.

"Nela, why are you here instead of in Munich with your father?" he asked.

"My father!" she exclaimed in shock. "My father is in Munich?"

"Yes, I saw him only a few weeks ago. He seems to be doing reasonably well, all things considered."

After excusing herself and hugging Mr. Greenblatt, she ran off to tell Isaac and Rachel the news and that she was heading for Munich. The distance from Bremen to Munich was about 580 kilometers, and it took more than a full day to reach the city. The first thing she did on arriving, was go to the Jewish Agency because they might have a record of his whereabouts. She was able to obtain his address and directions to get there, which was less than a 30-minute walk.

As she climbed the stairs to his apartment, her heart pounded and she felt her head spinning, but she pushed herself, finally reaching the third level. Standing in front of his door, heart racing, she knocked timidly, but there was no response. Then, after knocking more loudly, the door opened.

In front of her stood her father. Seeing her, his face paled and he placed his hand on the door frame to keep himself from falling. He pulled her to himself and wept into her shoulder, while she cried into his chest. Wordlessly they stood like this for a long time – there was nothing they could say. Finally, he kissed her forehead and took her into the apartment, their tears still flowing prodigiously.

Over the next hours that extended into days, they shared their stories.

"In the camp, I lost my religion," he said. "I don't even attend *shul* [synagogue] on the Sabbath anymore. I thought if there were a God, he wasn't a merciful one. He was malicious and toyed with us. Now, I think I may have been mistaken. This is a miracle."

"I, too, had lost my faith and identity, but I had friends who helped me through the worst times," she said. "Maybe there is a God, but I don't know that this miracle is of his making. Fate may have strange ways of making things turn around in unexpected ways. There are occasions when unexpected gifts come to us for no apparent reason. It's just happenstance."

"I suppose that's true," he responded. "The packages I had sent you might have seemed like miracles."

"The packages!" she cried out. "You sent the food packages? There was never any indication they were from you. I hadn't realized it since I thought you had been killed. Those packages kept me and some of the other girls alive, although many died despite the help. During my early days in the camp, I would daydream about being released. With time and loss of hope, I stopped daydreaming. However, when the packages began to arrive, I would daydream again — sometimes over trivial things, I admit, but the fact I engaged in this spoke to my determination to live."

They stayed together for the next two weeks. He had obtained a bicycle and as he peddled through Munich, she would sit on the handlebars like a little girl. He was involved in black market trading, exchanging German marks for US script, buying and selling cameras, and buying women's nylon stockings for which the soldiers paid handsomely, although he had only a vague notion of why they were so popular.

As the time to leave came, she told her father she had met a man who loved her and she was wildly in love with him. This gratified him immensely, and he told her he had met a woman whom he intended to marry, assuring Nela this woman couldn't and wouldn't replace her mother. She was kind and had a good head, and she, too, had lost her family, including two sons Yankele and Benyamin, and a daughter, Edgga. He told Nela he had become very lonely, and it was better to have someone with whom he could share a life. Nela accepted it and encouraged her father, yet at some level, it also bothered her.

Isaac had nervously anticipated her return. Before she had the opportunity to settle in, Isaac said, "Nela, I'd like to get married."

"Of course, that would make me so happy! When?"

"Tomorrow, as soon as possible."

"Tomorrow! I have to wait until then?" Only after did she tell Isaac about her time with her father. She had been slightly taken aback by his failure to ask after her father when he first saw her and attributed it as a reflection of his love for her rather than being selfish or self-absorbed.

The next day, taking Rachel with them, they went to see the rabbi at the local shul, who quickly arranged the necessary paperwork, dismissing some of the old customs that would have been necessary in their earlier lives. The rabbi arranged for the wedding to take place under a *chuppah* [canopy], as tradition dictated, and the groom broke a glass beneath his foot, a remembrance of the holy temples destroyed centuries earlier.

Over the next two years, she would ordinarily visit her father every six to seven weeks. One day, she appeared unexpectedly and told him that through Isaac's connection with an American hospital, they would be leaving for the United States within the week.

"So soon," he said. "I'm happy that you're happy, but I'm afraid I may never see you again." His eyes filling with tears, he added: "After finding one another, my heart hurts to lose you again."

Stroking his cheek, she said, "*Ojciec* [Dad], don't be foolish. You won't ever lose me. We'll be going to Chicago, where Isaac will complete his medical studies. Once we're settled, I'll send a telegram to let you know where I'll be. Forget about going to Israel. If you go to America, we'll be together again and we'll stay together. Two days later, she left her father, and as she descended the stairs, emptiness enveloped her, and her unbidden tears began to flow and continued as she walked to the train station, not caring about the people looking at her sympathetically.

The next Wednesday, they boarded the ship with the little luggage they had, and after a voyage of just more than six days, they arrived at Ellis Island in New York, excited by their future. Going through immigration and customs was simple. At immigration, an officer said to them, "Rosenzweig isn't an American name. Would you like me to change it slightly?"

Isaac's English, which had greatly improved, replied, "You can do that? That simple? Just the stroke of a pen?"

"You betcha. I do it all the time. Federowicz becomes Foster or Fraser, Chadlicki becomes Charles or Chad, and Rosenzweig can become Ross or Rose."

And so, Isaac and Nela Rosenzweig became Isaac and Nela Ross. She loved the country before they landed and looked forward to the freedom it offered and the vast opportunities that lay ahead of them. With her new name, she felt fully assimilated.

The next day they boarded the Streamliner, a slick train that took them to Chicago. During the train ride, they marveled at the landscape, the small towns and the mid-sized cities through which they traveled, the great rivers along which the train sometimes ran, and finally the edge of Lake Michigan. Nowhere were there bombed buildings, shattered trees, or decimated farmland.

Soon after arriving, they found an apartment near the University of Chicago where Isaac would be attending medical school. Nela found a job at a florist shop, and she was excited by being surrounded by living things and their sweet aromas. The elation she felt was tangible, a feeling she couldn't have imagined only a few years earlier. If only her father could be with her, that would make everything perfect.

One evening, when Isaac returned home, she greeted him enthusiastically, "Isaac, I have some good news. We'll soon be having a visitor."

"A visitor?" he asked, perplexed given that this was unusual. "Today? This isn't a good time for a visitor."

"Not today, Isaac. About eight months from now," she replied, patting her stomach.

It took him a moment to understand what she meant and said, "I'm so happy for you. That is very good news."

She puzzled over his response. He had said he was happy for her, not for them. Also, when he had understood she was pregnant, for the slightest moment, his eyes seemed to indicate something other than happiness. When she mentioned his reaction, he indicated she was being crazy as usual. Despite her certainty in what she saw, she soon dismissed these thoughts as being imaginary.

In due course, Nela gave birth to an apparently healthy son. However, within three months, the child exhibited signs of neurological damage, including an excessive startle reaction, difficulty swallowing, and apparent muscle weakness. The child was diagnosed as having Tay-Sachs disease, a rare genetic condition most often seen in the offspring of Ashkenazi Jews. He had a severe form and died at a little more than six months old.

She was disconsolate; Isaac seemed saddened but was able to compartmentalize his feelings and move forward. Nela was bitter. Looking upward she exclaimed, "I'm not Job. Stop testing me. I've long known our God is not merciful. I've said it before – how many times do you have to hear it?" Yet, she knew from her past she had to leave her grief behind and cope with the moment, so she did.

She heard from her father in 1949 that he and his wife couldn't gain entry to the US, but Canada had largely reduced restrictions against Jewish immigration, so they would be on a ship expected to land in Halifax on January 1, 1950.

Nela counted down the days for their arrival, excited to see her father and let him know that because of Isaac's earlier training, he would become a certified doctor that year, and that not long afterward he would be able to take up a residency in cardiology.

In late January, Nela and Isaac took a flight to New York for their reunion with her father. Isaac stayed only two days as he had to return to his duties in Chicago, but Nela remained with her father for two weeks. They explored the city, went to a delicatessen, visited Central Park, and even found a Yiddish theater, doing what a father and daughter are meant to do together.

For two years, Isaac and Nela's lives seemed to go along acceptably, but as Isaac's career flourished, strains in their relationship began to appear. Nela became increasingly aware his earlier adoring gestures had changed. He became increasingly demanding and controlling, overly critical of her, and at times brusque. One day in a restaurant during supper, he pointed at some elegantly dressed women and said, "If it weren't for you, I'd be with one of these modern girls." The first time he said it, she thought he was joking and laughed, but she took note of his comment. The second time, she knew he was serious and their marriage was coming to an end.

When she next met her father in New York, she told him what happened and he implored her not to do anything rash.

However, she ignored his advice and flatly stated, "I didn't survive the war to be held hostage by a narcissist."

As she became more insistent she would leave Isaac, her father became more adamant she stay with him. "He's a doctor, he's a good provider," her father said. "What more do you want?"

"I don't care he's a doctor. I wanted a kind husband. A life companion."

Her father was infuriated at her stubbornness. Even after boarding a train to Montreal where he lived, her father opened the window and called out to her, "When he was a nothing, you fell in love and married him, but now he's a successful doctor, you don't want him ... you do everything backward, Nela. Everything backward."

Her father's words kept coming back to her after she returned to Chicago. Maybe she was just being recalcitrant and could change her ways. Maybe she was just overly sensitive, as Isaac often said. Or maybe Isaac was manipulative and controlling, and needed power over her, and he did so through his words. Her father admonishing her had a marked effect, and she tried to follow his advice. However, Isaac became ever more critical of her every action – the way she dressed, spoke, and walked – without ever complimenting her. And he would never apologize for his disrespectful behaviors. She finally had enough and let him know she was unhappy and was leaving to live in New York. His mask had come off, as did the mask beneath his mask. He just shrugged and told her to do whatever she pleased.

She didn't have many salable skills and she berated herself for not taking academic courses while Isaac was in medical school. Even though she could readily obtain a job as a seamstress in New York's garment district, the memories of her work during the six years in the camp made her balk at the idea. She applied for a position as a switchboard operator with the telephone company and was immediately hired, probably because of her attractiveness as she certainly had no relevant skills or experience.

She became friendly with Pat, an attractive woman her age, who was hardened by life experiences. Pat knew how to play the game, while Nela was entirely naive about the new reality. Thus, while the work provided her with enough money, Nela became increasingly frustrated by the workplace sexism. The frequent comments, men brushing up against her or snapping her bra strap from behind as they walked by, angered her. They were taking liberties that appalled her, assuming women were helpless.

"They're just men being men, let it go," Pat said.

But Nela couldn't let it go. She confronted the abusers, and when it did little good, she filed a formal complaint with the bosses, which led to her dismissal as she was deemed a troublemaker.

As she sat in a coffee shop with her friend Lala, telling her what transpired, a man her age approached them. He was attractive, about six feet tall with jet black hair, dressed a little over the top, and used far too much aftershave lotion. "Hey, Lala, how ya doin'?"

"Fine, Sal, just swell. This here's my friend Nela."

"Nice ta meet ya, Nela. Ya from around here?" he asked.

"Not really. I live way at the other end of town. A long subway ride, but that's okay."

After sitting with them for a while, he rose, looked down at her, and said, "C'mon doll, I'm gonna give you a ride home."

"No thanks, Sal. I'm okay with the subway."

He was relentless. "What, you afraid of me? I ain't gonna bite. I'll just give you a ride home in a fine car. A classy dame like you don't need to ride on a smelly subway with the poor people."

Even though she disliked his attitude, she eventually relented, and he drove her home in his impressive red and white convertible Corvette. Once he knew where she lived, he would frequently come by and honk his horn to summon her.

One day, he said, "Lala told me you been lookin' for work. That right?" Before she could respond, he said, "My uncle Franco owns a car dealership. I can put in a word for you, and he'll hire you in a heartbeat."

Through this connection and her previous experience at the phone company, she became the receptionist and greeter at one of the larger car dealerships in the area. The price for the favor was Sal would pick her up in the early morning to drop her off at work.

She wasn't attracted to him, and the odor of his aftershave nauseated her. To her relief, he stopped wearing the "cologne" when she told him she had an allergy to some products with pungent aromas, which caused her eyes to water.

Eventually, his persistent attention wore her down and she began dating him despite his possessive and jealous behavior. Rather than his love-bombing warning her to stay away, she assumed his actions reflected his affection for her. There were several things she didn't understand about him, which eventually prompted her to ask, "Sal, what do you do for a living? It doesn't seem like you have a schedule, and you don't need to be anywhere at any specific time."

"Ah, I do dis and dat. I do lots of different things. I help take care of my grandma. She's always gotta go see the doctor and I'm the one who takes her. Mostly, though, I help my pop. He's gotten too old to do all the stuff by himself, so I'm always around for him."

His response smacked of evasiveness, and she asked, "What exactly do you do for your pop?"

This was met by an intense glare from him and a firm response: "I take care of business. You oughta take care of your business, too."

The truth of his activities emerged about six months later when the FBI, with the cooperation of the police, arrested Sal and his father. They were charged with racketeering, drug distribution, mail fraud, tax evasion, and running several brothels.

The FBI had been tailing Sal for months and was aware Nela had been dating him. So, she was brought in for questioning. Since she knew nothing of Sal's business dealings, she had nothing to tell them and was consequently unconcerned. This was America, after all, and there was no possibility she would be implicated in Sal's illegal dealings.

To her dismay, the FBI agents continued to put pressure on her.

"You've been dating Sal for months and you know nothing about what he did to earn a living, is that what you're claiming?" an agent asked.

"That's correct. I don't know anything at all, other than he was helping his father."

"With what?"

"With this and that he had told me. Nothing specific."

"He never confided in you, and you didn't ask?"

"I did ask, but he was evasive, and I didn't think it was a good idea to badger him since he made it clear my questions were unwelcome," she replied, naively assuming the agent would accept her response.

"So, his evasiveness didn't make you the least bit suspicious?"

"I thought his secretiveness was odd, but I thought asking more questions would be intrusive. As I said earlier, he had already made it clear it was none of my business."

After several meetings in which she repeated her innocence, the FBI agents felt they were getting nowhere with her and decided more aggressive steps were necessary. They leaked reports to a New York tabloid they were considering the arrest of Nela as the madame of several brothels. Moreover, they informed her she would never be able to obtain citizenship as her application would be placed on indefinite hold. However, if she provided evidence against Sal, they could make all this go away.

"I can't say what I don't know," she proclaimed to deaf ears.

In the meanwhile, Sal worried Nela would be coerced into saying something that would implicate him in crimes, even though he was sure she was oblivious of anything of the sort. However, he had to be certain she would stay quiet.

Two large men let themselves into Nela's apartment while she was asleep. She awoke to a large hand covering her mouth. "Nela, we have a message for you," a man said. "If you speak to the FBI about Sal, we'll be back and cut your tongue out, cook it, and make you swallow it. Do you understand?"

Terrified, she didn't respond, leading the man to squeeze her face. "Say you understand."

When she only nodded her head, he squeezed harder, saying through gritted teeth, "Say you understand."

With difficulty, she croaked out the words, "I understand."

Nela was terrified of what they might do to her. Just a week earlier, Lala, who had a severe heroin addiction, had jumped from the Brooklyn Bridge. It was assumed she had died by suicide, but Nela was now convinced Lala was thrown to her death. Owing to her drug addiction, Sal might have thought Lala would be pliable, and he wasn't taking the chance that Lala wouldn't keep her mouth zipped.

In desperation, she contacted her friend Pat, who had moved to California, and the very next day went to stay with her. It was apparent Nela had become exceptionally paranoid, taking unreasonable precautions to maintain her safety. Among other things, she slept in a small storage area beneath the staircase, only venturing out to discreetly peek through the living-room curtains to see if anybody was watching for her, and some nights she would go out for several hours to determine whether parked cars in the area had men watching for her. Moreover, Nela insisted the phones were bugged and microphones had been planted in the house to capture anything said, and every day she would thoroughly search through the house to find listening devices. Pat, who was pregnant, worried the distress created by Nela might affect her fetus, and she eventually asked Nela to leave.

Having no options, Nela returned to New York, where she remained alone and lonely. Fortunately, the FBI stopped harassing her once Sal and his father were prosecuted and given lengthy prison terms. Her life began to return to normal, but what she had viewed as an unmerciful God had other plans for her. In response to stomach pain, chronic constipation, and the presence of blood in her feces, her physician had a detailed examination performed, which revealed the presence of intestinal cancer.

She was convinced the distress and diet experienced in the labor camp were responsible for the cancer. Looking skyward, she said, "I've beaten so many other things you've thrown against me, and I'll get through this, too."

The cancer was diagnosed early and she was treated successfully. Having experienced trauma after trauma didn't weaken Nela. Instead, she had become more resilient and determined not just to survive but thrive. She seemed to have learned two critical lessons. The first was bad things happen, and not just to other people. The second was she had to be resolute in not relying on others. Thus, she sought ways to manage her life, including her financial condition, without being beholden to anybody, and certainly not a controlling man. Two bad experiences were enough.

Her father had toyed in the stock market for years, probably reflecting his inclination to gamble, but doing it in a socially acceptable way. Thus, the idea came to her of doing the same.

"The stock market could be the ideal way to attain the wealth to allow me to be independent," she said to her father. "As America prospers, so will I, and if American prosperity is reflected in the stock market, then that's where I'll place my bets."

She read voraciously about the market, signed up for all manner of stock news, and learned various investment strategies. Most importantly, before making any stock purchases, she learned everything possible about the company in which she considered investing. Using what she had learned, she placed small amounts of money into a diverse stock portfolio. Slowly and carefully, she amassed a good sum of money. Once her funds were substantial, she began to leverage her investments so she could wager progressively larger amounts on specific stocks. Of course, she understood a decline in stocks could set her back, but having been on a lengthy winning streak, her usual caution went by the wayside. Besides, her portfolio comprised both risky and safe stocks, so she thought the overall basket of investments would protect her. Over several years, her worth exceeded a million dollars. She credited her successes to her acumen while not ignoring the maxim "a rising tide lifted all boats." However, she seemed to have forgotten the corollary concerning the effect of the tide going out.

When the market crashed, her leveraged investments resulted in her losses being amplified. The bank called in its loans, forcing her to sell off most of her stocks, leaving her without her earlier paper profits. Still, she owned a mortgage-free house and continued to receive dividends from a few stocks she had been able to retain. She was able to maintain a modest if frugal lifestyle. For years, her lawyer told her she was eligible for monthly payments from the German government in the form of *Wiedergutmachung* [financial reparations] for the harm she endured during the Holocaust. She adamantly refused to accept this guilt money from angels with singed wings.

Much later, she told her friends, "I had resigned myself to a lonely life, but another unexpected reversal of fortune was in the cards. I met Charles, a tall, red-haired Irish guy who retired after selling his small hardware store. We were perfect together. Even my father didn't object to his not being Jewish, having been won over by Charles's apparent kindness and caring."

Nela and Charles formed a set of friends and she felt accepted. Every year, her father took them to Florida for the winter, and the time with him completed her small circle. With her father, she felt like the 14-year-old girl who romped through the parks in Lodz. When her father died from heart disease that probably started from the stressors experienced in the labor camp, she again felt as if she were adrift in an unstable boat. Fortunately, Charles was there to stabilize her. But when he died just a few years later, her persona changed entirely. She rarely went out and began a pattern of hoarding. She squirreled away every little item. Tchotchkes of every manner covered every inch of space within her home. It was almost impossible to find a route from one end of her home to another.

She would excuse her behavior by saying, "I'm aware my behavior is peculiar, but I can't stop myself from collecting. I don't know why I began doing this, but I believe it's a remnant from my time in the labor camp where every item found was kept in case it could have some use."

Perhaps that was so, or it might have been an early sign of the dementia that afflicted her in the last two years of her life. Unlike the cancer that she had beaten, the dementia progressed relentlessly, leaving her a shell of what she had been earlier.

She died peacefully but not happily – the dreams that brought her to America largely unfulfilled.

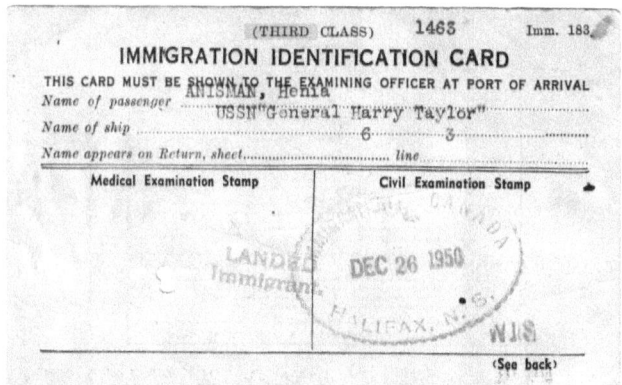

Once in Canada Chana and Shimon identified strongly as Canadians, treasuring every document they obtained from government agencies. The immigration card shows the date of their arrival in Halifax, which they celebrated every year.

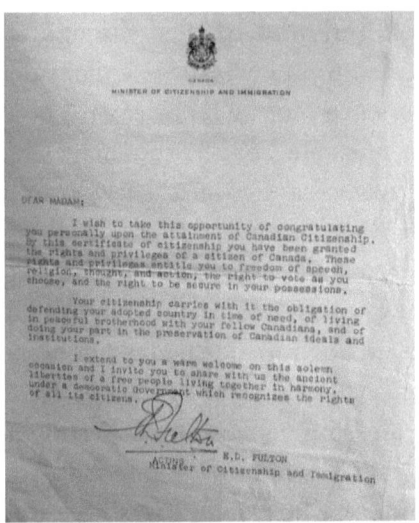

Along with their Citizenship papers, this letter was treasured because it assured Chana and Shimon that they entitled to freedom of speech, religion, thought, and action, which they had been denied for so long.

One of the pictures Pan Kowalczyk had given Nela in the tin box. The picture is of her father as a boy, probably taken at the time of his Bar Mitzvah in 1915.

Shimon in New York City in 1953 on a business trip and to visit Nela.

Shimon in London in 1955 on a business trip to obtain machinery for the family's growing business.

Nela and her father Shimon during better times. The picture was taken in 1963 during one of their winter stays in Florida.

Nela before marrying Charles (about 1968)

Shimon and his cousin in Jerusalem early in the 1960s. Other than Nela, this cousin and two who lived in the Soviet Union were the only survivors of Shimon's extended family.

6

YOSSI AND SASHA: THE KINDERTRANSPORTS

> We are caught in an inescapable network of mutuality, tied in a single garment of destiny. Whatever affects one directly, affects all indirectly.
>
> – Dr. Martin Luther King, 1963

One day, Chaviva was interviewed on the radio about the Holocaust by a prim British woman who had previously been with the BBC. At times, the exchange was tense.

"When the National Socialists came to power in 1933," Chaviva said, "many Jews in Germany immigrated to neighboring European countries, and a few were able to reach the US and Canada. Those who had been politically aware were most likely to leave, as were civil servants who were dismissed from their positions. They typically sought asylum in other countries based on the threat of racial, religious, or political persecution. My family had at first considered trying to leave but then reconsidered, thinking it was too early to panic. They just couldn't accept the Nazis intended to exterminate all Jews. Despite the history of pogroms and mass killings, the notion of Jews being exterminated was just too absurd. By the time we realized how bad the situation was, more countries became reluctant to accept Jewish refugees."

Scowling, she added: "The Nazis were only too happy to see the pesky Jews leave, and they gained by heavily taxing emigration and subsequently confiscating their possessions. Our inability to leave wasn't because of the Nazis blocking us as much as the unwelcoming behavior of so many other countries."

The interviewer attempted to push back mildly. "Well, recognizing the danger posed to Jews, US President Franklin Roosevelt organized a conference at Évian-les-Bains in early July 1938 to address the issue," she said. "Representatives of 32 countries who attended were in favor of taking actions to help Jews."

"Yes, President and Mrs. Roosevelt were very honorable, and I believe they did what they could," Chaviva replied. "At Évian, the representatives of many countries said all the right things, as diplomats typically do. In the end, most of these countries were resistant to accepting Jewish immigrants."

"Do you believe there were specific events that fomented the hatred of Jews by the National Socialists?" the interviewer asked.

"As I'm sure you're aware, the hatred of Jews was long-standing, and haters have given diverse reasons for it. It's like a horrible virus for which there is neither a vaccine to prevent it nor a therapy to eliminate it once it has taken hold. For the victims of antisemitism, it doesn't matter why it occurred, only that it did."

"What do you suppose made Hitler so effective in promoting this hatred?" the interviewer asked.

"What Hitler did successfully was normalize the hatred directed at Jews, allowing intense animosity to emerge without consequence to the haters," she replied. "The treatment of Jews was abhorrent from the day they took office, and the National Socialists spread the loathing in whatever countries they dominated. No matter how much they succeeded in suppressing the rights of Jews, it never seemed to be enough. Hitler and Goebbels had been waiting for an opportunity to mobilize German and Austrian people to increase their attacks on their Jewish citizens. A 17-year-old Jewish refugee gave them the perfect excuse when, on November 7, 1938, he entered the German Embassy in Paris and shot a German diplomat who died two days later. This was sufficient to prompt Kristallnacht. There were hundreds of synagogues destroyed, thousands of Jewish-owned businesses vandalized, and thousands of Jewish men were transported to concentration camps, and many more were severely assaulted."

Sympathetically, the interviewer said, "The fear created after that night no doubt caused many Jews in Germany and Austria to redouble their attempts to emigrate through authorized channels, or perhaps they found alternative ways of leaving given that the doors for immigration to many countries were firmly closed?"

"Well, anybody who had been sufficiently naive to think they were safe had their eyes opened by Kristallnacht," Chaviva responded. "Unfortunately, the flood of immigrants proved to be a challenge to many countries, so those that had been accepting Jews earlier ultimately closed their borders. Still, by September 1939, thousands of Jews had reached the US, Britain, Palestine, various South American countries, and even parts of China."

"I'm very proud my government played a critical role in saving children from the Nazis," the interviewer said.

Pausing, Chaviva seemed to debate with herself about how to respond. Finally, she said, "Yes ... yes, I suppose that's accurate. Reading the writing on the proverbial wall following Kristallnacht, several individuals and groups mobilized to save Jewish children. Given their obvious plight, Britain promptly agreed to take in children on Kindertransports [children's transports], provided they were younger than 17 and wouldn't be a financial burden on the country. The notion at the time, however naive, was that once the crisis had passed, the children would be repatriated to their home countries to be with their parents. The Kindertransports began in March 1939 and ended on September 1, 1939. About 10,000 children had been rescued by the time the war began, after which transports were no longer possible. While most children were sent to Britain, some ended up in other European countries that were later conquered, and many of these children likely died with other Jews."

"Did Britain decide which children would be allowed entry, or were others tasked with this?" the interviewer asked.

"As you can imagine, choosing who would live and those who

might suffer miserably and perhaps die was a horribly painful task, yet it needed to be done, and done without delay," Chaviva said. "Jewish organizations quickly formed lists of children who were at greatest risk for retribution by the Nazis, particularly the children or grandchildren of those who were politically threatening, as well as some children who had been in orphanages. Individuals such as Florence Nankivel and Wilfrid Israel worked diligently to extract children from Germany and Austria, arranging their transport by boat or train.

"Similar activities were undertaken in Poland and the Netherlands. Nicholas Winton, who had become involved with left-wing politics and understood the dangers posed by appeasing the Nazis, traveled to Czechoslovakia and, with others, was successful in transporting 669 children to Britain. Winton lamented that if the invasion of Poland had occurred even a few days later, more children would have survived. Indeed, the transport of 250 children who were to leave was canceled the very day Germany invaded Poland and, as far as we know, ultimately only two of these children survived. Many more could have been saved if the US had been willing to accept children. An effort was made to have the US absorb 20,000 endangered children, but congressional approval wasn't obtained."

Sensing that although the interviewer was sensitive to the plight of Jews, she was more intent on pointing to the critical role played by Britain in saving children, Chaviva chose to direct the conversation the way she wanted it to go.

"There was little question the Kindertransports saved the lives of many children," Chaviva said. "What is too often overlooked is the trauma created in the children and their parents. Just for a moment put yourself in the heart-wrenching place of parents who gave up their children so they could survive. The children, of course, experienced considerable trauma upon being separated from their parents, especially older children who were likely aware they might never see them again."

"I'm sorry, Chaviva, it wasn't my intention to be insensitive," the interviewer said. "I just want our audience to understand that while

Britain hasn't always been perfect, it has done many good things for Jews of which many people aren't aware."

"No need to apologize, yet the account of the Kindertransport must be accurate. Homes were found for most children who arrived, and when homes were not immediately available, children were temporarily housed in schools and hostels. As well-intentioned as the efforts were, in many cases, siblings were separated from one another, depriving them of the little support they had. Moreover, due to the understandable rush to find places for the children, many homes were not vetted as well as they should have been and, consequently, some ended up being placed with families who used them as servants, and, more distressing, some experienced abuse."

"I've heard of such events, but I assumed they were infrequent," the interviewer doggedly insisted. "The British people were overwhelmingly supportive of allowing Jewish children into the country, and this was broadly shared by politicians."

Shaking her head to signify doubt, Chaviva said, "That's mostly accurate, although a considerable number of people wanted to keep Jews out of Britain. Arguably, Clement Attlee the prime minister of Britain at the end of the war, harbored antisemitic feelings, and his loud-mouthed foreign secretary Ernest Bevin made it widely known he was no friend of Jews. Even Neville Chamberlain, who was instrumental in the establishment of the Kindertransports as prime minister, said, 'I believe the persecution arose out of two motives: a desire to rob the Jews of their money and a jealousy of their superior cleverness.' Undoing his complimentary comments, he went on to say, 'No doubt the Jews aren't a lovable people; I don't care about them myself – but that is not sufficient to explain the pogrom.'

"Such ideas were all too common among some British people," she added, "resulting in adamant protests against Jews being allowed to immigrate, regardless of their age, and it wasn't unusual for Jewish immigrants to be ostracized in schools."

"That may be true, but you're not suggesting those children who came were poorly treated?" the interviewer asked, becoming a bit defensive.

Shaking her head, Chaviva said, "I appreciate the times were very uncertain, and in the spring of 1940, paranoia took hold in Britain about a 'Fifth Column' that supported Nazism. Consequently, individuals of various nationalities, including Jews who had immigrated, were interned by the government. Remarkably, more than 1,000 children over the age of 16 who had arrived on the Kindertransports were deemed to be 'enemy aliens' and were treated as such. Some of these children were sent to Canada to be interned and found themselves on the same ships that were transporting German prisoners of war as if there were some equivalence between the two. Only after a great outcry were they separated from the Nazis and not interned in the same camps in Canada."

As the radio program was coming to a close, the interviewer wanted to end on a positive note, saying, "I'm delighted to say many of the children who were saved through the Kindertransports later went on to become highly successful historians, mathematicians, writers, artists, architects, journalists, entrepreneurs, and scientists, two of whom received the Nobel Prize in chemistry and physics. We can count on many of the children of those saved through the Kindertransports likewise going on to do great things. The world has benefited immensely from them."

"That's so true, and thank you so much for your comment," Chaviva said. "I can't help but think about what else might have been achieved for humankind if all of the six million had survived."

Seeing the situation for Jews in Czechoslovakia had become increasingly dire, Gilda Fried decided to try to have her ten-year-old son Yossi join a transport that would take him to Britain. Since his father had been a devoted member of a left-wing group before he was arrested by Nazi police, the boy had been put on a priority list for a spot on a Kindertransport. With the loss of her husband, it was much more difficult for Gilda to send her son off. She hoped she would have the opportunity of immigrating to Britain later to join him but was aware of its unlikelihood. Still, the rationalization gave her the courage to do what was necessary.

Hesitantly, Gilda and Yossi walked to the train station holding hands, and he carried a small knapsack containing a few belongings. He repeatedly implored her not to send him to Britain, and repeatedly she found ways of diminishing his anxiety. She had intended to stay with him until it was time to board the train, but when they reached the station entrance, she was barred from going in.

An officious soldier said, "Only children may pass this point. Parents cannot accompany them."

When she objected, he glared at her menacingly and said, "Send him off now as the train will leave shortly. If he is not on board, rest assured he will not have the opportunity of leaving on another train."

She pulled Yossi aside, who again pleaded with his mother not to send him off. "What if I never see you again?" he asked. "If you couldn't even take me into the station, how will you ever get to me later?"

Her determination almost faltered as she gazed into his large brown eyes, but in the end, she said, "Oh, don't be a silly boy. Where you'll be going, it will be like a summer camp and you'll be with many other children. As soon as I can obtain the proper exit papers, I will join you in Britain. By then, your father will also be free, and we'll be a happy family again in a better place."

Reluctantly, he agreed, and she added: "As the train leaves the station, look out the window and you'll see me waving to you."

He took a seat next to a window, listening to the sounds of crying children from all sections of the train car. He was determined to be brave, although his eyes were brimming with tears. As the train moved out of the station, he looked for his mother. He spotted her waving and smiling, which briefly lifted his spirits, unaware she couldn't see inside the train and had been putting on a show in hopes he would see her. Once the train passed, Gilda walked away slowly, her body wracked by unrestrained sobbing, and dropping to her haunches, mournfully cried, "The light of my life has been extinguished."

On arriving in Britain, the children were divided into groups based on whether homes had been found for them. Yossi was among those for whom a home hadn't yet been arranged, so he was transferred to a hostel along with 14 other children. Even though he was well looked after, he missed his parents terribly and was lonely and depressed, had difficulty sleeping, and entirely lost his appetite. His frequent periods of wistfulness, accompanied by intensely dwelling on his feelings, led him to become introverted, spending long periods alone reading some of the few available books.

While sitting on the floor leaning against a wall of the main common room, a book on his lap, a nicely dressed man and woman accompanied by a young girl who had been staying at the hostel walked through the room. The girl whose hand was being held by the woman looked at Yossi and greeted him. He, in turn, said, "Hi, Sasha. Are you leaving?"

"I think so," she replied uncertainly, looking up at the woman holding her hand. "I hope I'll see you again."

When the woman looked over at Yossi, he met her eyes and smiled. Continuing to hold Sasha by the hand, she went over to him and bent to her knees. "Hello, what are you reading so intently?" she asked in Czech. Upon showing her the book, she said, "I read that book to my children a few years ago when I lived in Prague. It's a very nice book for children."

"Yes, it is. But really, I'm too old for this book and I'd like something more suitable."

"Are there certain authors whose work you like reading most?"

Thinking aloud, he said, "I very much liked *Babička* [The Grandmother] by Božena Němcová. I was also fond of Eduard Bass's book *Klapzubova Jedenáctka* [Klapzubova's Eleven] since I loved playing soccer, and in my imagination, I was part of Pane Klapzubova's team."

"Those are both classic Czech books. You seem to have an appetite for reading."

"I do. I would often read books that belonged to my mother. She had several books by Karel Čapek I enjoyed. I also like books by Jaroslav Hašek and especially Franz Kafka."

Utterly surprised by these choices she replied, "Those are books for adults. Aren't you a bit young to be reading books like that?"

"I suppose so, but I like history and stuff like that. I'm also attracted to satirical works and the absurd situations Kafka writes about."

"What's your name, dear boy?" she asked gently.

"Yossi. My mama says I was named after her grandfather, who she said was a great scholar."

"And do you want to be a scholar like your great-grandfather?"

He was slow in responding, finally saying, "I suppose so, although I hadn't thought of that. It would be wonderful to be able to read as much as I liked." Then after a brief pause, he added: "I'm not sure what makes a person a great scholar. I just like learning new things."

Placing her hand on his outstretched leg, the woman turned to the young girl who was about Yossi's age, saying, "Sasha, stay here with Yossi for a moment. I'll be back in a jiffy."

She walked over to her husband, Desmond, and quietly whispered, "That little boy is an absolute charmer and so very, very bright – brilliant. I don't want him to stay here any longer. Our house is big enough, so let's take both Sasha and him. It will be good for both of them."

"If that's what you'd like Margaret, then it's fine with me. I promised Nicky Winton's people we would take one child. If we took two, they would be doubly pleased."

Smilingly broadly, she returned to the two children and bent to her knees again. "Yossi, how would you like to come home with us? I think you'd be very happy being with Sasha and my two children."

He glanced at Sasha who was vigorously nodding her head and said, "That would be wonderful. You're very kind. Thank you so very much."

"It's settled then," she replied and stood up. Hand in hand, they all walked back to the administrator of the hostel and informed him of their decision, signed the necessary papers, and went off.

Yossi and Sasha were awed by the grandeur of the Ashwood home. They were introduced to their children, nine-year-old Jane and ten-year-old Trevor. The four children took to one another immediately, and they soon formed an inseparable bond.

Over the next days, Yossi learned Desmond and Margaret

Ashwood came from what was referred to as the upper class and had a long family history of serving in the diplomatic core. They and their children had spent three years in Czechoslovakia and, before that, had been in Canada for a similar amount of time, where Desmond served as a military attaché. Margaret told them they would receive a new posting soon. Until then, Yossi and Sasha would accompany Jane and Trevor to the private school they attended.

Not understanding English well made it difficult for them at first, but they quickly were able to understand the language, and not long afterward could speak fluently. Even though Yossi and Sasha initially had been more comfortable speaking in Czech, they increasingly spoke to one another in English.

Eight months later, Desmond was posted to Argentina, and the family traveled there a month later. Soon after they arrived in Buenos Aires, the children were taught Spanish by a private tutor, and by the time school started again, they were sufficiently well-equipped to participate in classes.

To their pleasant surprise, Yossi and Sasha found Buenos Aires had a large Jewish community that comprised immigrants who had come to the country over the preceding two decades. At supper, Sasha said, "With so many Jews here, I hope Yossi and I will be safe. Still, there were lots of Jewish people in Czechoslovakia and look what happened there."

With little hesitation, Desmond said, "You needn't be concerned. As part of the British delegation to this country, no harm will come to any of us. The current government is neutral concerning the war in Europe, and Britain has a strong relationship with Argentina. There has been a push to have Argentina join the Allies in fighting Germany, but they've been holding fast in remaining neutral. Several officers in the Argentine army support the Axis, but they are the minority. That said, many Germans have located here in the past years, and large sums of money are being transferred from Germany. It's unlikely the present government will fall. If it does, then depending on who takes charge, the ties between Argentina and the Reich may strengthen and it would become more uncomfortable for us here."

While his words soothed them to an extent, having already been victimized by the Nazis, Sasha and Yossi remained wary. Besides, they had already been keenly aware that some of their classmates who were of German descent were brazenly ostracizing them. Despite their safety concerns, they wouldn't allow themselves to be intimidated and openly mingled with other members of the Jewish community. Encouraged by Desmond and Margaret, they attended holiday services and became involved in other activities sponsored by their synagogue. Margaret explained, "It's very important you maintain your identity and take pride in who you are."

Later, she surprised the rabbi at the synagogue, asking him to tutor Yossi and Sasha in Bible studies as well as Jewish customs and history, which he did happily. When the time came, he also prepared Yossi for his bar mitzvah and Sasha for her bat mitzvah, although this was ordinarily done among girls when they turned 12 years of age, which had passed months earlier. Their family celebrated with the Jewish community, which took great pride in welcoming Desmond and Margaret as honorary members of the fold.

That evening, Sasha whispered to Yossi, "Like you, I miss my mama and papa terribly. Our parents would have been so very proud today, and your parents would have been overjoyed to hear you read from the Torah today."

Tearfully, he replied, "I had been thinking exactly that, and it's with mixed emotions we both celebrate this day."

At supper, Desmond announced, "Well, my little family, our days here in Argentina are coming to an end."

"We're going back to Britain!" Jane shouted in excitement.

"No, I've been posted to the United States, and we'll be going there directly within a few weeks."

Yossi expressed concern. "I'm glad we'll be going to America, but, with all our moving around, how will our parents be able to find us?"

Although she knew better, Margaret said, "Don't worry about

that. When this miserable war ends, our government will have a pulse on the situation, and reunifications of families will be possible."

When they arrived in Washington in late 1943, the US was simultaneously at war against Japan in the Pacific and alongside the British and Canadians against the Nazis in Europe. Desmond's position had him coordinating with the Americans in transporting munitions and soldiers to Britain and was instrumental in the transfer of weapons to Russia.

After years of witnessing the success of the Nazi war machine, Desmond was growing optimistic about defeating the Axis powers.

"The success of the German U-boat campaign has been diminished by the US forming convoys to reach Europe and by greater protection from aircraft," he told his family. "Among other things, it has allowed us to get arms to Britain more readily. The Russians are methodically pushing the Germans back, and Italy will soon be eliminated as a German ally. Hitler keeps insisting the war could be salvaged and has begun taking extreme measures to sustain his overextended armies. He is likely fooling himself, and communications we intercepted indicated several of his generals have given up on this idea and their morale has declined."

"And what's the status of the people being held in concentration camps?" Margaret asked, which perked the attention of the children even more.

Aware of Yossi and Sasha's apprehension, he debated how to respond, wishing Margaret hadn't raised the issue. He opted to be upfront yet put a hopeful spin on the situation.

"In several respects, what we've been seeing has been promising, although I had hoped for better," Desmond said. "The Nazis continue to transfer Jewish people, Roma, and political prisoners from across Europe to the camps. There have been indications of resistance from inmates of camps as well as in some ghettos, especially within Warsaw, although it's hard to imagine this will have much of an effect." Then looking at the children directly, he added: "I've been pushing for action to bomb the rail lines in the hope of slowing down the transfer of prisoners to these camps. Admittedly, I can't say how successful I'll be."

Frustrated, Margaret said, "Oh for goodness' sake! The Allied governments have known about the treatment of Jews in these camps for some time. It's no secret! Why hasn't anything been done? Surely, the rail lines could easily be destroyed."

Seeing Yossi and Sasha's lowered heads and distraught expressions, he was annoyed with Margaret for distressing them more than they already were. But always the diplomat, he put his arm around Margaret before reaching across the dinner table and, placing a hand on each of Sasha's and Yossi's, said, "I know how concerned you are. I agree with Margaret the situation is grim, though as I said earlier, I'm hopeful things will soon change."

"Soon?" Yossi said. "I'm afraid it may already be too late."

Throughout 1944, the tide of the war flowed against the Nazis and the Allies progressively throttled the Wehrmacht. Nazi generals were making secret plans to surrender, and many officers were busy enriching themselves and seeking to ensure the wealth they looted would remain safe. Some Nazi officers made plans to assassinate the Führer and his close circle, but success eluded them. In July 1944, an attempt was made to kill Hitler. Supported by several generals and others in a resistance movement within the Wehrmacht, Colonel Claus von Stauffenberg placed a bomb within the Wolf's Lair field headquarters near Rastenburg. To the dismay of the resistance movement, through sheer luck, Hitler escaped death. In the weeks that followed, the leaders of the movement were executed, as were several thousand members of the resistance within the Wehrmacht.

Desmond confided to Margaret, "Even though there has been some opposition to Hitler's efforts and the Nazis have been retreating on multiple fronts, they're not fully vanquished and have undertaken several large-scale counteroffensives. I keep expecting Hitler will pull a rabbit out of a hat in the form of a superweapon, such as an atomic bomb that can be mounted on one of the V-2 rockets they've used to attack London. Our information is they've been working on this since 1939 or 1940, but I doubt they advanced far enough to create this weapon despite having several skilled physicists."

In May 1945, shortly after Berlin fell and Hitler died by suicide, the Nazi armed forces unconditionally surrendered. The news was met with jubilation, yet much more needed to be accomplished in hopes of producing lasting peace. At the end of July through early August, Soviet, American, and British leaders met at the Potsdam Conference to decide on the spheres of influence that would be maintained by each country. Many disagreements arose among the victors, and in the end, it was the Soviets who gained the most.

Feeling defeated, Desmond said to Margaret, "I had passionately anticipated the end of the war but hadn't reckoned on politics undermining my capacity to make important contributions to British foreign policy. When Harry Truman assumed the role of the president after Roosevelt died, I had assumed a much harder line would be taken with Stalin. However, French President Charles de Gaulle, who might have been a challenge for Stalin, wasn't included in the conference."

With the change in government during the Potsdam negotiations, Attlee and Bevin replaced Winston Churchill and Anthony Eden. Desmond expressed disappointment he could do little to affect their positions.

"I'm unhappy and bitter about this, although truth be told, I suspect my having a voice behind the scenes wouldn't have made any difference given Russia was resolute in not being displaced from the regions they occupied after the war," he said. "Besides, the concessions made by the US and Great Britain five months earlier at the Yalta Conference couldn't readily be undone. I'm still shocked they agreed to allow Poland, Czechoslovakia, and Romania to become part of the Soviet orbit, which these countries perceive as a 'Western betrayal.' Frankly, like many of my colleagues, I think Yalta and Potsdam may be a prelude for a different type of conflict between the Russians and Western countries."

When his term ended in 1946, Desmond chose not to maintain a diplomatic position and instead accepted an offer to serve as a university professor teaching political science. He expected his children would attend the same university in Washington the following year. But that wasn't to be.

Soon afterward, in a discussion with Desmond and Margaret, Sasha said, "I'd like to go to college in New York City, and both Yossi and Trevor would like to do the same. Next year, when Jane is old enough, she can join us there. How do you feel about that?"

Somewhat taken aback, Desmond said, "I had hoped you would stay here in Washington with Margaret and me. Several fine universities would certainly welcome you."

The young people seemed crestfallen until Margaret interjected. "I think that's a splendid idea," she said. "Desmond, they need to find their way, and if we keep hovering over them, they'll never be able to do that."

Margaret's intervention brought Desmond around to her way of thinking. Their excitement over going to college, however, dissipated several days later.

Desmond took Yossi and Sasha aside, and as they sat across from him in their living room, he said in a quavering voice, "I've heard from our embassy your parents did not survive the war. I'm so terribly, terribly sorry."

They sat quietly collecting themselves. With tear-filled eyes, Sasha said, "We pretty well figured as much. Very few Jews survived, and if our parents had lived through it, we would have received word by now. Yossi and I have discussed this frequently, and though we were pessimistic, not knowing with certainty has weighed on us. At least our parents knew we were being well looked after and would have been so grateful to you."

He had difficulty responding given the lump in his throat. Realizing it, they both went over and hugged him. Finally, when he felt able to speak, he told them, "I think it has been apparent you've been like my own children and my love for you is as great as it is for my biological offspring."

"We know that," said Yossi. "We're your children as much as Trevor and Jane, except we aren't a random assortment of your genes and those provided by Margaret. You got to choose us."

Sasha, Yossi, and Trevor arrived in New York in mid-August and went directly to the apartment that had been leased on their behalf by a good friend of Desmond's. He arranged for a bed, a set of drawers, and a small desk for each bedroom. He left a note behind providing his phone number, adding he would check in periodically to make sure the desks were being well used.

The following week was bittersweet. The excitement of entering college was tinged with the knowledge this would be the first time in years the family would be separated. Soon after Desmond, Margaret, and Jane left to return to Washington, the three young people began their studies. Trevor planned to major in political science, hoping to join the diplomatic corps eventually. Sasha would major in sociology, intent on understanding group behaviors. Yossi chose psychology, wanting to study the immediate and long-term consequences of early-life stressful experiences.

They looked forward to Jane joining them the following year, but when the time came, she chose to stay in Washington, saying, "Somebody has got to stay and look after Mum and Dad – otherwise they're bound to get themselves into trouble."

Although Jane had said this in her usual jovial way, it was understood the comment reflected her concern that their aging parents would need assistance soon.

While in their third year at the university, they heard about an upcoming lecture by a well-known historian on issues related to the Holocaust, which they attended together. Yossi was enthralled by the lecture and afterward approached the speaker for more information. Zosha was delighted to meet Yossi, as well as Sasha and Trevor. Always open to students, she described in greater detail over coffee what she had been doing, and she learned about their goals and aspirations. Over the ensuing months, Yossi met with her frequently, sometimes at her office at Yeshiva University and sometimes at a comfortable café.

Invariably, she would begin the conversation by asking, "So Yossi, how is your research going?"

Typically, he would respond with something to the effect of, "It's going. It's slow, but it's going."

On this Thursday afternoon, he repeated the same thing but had more to add. "What we've been seeing, as have others, is that adverse early-life experiences will have some very bad consequences in many people," Yossi said. "Still, there are enormous differences among individuals, and in a few, these experiences might enhance their resilience. Many factors contribute to the profound differences that occur between people. I've been able to identify a few, but there's certainly much more going on to produce these different outcomes. I suspect biological processes may play into them, but I don't have the skills or tools to dig into these factors. What irks me is I'm bewildered by what can be done to mitigate the adverse effects of toxic early-life experiences. So, I feel a bit disillusioned and frustrated. I'd like to do something bigger, something much more significant."

"I can appreciate what you're saying, Yossi," Zosha said. "I've been there myself – more than once. It's too soon for you to despair. I'd guess that as you collect additional data, the fog will clear and certain fundamental factors will emerge that account for the differences you've been seeing. Does it have to do with the age at which the trauma occurred or the availability of adequate familial support that can buffer the effects of the trauma? From my vantage, I wonder whether the trauma of adverse early-life events will have carryover effects on the next generation of children."

"I had considered trauma could have intergenerational consequences, and several research reports have pointed to this possibility," Yossi replied. "I suppose that if traumatized individuals continue to carry their baggage with them, they could affect the psychological functioning of their children. If I decide to do graduate work, that would be an ideal project to pursue. It would take forever to complete that sort of research, and I have no idea where I would obtain research participants."

"That shouldn't be a great obstacle," Zosha said. "The world is a terrifying and deadly place, often without mercy. Wars frequently occur worldwide, and so do famines and numerous other catastrophic events, so it should be possible to evaluate the consequences for those who encountered them as well as their children. You might consider working with large organizations that have access to these populations. For instance, think about partnering with specific United Nations organizations, although I perceive considerable biases present may become more prominent in the coming years that might be difficult to navigate. Nonetheless, segments of the UN, such as the World Health Organization, may have information that would be useful. Alternatively, a good starting place would be to look into Holocaust survivors and their children."

Yossi registered in a graduate program in psychology at Yeshiva University the following year, and Sasha similarly accepted an offer to enroll in sociology. Sadly, Trevor left them after being accepted into a program on international studies at Harvard, although he assured them he would continue to see them often.

In evaluating the available research, Yossi found appreciable information on the immediate and lasting impact of severe trauma. In contrast, data that focused on the intergenerational effects of early-life adverse events were sparse, although several studies conducted in Israel indicated the effects of trauma could affect the children of survivors. Likewise, it had been reported that a famine in parts of China could have intergenerational health consequences, and the children of those who survived the "Dutch Hunger Winter" – the Nazis cut off food supplies in the Netherlands in 1944-1945 in retaliation for the exiled Dutch government supporting the Allies – similarly experienced health disturbances. He had hoped to obtain more data through the United Nations, but surprisingly little information was available. Even the UN peacekeeping operations in many countries failed to conduct follow-up analyses on survivors, let alone on the children of survivors, and UNESCO had little to offer despite its focus on the welfare of children.

The lack of information puzzled Yossi.

"Given the number of traumatic events experienced by collectives, I'm astounded by how little research has been conducted to evaluate the intergenerational effects that might ensue," he told Zosha. "Surely, data must have been collected concerning the long-term consequences of the Holodomor [the starvation of millions of Ukrainians due to Stalin's policies in 1932-1933], the Armenian genocide by Turks, as well as the multigenerational trauma experienced worldwide by Indigenous People at the hands of European colonizers."

"I'm surprised you're surprised," she replied. "The Soviets have been suppressing anything related to the Holodomor, and the Turks have made great efforts to eliminate efforts to study an Armenian genocide they claim never occurred. Researchers within European countries, as well as the US and Canada, have only recently begun to assess the impact of colonization on Indigenous people, but for a variety of reasons, it has been happening too slowly."

"Surely, however, groups affected by these cover-ups have attempted to make their voices heard," he said.

"Oh, some certainly have. But, the international power and influence of the transgressors, including within the UN, have assured that the voices of victims are muted. I expect eventually some of these issues will come to the surface within democratic countries. In contrast, where autocrats rule, these issues will remain buried. At the moment, it seems the will to help victims of earlier severe injustices isn't present.

"Closer to home, we've already witnessed the Shoah being minimized, and claims have even been made it never happened," she added. "People seem adept at picking and choosing to make events fit their common narrative. Like you, Yossi, I'm grateful to Britain for agreeing to the Kindertransports. Many British people are understandably proud of doing what they did and justly commemorate their actions. Yet they conveniently forget how little they did for Czechoslovakia and Poland and have amnesia about their failure to accept Jews earlier and their determination in preventing them from migrating to Israel when it could have made such a great difference."

Nodding, Yossi said, "You made exactly that point in the context of the Nuremberg trials in the first of your lectures I attended. I suppose it was inevitable the actions taken by the UN would be politicized and will continue to be in the future.

"That's a shame," he added. "It's hard to get by the potential benefits the United Nations could promote in the absence of self-serving motivations."

"You and I might know that," Zosha said, "but most people still believe the UN will be a panacea to prevent wars and help underserved communities everywhere and are often ignorant of the political intrigues and corruption that have become endemic to large segments of the organization.

Yossi was gratified by the increasing interest from other scientists in the intergenerational effects of early-life adverse experiences. In a discussion with Gloria, a fellow graduate student who was the daughter of a Holocaust survivor, he talked about how most researchers had adopted the view that survivors of trauma and their children are at elevated risk of subsequently developing diverse disorders.

"I don't fully buy into it and find it perspective demeaning," Yossi said. "It paints people like us as somehow lacking. My sense is that although many Shoah survivors seemed to be at risk for pathologies, many others were resilient and were able to get through later adverse experiences. I don't know what makes for the enhanced resilience, although it seems having a shared identity and obtaining adequate social support may have fostered it."

Gloria had an alternative view. "While I don't disagree, I suspect the biological changes brought about by trauma experiences, or perhaps the presence of innate dispositions, made some individuals more vulnerable and others more resilient," she said. "This is in keeping with a Darwinian view of what promotes resilience. Given how few Jews survived the Shoah, one needs to question whether there was something unique among survivors. Is it possible some of the survivors were those who were most hardy, crafty, or had effective cognitive methods of coping? In effect, they might have inherited their resilient capacity and in some manner passed on these characteristics to their children?"

Given their shared interests, Sasha continued to be Yossi's

sounding board while continuing with her research on the links between diverse psychosocial factors and the occurrence of communicable diseases. She considered Yossi's approach viable and added her own views.

"When we assess the consequences of trauma, it might be important to consider resilience from a broader perspective," Sasha said. "A person could, after all, be resilient in overcoming certain types of challenges but still be more vulnerable to some diseases. As Gloria said, biological selection pressures among some might have resulted in their offspring being better able to contend with stressful events. At the same time, the earlier trauma may have disturbed immune functioning and made them more vulnerable to specific diseases, and perhaps the biological changes could be inherited by their children. I suppose our genes and environmental events could interact to produce diverse outcomes in ways we still don't understand."

With the ideas from Gloria and Sasha in mind, he turned his research to determining whether some Holocaust survivors and their children were, in fact, vulnerable to diverse diseases while others were resilient and how individuals coped with adverse events. Over the next two years, he collected data from survivors and their children in Israel and did the same in the US and countries in South America. He hypothesized the intergenerational effects of the Holocaust might vary with lifestyles, including poverty, as Sasha insisted, which might determine the outcomes. He would have liked to obtain similar data from Jews in the Soviet Union, but collaborations of this sort were limited by the politics of the time.

The information he collected was instrumental in showing the many physical and psychological conditions associated with trauma and pointed to the possibility that both resilience and vulnerability could be transmitted to the next generation. Sasha's research added to his work by demonstrating that while the effects of trauma could have marked effects on people of any age, the effects of these experiences were most profound if they occurred in children. Yossi and Sasha received their doctoral degrees together and had the enormous pleasure of having Desmond, Margaret, Trevor, and Jane at their graduation ceremony.

In later years, Yossi witnessed the evolution of a novel way in which trauma was considered. The theory was that adverse experiences and environments could influence the actions of certain genes without altering the genome itself, a phenomenon referred to as epigenetics. As a result, either increased vulnerability to illnesses or enhanced resilience were more likely to develop, and these effects could be transmitted across generations. Unbeknownst to Yossi, his research played a role in affecting that of a young scholar in Israel who was a third-generation Holocaust survivor. The researcher, Jake, had been studying epigenetics, which ultimately was fundamental in showing how the altered actions of genes promoted by cumulative, historical trauma could affect the lives of underserved Indigenous people.

Although consumed by his research, Yossi couldn't let go of his conversations with Zosha on the ineffectiveness of the United Nations and how easily its mission could be corrupted. Even after she moved to Israel, they stayed in contact, and through her network, he was able to receive inside information from within the UN. With his increasing expertise in international studies, Trevor also was a font of information on several political intrigues and facilitated Yossi's investigation into the organization. To be sure, considerable information was available publicly, with reports released by the UN regarding its efforts to curb corruption. The self-congratulatory flow of supposed facts released by the UN was no doubt scrubbed clean, and Yossi assumed more telling material could be unearthed that had gone under the radar.

Yossi debated whether he should pursue his research or turn his attention to the duplicity he believed was endemic within the UN. He decided to pursue both even though achieving just one could be all-consuming. He decided the best way to investigate the UN was from the inside. Fortuitously, an opening appeared with UNICEF and he was able to obtain the position. At the outset, he thought working for UNICEF would be less than ideal in a hunt for corruption. After all, if any organization would be a boon to human welfare, UNICEF would likely be it. His attraction to UNICEF was reinforced by its mission to defend children's rights and helping them reach their potential. He anticipated working at UNICEF might provide a way of evaluating interventions that could enhance well-being among children who experienced traumatic early-life events.

To his dismay, things didn't work out as he had hoped, he told Sasha.

"It took less than a year for me to become disillusioned with UNICEF as well as several related UN organizations," he said. "Upward of ten million children worldwide had died of preventable diseases such as measles, polio, and diarrhea. As you know full well, these illnesses could have been greatly diminished simply by providing clean drinking water, a healthier diet, adequate shelter, and immunization against diseases. I discovered that after many years and billions of dollars being thrown at the issue, the number of children that continued to die yearly was only modestly reduced."

"Yeah, it's disheartening," Sasha replied. "Infant mortality declined by a scant 14 percent, and maternal mortality has remained inordinately high, surpassing half a million women each year, and it's much worse in sub-Saharan Africa. Remarkably, in some countries, such as those within the Soviet Union, the frequency of infant mortality has actually increased, often due to diarrheal illnesses that could be attenuated by rehydration tablets at a cost of about 25 cents."

Taking time off from work, they visited Trevor in Boston. Yossi's brain, as usual, seemed to have remained in New York as he continued dwelling on the disappointments he felt in working with UNICEF as well as the corrupt behavior in other UN organizations.

"If nothing else, some UN agencies have gained expertise in the art of covering up misdeeds," Yossi said. "Many employees before me were aware of the situation, but knowing the fate of those who rocked the boat, they walked away from doing anything. I met quite a few people who were as appalled as I was. Many with considerable experience concluded what they witnessed weren't isolated events and concluded corruption, abuse, and cover-ups were endemic within the organization. Perhaps hoping I might take some type of action they wouldn't or couldn't, a few people spoke to me openly, provided I would keep their identities confidential."

"And yet the roadblocks kept appearing," Trevor said, figuring the UN was practiced in shutting down investigations.

"That's an understatement," Yossi replied. "As Sasha knows, when upper management got wind of what I was doing, which I knew they inevitably would, they pulled their usual routine to get rid of undesirables. They decided the department required restructuring and I was declared redundant, and so with little notice, I was gone. What they hadn't reckoned on was that many frustrated and disgruntled employees would keep feeding me information."

"I would have thought employees would be daunted once they saw you being dismissed so readily," Trevor said.

"Quite the opposite," Yossi said. "I was astounded by how many people wanted to divulge information, and they came from multiple sectors of the UN. Granted, most of the information passed to me comprised unsubstantiated allegations that needed verification, which wouldn't be simple. What I was told nonetheless provided multiple avenues for analysis."

"So, with more time on your hands, you decided to follow the trail wherever it would lead. I suppose this then gave you the impetus to write a book-length exposé of the UN?" asked Trevor rhetorically, knowing Yossi had started to do just that.

"In part, I suppose, but not entirely," Yossi answered. "It was the confluence of several experiences that gave rise to the idea. My discussions with Zosha had a lot to do with it, and I considered Dad's frustration in having his hands tied and not being able to do much at the Potsdam conference. The thought of Nicholas Winton being able to do so much for children he saved through the Kindertransports also played into this, and I recalled the many others who put their well-being on the line to save others. Aristides de Sousa Mendes, the Portuguese consul in Bordeaux, France, defied his government by providing visas to 10,000 Jews as well as many others. For his empathy, he and his family became pariahs, he was removed from the foreign service, and he lived in poverty until he died in 1954. With such knowledge, I couldn't just sit on my hands, and if I did, I would eventually become just another embittered person."

"Once the book has been completed, you might find it difficult to have it accepted by a major publishing house," Sasha said. "They might be cowed by the significant and broad influence of the UN."

"I had initially been concerned by that prospect," Yossi said. "Even so, I couldn't let it deter me from doing the right thing. As it turned out, many people outside of the UN had been aware of the problems, although most hadn't realized how pervasive they had become. As word spread within Zosha's circle about what I was up to, interest increased, and I was approached by several publishers that offered to help me put the work together and publish the book once it was completed."

Concerned, Sasha said, "If word spread in this circle, then you can count on certain people at the UN having heard the same things, and they may take measures to silence you."

"They've already started, Sasha," Yossi said. "Most of my friends working at the UN have been questioned by their bosses and warned not to assist me in any way. They've gone so far as to hint everyone has skeletons in their closets that could be exposed. Approaches were likewise made to several publishers informing them I was just another attention-seeking, bitter ex-employee seeking revenge. I believe I'm being monitored, and it isn't simply delusional thinking on my part."

"Really, what makes you think that?" asked Sosha worriedly.

"I hadn't told you earlier knowing you would react like the sky was falling," he said. "At first, there were little things that aroused my suspicions. I would see the same car pass me on the street repeatedly, and on several occasions I spotted people, usually two or three, who would alternate their positions, taking turns to stay close to me. Also, on several occasions upon returning home, I sensed some items had been moved about. I had initially assumed I was being paranoid over several small coincidences. Nonetheless, to diminish my uncertainty, I placed tiny pieces of thread along my desk drawers, and on two occasions they were dislodged. I also arranged for friends working with publishers to send me letters with small marks along the seal of the envelope, which allowed me to detect they had been opened before getting to me. After that, I thoroughly searched my apartment for hidden microphones and miniature cameras, but I haven't found anything. Still, as we know, the absence of evidence doesn't necessarily imply evidence of absence."

"Are you worried about your safety?" asked Trevor, now as disquieted as Sasha.

"To some extent. I'd have to be nuts not to be," Yossi replied. "Still, if they wanted to harm me, they would already have done so. Given how simple it was to discover what they were up to leads me to believe their malign intents are limited to scaring me off."

Yossi signed with a publishing house he felt would best represent him and had the clout to widely distribute and advertise his book. They assigned him an editor, Judith Blumfeld, a middle-aged woman who was highly experienced. When they first met in Judith's Manhattan office, she introduced herself, and after having coffee brought in, immediately got down to business.

"Yossi, Sasha, I'm very excited to be included in this project," she said. "I'll begin by saying I don't intend to get in the way of what you'd like to achieve. My contribution will be limited to making sure the message you'll be delivering is as good as it can be. The reality is you're a first-time author and we can reasonably expect there will be a bit of a learning curve to get the book just right."

Nodding vigorously and grinning, Sasha said, "He's stubborn, believe me, but he follows instructions well."

"Okay, I'll take your word for it," Judith said. "Before we begin, would it be acceptable if I brought in another agent from our firm?"

With their assent, she called another agent, who appeared shortly. "Yossi, Sasha, please meet Leah Belzer," Judith said. "She has represented many of our writers who have focused on the Holocaust, and I expect she will be helpful to you."

"Thanks, Judith," said Leah, an older woman. "I should explain

I'm not a writer, although I might be better if I were writing in Polish. At any rate, I do know when historical novels are having the desired impact. When Judith informed me what you were up to, I insisted on being included."

Turning to Yossi, Judith continued, "Before we begin, tell us how you came to this project, what motivated you to undertake something so challenging, and where you see this going in the long run?"

"Sure, but I won't bore you with the early history of...."

Holding up her hand, Judith interrupted, "No, Yossi. Please start at the beginning. We have lots and lots of time and we definitely won't be bored. I've been told the two of you were on the Kindertransports out of Czechoslovakia. If you would, I'd appreciate you beginning there. Both Leah and I are very interested in this topic and your history may be pertinent to the book. So, however long it takes, that's what it will take."

As the story unfolded, Judith and Leah listened intently without interruption, often vigorously taking notes. While they had a professional demeanor, there were times when it was difficult to contain their emotions, particularly upon hearing about the death of their biological parents.

When Yossi mentioned his affiliation with Zosha, Leah interrupted. "I had heard of you and Sasha through friends of Zosha. I had a relationship with Zosha since 1945 when we met on a US transport truck taking us out of Poland. It was through her influence I came to do what I am now. Over many years, she and I had many opportunities to collaborate, and I hope she benefited as much as I did. A piece of me was lost when I heard of her passing."

"It's been the same for us," Sasha said. "She was not only our mentor but also our inspiration."

"I've known of Zosha's work and respected her greatly for everything she's done," Judith said. "I'm sure her work will continue on multiple fronts, and this project may be one of those." Then, acknowledging Yossi's scientific research, she added: "In a sense, it will be the transmission of efforts across generations, even if you aren't directly related to her."

Yossi then described his motivation for the book and what he hoped to accomplish.

"Frankly, like most people, I had at one time thought the UN was an honorable and worthwhile organization focused on maintaining peace between nations and helping people who couldn't help themselves," he said. "Admittedly, Zosha had warned me in her subtle way I might not like what I discovered. Perhaps she was too subtle, so I was astounded by the things I saw for myself and what I heard from others. There's no question the UN could have much to offer, and I continuously vacillate between wanting to write a book that points to the goodness of the UN and one that exposes some of its evils."

Only slightly taken aback by Yossi's indecision, Judith leaned back, lit a cigarette, and said, "Yossi, as I said earlier, our job will be to help you shape your story and not interfere with how you tell it. So, with your consent, I'll offer a few pieces of advice."

Receiving their nods of approval, she said, "Good. First, understand while you're not writing fiction, to get your message across you need to be telling a story to engage your readers. Second, it's essential to provide an account that doesn't smack of self-interest and preferably doesn't lecture or hector the reader. Provide facts and avoid vitriol. Finally, you evidently are torn about how you feel about the UN. Your antipathy is mixed with hope for the UN, which will probably serve you well in writing this book. As you expose duplicity that might be present within the UN, you should also acknowledge in what ways it has been useful. Failing this, readers might see you as a malcontent tilting at windmills."

Yossi was meticulous in following Judith's advice. He began his book by describing how the League of Nations came about following the First World War and pointed to its laudable goals of improving global welfare, promoting disarmament, settling disputes between countries through diplomatic means, and preventing wars by collective security. However, the league couldn't force countries to enforce the rules it set out. It had no armed forces, and member countries were reluctant to become directly embroiled in conflicts. It couldn't even maintain the economic sanctions that were recommended. At the time, most countries focused on national interests, so several of the initial members left the league. The US largely abdicated its influence on international affairs, never joining the organization. In the end, the League of Nations was incapable of thwarting the National Socialist movement and the subsequent outbreak of World War II.

As much as the League of Nations failed in its primary objective, it showed that diverse nations could be brought together, and its failures might have turned out as a template for what not to do. On the surface, the UN appeared more successful than its predecessor. It initially had just 51 members, but by 1970, its membership reached 127 and would expand further over the ensuing years. Some of these countries formed coalitions to impose their will on the UN, and the influence of the United States diminished accordingly. With the collusion of the Soviet Union and the Third World bloc, the UN passed a resolution in 1975 declaring Zionism to be a form of racism, although it was rescinded with the end of the Cold War. By then, however, cracks had become notable between Western countries and those of the rest of the world, a divide that would be difficult to breach.

With Judith's guidance, the early chapters included a recitation of the challenges the UN overcame in attempting to remain relevant and gave credit to UN organizational successes. He lauded UNICEF despite its limitations as well as the United Nations Development Program and the UN Refugee Agency, although he pointed to the latter being plagued by individuals exchanging asylum for cash. He was effusive over the role of the World Health Organization but didn't hold back in criticizing it for not paying enough attention to limiting the spread of new communicable diseases and for not doing enough to spread the message that poverty, overpopulation, and destruction of animal habitats were instrumental in these diseases' emergence. Furthermore, he detailed the factors that promoted antibiotic resistance, which would ultimately be among the greatest threats to the spread of bacterial infections, saying the WHO was largely ineffective in curbing the threat. Surely, the WHO ought to have invested more to prevent the spread of infection across national borders, especially as many countries couldn't detect and investigate communicable diseases, let alone report on them.

In describing one of the primary functions of the UN – maintaining peace between nations – Yossi described some successes, particularly in the development of international peacekeeping forces. The interventions of the UN in the Congo and Cyprus were described as major wins, and the UN intervention in Korea was viewed as a military success even though it was a strategic failure that heralded the increasing influence of China.

At the same time, with encouragement from Leah, he pulled no punches concerning several notable failures, including Somalia and, initially, Bosnia. He was resolute in pointing to disagreements among members of the Security Council resulting in the UN being incapable of doing anything meaningful about the genocides in Cambodia and Bangladesh. Yossi argued persuasively these failures were only the start of many others that would follow. The UN had become a paper tiger.

Trevor was frustrated with the book's direction. He felt Yossi wasn't sufficiently pointing out the source of the failures of the UN. "It's indisputable most states operate to meet their needs and may resort to war if they deem it necessary, paying no heed to an emasculated international organization," Trevor said.

"Maybe I'm being too soft," Yossi said. "I'll work on revising that section of the book, even if it's no secret the permanent members of the Security Council are exceptionally biased. There's no question the Security Council is more powerful than the General Assembly, which is supposed to be the most representative organ of the UN, but ultimately it became too politicized. Blocs of countries formed that support one another and denigrate any countries they choose. Ironically, some of the same countries that are quick to chastise others have themselves been among the greatest human rights abusers. Simply look at which countries sit on the UN Commission on the Status of Women. Again, it's an instance of the fox guarding the hen house."

"That's not half of it," Trevor said, his set jaw emphasizing his annoyance. "UN officials have been fully aware that arms smugglers have been profiting enormously by supplying all sorts of weapons to rebel groups in African countries such as Angola and Liberia. At best, weak efforts have been made to deter this smuggling, but as long as arms flow, the fighting will continue, often promoted by third parties with their own agendas. In essence, countries have engaged in proxy wars, and I don't see an end to it. My sense is the will to stop the arms supply isn't there, perhaps due to political factors."

"I'd bet financial interests are probably also at play," Sasha said. "I think financial corruption is widespread within diverse UN agencies, and this exposé ought to focus on it. If we dig deeper, we'll find the financial corruption is widespread."

"We don't have to dig very deeply to come to that conclusion," Yossi replied. "My informants at various UN agencies have made that apparent. In addition to its core funds, which amount to a few billion dollars, specific agencies within the UN receive far more for specific projects, much of it coming from wealthy donors. However, there may have been strings attached to the donations. Moreover, keeping track of where the money was going and who benefited wasn't high on the UN agenda, and in the absence of proper oversight and accountability, those with special interests have been having a hay day. An investigation a few years ago revealed fraud had increased over the years, and deficiencies existed in the way UN agencies interacted with nongovernmental organizations [NGOs], including bribes to obtain favorable recommendations for specific projects."

"That's fairly predictable and fits with everything else we know," Trevor said.

"It certainly does, even if it doesn't fully portray the extent of the financial wizardry endorsed by UN officials to make large sums of money disappear," Yossi said.

Then he thought of someone who could buttress the point. "Sasha, do you remember Adam Gluman?" Yossi asked.

"Of course, I do," she said. "He was with us on the

Kindertransport. A nice boy who was withdrawn and suffered miserably being away from his family. I don't know the details, but I think he eventually ended up in Canada."

"That's right," Yossi said. "He flourished there and eventually received extensive training in economics and accounting, eventually developing expertise in forensic accounting. He is often consulted to look into cases of financial malfeasance, and on several occasions, he was brought in to audit government books. I had several chats with him and, although he was careful not to say too much, he confided he was well aware of financial intrigues within UN agencies."

"Was he able to point you to more than we already suspected?" she asked.

"Yes and no," Yossi answered. "He never named names and was scrupulous in not specifying agencies that were most tainted. Yet he indicated the web of intersecting interests made it exceptionally difficult to track and uncover most of the transgressions, although he alluded to bribery, outright theft, and bid-rigging not being unusual. After a few experiences working with the UN, he distanced himself from the entire organization. He claimed that while promises had repeatedly been made to look into the corruption, the efforts were meek, and even when information was available that pointed to deceit, deception, and duplicity, the data were largely ignored. He didn't need to add that when whistleblowers came forward, they were fired and even arrested to make it seem as if they were the source of nefarious dealings. He quoted one of his associates in saying the UN had developed 'a culture of impunity' that operates in secrecy and is shielded by diplomatic immunity."

Both Sasha and Trevor felt the descriptions of financial finagling at the UN were important for the book because it may have undermined human rights efforts.

"Aside from being ineffective in helping countries and people who experience poverty and disease, basic human rights have often been sidelined despite the UN making a big deal of their effectiveness on that front," Sasha said. "The Universal Declaration of Human Rights was not signed by the Soviets and several other countries within their orbit. Even some countries that signed on to it have been guilty of abusing human rights, political rights, and civil liberties."

Chiming in, Trevor acidly said, "The UN's Human Rights Council was established to replace the UN Commission on Human Rights because of biases that allowed countries with poor human rights records to become sitting members. From where I sit, a change in name of the group was all that was achieved. The council has been castigated for having members include countries that have been engaged in multiple human rights abuses and been taken to task for their behavior toward women or people who are gay. It's been argued these countries become members of the council for the express purpose of avoiding censure. Impartiality and objectivity have been sorely lacking."

At a later meeting, the three conspirators, as they thought of themselves, were debating about what should be included and excluded from the book when a phone call came from Chaviva, who had been kept in the loop about their work. After being told about their most recent discussion, she said, "I confess my gripes about the UN go beyond financial corruption and incompetence and extend to willful efforts to castigate and slander specific countries, especially Israel. I've heard it again and again from Israeli government officials and various Jewish agencies within the US. I'm especially outraged by the work of NGOs and by that of special rapporteurs, as they're called. These people are assigned to various human rights issues on the assumption they are knowledgeable concerning international human rights and humanitarian law, as well as being experienced in the field of human rights. It is understood, of course, those who nominate themselves for such a position should display independence, impartiality, and objectivity and be of unquestionable integrity. Yet it has been obvious they often have a score to settle, which ought to have disqualified them for such a position. Some have unquestionable anti-American or anti-Israeli biases and behave without shame, guilt, or remorse."

On a different issue, you're aware that Zosha hadn't been impressed by the outcomes at the Nuremberg trials," Yossi said. "Yet I had hoped the creation of the International Law Commission might be an effective way of bringing individuals to justice. It seemed unfortunate this commission was largely abandoned during the Cold War. Now, with all the political machinations in both the Security Council and General Assembly, it's probably good it never developed more fully since it could be used as a tool to bludgeon individuals who would serve as a proxy for attacking nations. For years there have been efforts to replace the commission with an International Criminal Court. So far, its creation has been unsuccessful, although I'm certain it will be established. I'm concerned it will be entirely ineffective and only be symbolic. Time will tell, I suppose."

At one of his periodic meetings with Judith and Leah, Yossi confided he was torn about how far to take the book and even how critical he should be. "I don't want to be perceived as standing on a soapbox," he said.

"All you can do is dispassionately point to corruption, biases, and nefarious behaviors wherever they exist," Leah responded. "We need to hope with time more people will become aware the UN is a failed organization and make efforts to reform it."

"The simple fact is contrary opinions have been expressed concerning the value of the UN," he said. "Going back some time, President Dwight D. Eisenhower recognized the UN had many flaws but held fast to the position it was the best that could be offered to 'substitute the conference table for the battlefield.' Historians have similarly suggested that while the UN never fulfilled initial hopes, it has nonetheless served important functions. On the other side, the UN has not only failed to meet its intended role in world affairs but was instrumental in limiting actions that could have prevented genocides."

"So, what are you saying?" asked a confused Sasha. "Do you think it's premature to publish the book?"

"Not at all," he replied. "I just would like it to end on a hopeful note. There have been frequent calls for the UN to be reformed, often without suggestions for how it could be achieved. I've struggled with this for some time and wonder whether the mission of the UN should be restricted to humanitarian work."

"That's certainly one option," Leah said. "From there, the UN can be rebuilt adopting its best aspects while avoiding the politicization that has been so problematic. Whether it will ever be able to limit wars between and within nations is doubtful. Frankly, the efforts to reform the UN from the inside have failed miserably. There are too many vested interests in keeping things as they are. Regardless of what you write, your book won't change the culture of the UN or alter the opinions of intransigent people and countries. If any progress is to be made, it will occur in small increments. Hopefully, others will insert themselves into the process."

"Maybe so, but I don't see that happening any time soon," Yossi replied. "Then again, if nobody takes up the gauntlet, then nothing will ever change."

It was only years later that Yossi and Sasha were witness to the further multiple failings of the UN and its allied agencies, plagued by nepotism, cronyism, biases, and much greater financial corruption. While they expected wars would occur, they were astonished the UN was hapless in dealing with rebels within Africa who kidnapped young people who were used as child soldiers to murder thousands of people. They were equally appalled that peacekeeping forces used local women as sex slaves and were guilty of pedophilic rape.

They weren't isolated events, having also been documented in Haiti, Liberia, Congo, Sudan, Burundi, and Côte d'Ivoire. Like the Catholic Church that covered up abuses by clergy members, the higher-ups in the UN were successful in keeping secrets buried. In the end, many reports and several books would be published documenting the remarkable inadequacies and misrepresentations of the UN. Still, as Zosha had predicted, the general public remained willfully ignorant and accepted whatever they were inclined to believe before.

7

RACHEL: MYSTERY OF FATE

> Destiny is a good thing to accept when it's going your way. When it isn't, don't call it destiny; call it injustice, treachery, or simple bad luck.
>
> – Joseph Heller, *God Knows*

Rachel was happy for Nela and Isaac and hoped their new life in the United States would be everything they wanted. Although Rachel had spent many nights in the apartment alone, the permanence of Nela's absence made the loneliness that much stronger and more persistent. They had a shared past that had tied them together. Without Nela, she felt bereft of anyone close.

Over the preceding two years, she had applied for immigration through various embassies. Her first choice, Israel, wasn't possible because of the British blockade. Her application for the United States went unanswered, and efforts to other countries were rejected. Months and years passed without a hint of interest from any desirable country. She had no special talents that would have facilitated her immigration, but she couldn't bear staying in Germany, and returning to Poland wasn't an option.

She recalled that her mother had a cousin with whom she was very close who had immigrated to Canada several years before the war. His surname was Prager, which had been her mother's maiden name. She wasn't sure of his first name. It might have been Moishe, Mottel, or Menachem – some name beginning with the letter M. She had no idea where in Canada he lived. It was a large country and all she knew was the name of the city sounded odd.

Even though the Jewish Agency focused on future immigration to Israel, in desperation she contacted their office asking for help, which they were happy to provide. By going through a list of Canadian cities together, she thought Winnipeg was the one her mother mentioned. From there, the agency worker readily found that only one family with the name Prager lived in Winnipeg, and the first name of the person listed in the file was Mordechai. The agent gave her the address and wished her well, mentioning that within a year entry to Israel might be possible, so if things didn't work out with going to Canada, Israel might remain an option.

That same day she wrote him a long letter, introducing herself and indicating he may be a cousin of her mother Channah, who had likely been killed during the war, although she wasn't certain. If he was, indeed, her mother's cousin, would he be willing to sponsor her immigration to Canada?

About ten days later, she received a letter from him. He indicated how saddened he was to hear about Channah, who not only was his cousin but also his best friend during childhood. Not having heard from Channah since the war began, he expected the worst, but having it confirmed by Rachel was devastating. The main thing was his willingness to sponsor her immigration to Canada and his excitement at the prospect of Rachel joining his family. He had contacted his lawyer to determine the necessary steps and would write her as soon as he received word, which would only take a few days.

She felt more than simple relief. She was overjoyed and could have danced in the street. Looking toward heaven, she said, "Oh, God, please let this happen. Let this happen. Don't take me to the Jordan River and then not let me enter the Promised Land."

A large envelope arrived two days later containing copies of several documents from Mordechai's lawyer. The documents were certified affidavits indicating Rachel was the daughter of Channah Freiberg, née Prager, who was the cousin of Mordechai Prager. Furthermore, he was acting as a sponsor for Rachel's immigration to Canada. He attested Rachel would be fully employed at the Prager Department Store in Winnipeg. A letter from the lawyer included in the envelope instructed her to make an appointment with the attaché responsible for immigration at the Canadian embassy in Berlin and to present the enclosed documents to the attaché. The lawyer indicated he would do whatever was necessary on his end. Finally, a handwritten letter from Mordechai repeated his delight at the prospect of her coming to Canada, and that his wife, Sonia, and their children were equally enthusiastic. He added that if she needed any money to obtain a berth on a ship or for any other reason, he would wire transfer it to her.

The next morning, after mailing her letter to Mordechai thanking him and indicating how excited she was, Rachel headed to the train station to travel to Berlin.

She was filled with anxiety until she boarded the train. The distance to Berlin was a little more than 300 kilometer and the ride would take slightly more than five hours. Ordinarily, the monotony of a swaying train would have put her to sleep, but her excitement and churning mind kept her awake. Once she reached Berlin, it was too late to go to the embassy, so she found overnight lodging nearby. She awoke early the next morning and arrived at the embassy an hour before it was open. A small line of people had already assembled, and many others arrived afterward. The woman behind her in line said most of the people waiting were Jews from cities across Germany, all of whom had waited days just to make an appointment. It was then that panic set in because she had forgotten to make an appointment despite the lawyer instructing her to do so.

The embassy door opened punctually at 9:00, and the line slowly moved forward. Their first stop was at a desk where a young woman behind a counter asked the reason for their visit. When it was finally her turn, Rachel indicated why she was there but, when asked for her appointment card, said she hadn't realized she needed one. If she had, she would have called from Bremen to make arrangements.

The young blonde-haired woman shook her head and said, "It's unfortunate you came so far, but without an appointment, it's impossible to see the attaché. He has appointments scheduled every 15 minutes throughout the day. I'm so sorry."

Rachel was beyond despondent. She started to walk away, but then she turned to the woman and said, "Fraulein, I spent more than three years in concentration camps. Every day we had to line up for food and water, for work assignments, and now I have to stand in line here. Every day I wondered whether I would live to see the next morning. The uncertainty nearly pushed me into insanity. Please, Fraulein, I can't bear any further torture."

"I'm sorry about what you went through," she replied. "Most of the people in the line have had similar horrid experiences. But unlike you, they have appointments to see the attaché."

With her head bowed and tears brimming, she stepped away from the counter, bumping into a man who had been standing behind her while she spoke to the clerk.

"I'm so sorry," Rachel exclaimed. "I hadn't realized you were there."

"No, no. It's entirely my fault. I thought I recognized you, so I came over, and then I became curious about the conversation you were having because it seemed very intense."

Rachel looked at him slightly confused but feeling she had met him previously. "You do look familiar," she said. "Have you been in Bremen during the last few months?"

He began to reply and then stopped, looking at her quizzically, half smiling as he could see her struggling to recognize him.

She suddenly remembered and said, "You're Graham, the wounded Canadian pilot that Isaac treated. We met when you came by to thank him for taking care of you."

"You remembered, which confirms I'm unforgettable," he said grinning.

"How are you now? I trust your wounds have healed," Rachel said.

"For the most part they have, but I won't be flying for a while. So I've been assigned to work here at the embassy."

He looked at her pensively for another few moments before saying, "I don't mean to be bold, but please come with me."

Together they took the stairs to the second level and stood outside a door with a small plaque indicating it was the office of John Munroe, attaché. When the door opened and a young woman came out, Graham held the door open for Rachel and they entered.

He addressed a man behind the desk and said, "John, I've brought this young woman, a friend of mine from Bremen, who needs to obtain papers to immigrate to Canada."

"Certainly, John. I can do that if she has the needed paperwork."

"I do," she said in excitement, passing the envelope to him.

He glanced at the contents of the envelope perfunctorily, and after a few minutes, he said, "Everything looks fine. Very professionally done. There won't be any problem, and on Graham's behalf, I'll expedite this. Now, my assistant will take several photographs of you that will be appended to the document, after which you can be on your way. You should receive all the necessary documentation within five days at the address shown on the papers. Have a very good life in Canada."

Graham walked her out and promised to visit her in Winnipeg if he visited the city.

She wrote Mordechai as soon as she returned to Bremen, letting him know her trip was successful and she would write him once she received her documents and arranged for travel to Canada.

As promised, Rachel's immigration and travel papers arrived within a few days. She sat gazing at the official documents, covered by stamps and signatures. These few pages of paper would turn her from a displaced person into one with a new home. She wrote Graham in Berlin, letting him know that all was well and that if at some point she reunited with Nela and Isaac, she would tell them about their providential meeting at the embassy.

She hurried to book a berth on a liner traveling to Canada. The ship would leave Bremerhaven in two weeks and take her to Halifax, a voyage that would take about 12 days.

What would she take with her? Clothing, her little stash of makeup, and the two pictures she obtained from Panye Kowalska years earlier. What else was there? Even if there was anything, she didn't want it since the objects would only bring back memories she wanted to escape. She brought what little of value she had in the apartment to the synagogue so it could be donated to orphaned children.

Two weeks later, carrying her belongings in a backpack that had been used by an unknown American soldier, she arrived at the ship docked at the Bremerhaven port. She was directed to a long single-story building about 200 meters down the pier. There, she stood in line along with others who would be boarding the ship – another line, she thought, as she wondered whether there would ever be a time when she and the other Jews would no longer be treated as cattle. Tiring from standing on a single spot, she put her rucksack down and sat on it. The voices around her were Polish, Ukrainian, Czechoslovakian, Lithuanian, and Yiddish. They were all Jews who had gathered from across the continent, all looking forward to leaving a place they didn't want to be.

After about an hour, the line slowly began to move, a few feet forward and then a delay, another few feet, and yet another delay. So it went until she reached the structure, where two officious employees sat behind desks while she, like the others, stood in front of them submissively. Rachel recalled the fate of people who would be sent to the left or the right.

The blond Aryan woman sitting behind the desk scrupulously and slowly examined her papers. She looked at the pictures and then at Rachel, and then again, after which she examined each line of each page, not saying a word. Rachel wondered what this woman's job was during the war. Catching the eye of the elderly man standing at the next desk, he seemed to sigh, shrugging his shoulders and wordlessly signaling, "What can we do?"

Finally, satisfied everything was in order, the woman handed back

Rachel's papers and a boarding pass and wordlessly pointed her to the right.

When she left the building, she walked to the pier where the ship was docked. Having gone through this long process, she could barely contain her laughter upon coming to yet another line of people waiting to board the ship.

The line moved relatively quickly. They were greeted at the gangway, and after showing their boarding passes, the travelers were given their assigned cabin and given directions there. She reached her cabin, placed her knapsack at the end of one of the two beds, and then sat down exhausted from standing and waiting. The unadorned room was clean and seemed comfortable.

Shortly afterward she heard a soft knock and the cabin door opened hesitantly. The head of a woman appeared who smiled and said in Polish, "Hello, I think we will be roommates for the next few days."

Rachel enthusiastically greeted the dark-haired woman, who was about her own age. "Hello, I'm Rachel. Please take whichever berth you like," she said.

"Thank you, that berth is fine," the woman replied, pointing to the one without Rachel's knapsack on top. "I'm very glad to meet you, Rachel. I'm Mayim."

"Mayim! What a beautiful name," Rachel said. "Mine is so dull and yours is so, well, creative."

Smiling, Mayim suggested they go on deck. "I don't want to spend the voyage in this gloomy cabin and would rather watch the sea," she said. "Besides, I want the pleasure of seeing the ship pull away from the harbor. I never want to see Germany again. Never, ever again."

Along with many other immigrants, they leaned against the rail facing the port. When they heard the propellers begin to spin, they all stood still, and as the ship began moving, a cheer erupted. Nobody moved from the rail until Bremerhaven was out of sight.

Over the ensuing days, the two young women shared their experiences. Rachel recounted her time before the war and the long wretched days as a slave laborer in a work camp, including the beastly treatment she received from the SS guards and kapos. She didn't spend long describing her experiences as they were too painful and would trigger feelings of depression and signs of PTSD. Instead, she focused more on the time with Nela since they were liberated, as well as her discovery of a cousin in Winnipeg, which was now her destination.

Unlike Rachel, Mayim hadn't been in one of the camps. She had lived in Krakow with her parents, who were both musicians. After her parents were detained and sent to Theresienstadt, she was hidden in an attic of a Catholic family who knew her parents well as they had also been musicians. They worked hard to keep her safe, even building a false wall behind which she could hide if the Nazis searched the attic, although she was certain that if there was a raid, the Nazis would find her.

"Of course, I'll always be grateful to them for their kindness and bravery in defying the Nazis," Mayim said. "But living in an attic without seeing light and only being able to come out when it is dark can damage a person's sanity. Aside from the discomfort, isolation, and loneliness, the constant fear of discovery by the Nazis wore on me. The Catholic family was very careful, and I don't think any of their neighbors ever learned I was being hidden. If they had, it was likely they would inform the Gestapo. It was a relief when the Nazis left and the Russians arrived soon afterward. With liberation and learning my parents likely hadn't survived, I left Krakow and made my way to Bremen, where I supported myself teaching children to play the violin."

"And why did you choose to immigrate to Canada?" Rachel asked.

"My father had an older brother who left for Canada years before the war. He established a small, moderately successful music school in Toronto. I contacted him two years ago and he was delighted to sponsor my entry into Canada, but the government wasn't keen on taking in new immigrants. So I didn't have any option but wait for Canada to loosen its policies, and even after they opened their doors, it was a struggle to get papers. Unless one is very special or has a champion who will push their application, nothing happens quickly."

Rachel said, "When I was attempting to obtain my papers, I ran into difficulties. Fortunately, a friend of Nela's husband worked at the embassy, and when he recognized me, he was able to shepherd my application through the system with ease. Like anywhere else, I suppose favoritism and connections may be the currency in Canada."

"I'm certain of that, especially as Canada has historically not been a friendly place for Jews," Mayim replied.

Shocked, Rachel could only say, "Really! But Canada was an ally during the war."

"Yes, Canada was an ally of the British and Americans, but not for Jews. In the years I waited in Bremen, I spoke to many people and read what I could about Canada. It seems from Hitler's rise in 1933 until recently, Canada accepted only 5,000 Jewish immigrants, fewer than any Allied country. Many refugees who arrived during the war were mistreated and often kept in internment camps."

Rachel responded, "Was this attitude an isolated one or was it generally so?"

Sighing heavily, Mayim said, "I wish it was otherwise, but I believe the negative attitude toward us is widespread. My understanding is antisemitism in Canada became socially acceptable, so Jews were restricted from many professions. For that matter, our people weren't even allowed to enter certain properties, being met by signs saying, 'No Jews or Dogs Allowed.' This attitude was particularly prominent in the province of Quebec, where the Catholic priest Lionel Groulx, who was very influential, preached in writing, on the radio, as well as from the pulpit about the dangers of immigrants, especially Jews.'

"And the government did nothing to curtail this?" Rachel asked incredulously.

"Apparently not. Antisemitic attitudes were present in the federal government of Prime Minister William Lyon Mackenzie. Irrespective of their nationality, Jews were considered the 'least desirable' immigrants. In 1939, at the outset of the peril to Jews, upon being asked how many Jews would be permitted entry to Canada, a prominent government official said, 'None is too many.' I'm not sure why the government reversed course and opened its doors a crack so people like us can gain entry to Canada. Perhaps it was due to international pressure."

Throughout the passage, they were inseparable and dreaded when they would have to go their separate ways. Once they debarked at Pier 21 in Halifax, they discovered they would be taking the same train westward. Mayim would get off in Toronto, a distance of about 1,300 kilometer, while Rachel would travel an additional 1,900 kilometer to Winnipeg. When they reached Toronto, they tearfully exchanged information so they could keep in touch.

Mordechai and Sonia were there waiting for her when the train reached Winnipeg. His first words, speaking Yiddish, after embracing her were, "You look exactly like your mother. I miss her dearly, *olav hasholem*, may her memory be a blessing."

Sonia stepped forward, hugged Rachel, and said, "I'm so sorry for what you've been through." Then tearing up, she continued, "So few survived. So few. We've been so worried about the family. But now, at least, we have you. It's a miracle."

"Thank you so much, Sonia. It is a miracle. Despite what I went through, today I feel blessed."

Sonia reached into a large bag at her feet and pulled out a heavy red coat.

"I knew you wouldn't be dressed for our winter, so I brought along this warm coat," she said. "I didn't know your size and picked a large one that would definitely fit. If it were too small, that would be a problem."

The coat was several sizes too large. Laughing, Rachel said, "Hmmm, this could fit a Cossack, but it will do nicely."

"Yes, today you'll wear it and tomorrow you and I will go shopping for a new wardrobe,' Sonia replied. "The store Mordechai and I own has a very nice women's section, so we can start there. We don't carry high fashion, so we'll visit other shops as well."

Laughing again, Rachel said, "High fashion! No, I've never worn high fashion. In the camps, we were lucky if we had anything that wasn't threadbare. I'm not picky, believe me."

Mordechai went off to get the car while the two women waited arm-in-arm inside the station. When Mordechai pulled up in a large black vehicle, Rachel was awed. "For years I've only been in trucks of one sort or another," she said. "This will be a new experience for me."

"Mordechai loves his Cadillac," Sonia said. "On Sundays, he makes me take drives with him so we can look around. We've seen everything there is to be seen; he just likes driving the Cadillac. He calls it his Caddy and fusses over it as if it were a child. I once wanted to drive it myself, but he wouldn't let me. He told me nobody is allowed to touch the Caddy. *Meshuga* [crazy] or what?"

The drive in the Cadillac was exciting, and all the way home Sonia kept on talking while Mordechai sat quietly, occasionally making eye contact with Rachel through the rear-view mirror. With a head motion, he conveyed, "Let her talk."

They reached home in a Winnipeg suburb and pulled into the driveway. Each of the houses was distinct yet had a similar feel, with a yard in the front and a two-car garage. They quickly entered to get out of the bitter cold. They were greeted by 12-year-old Shimon and nine-year-old Talia. The young girl immediately pulled Rachel to her room to show her collection of dolls.

Returning to the dining area, Rachel said, "That was interesting. I met Trudy, Isabel, and Judy. They were all very polite and well-behaved." Then she turned to Talia, saying, "I'm not so sure about Rose, she looks like she can be a handful," which elicited giggles from the young girl.

Sonia gave Rachel a tour, saying, "This style of house, with different landings separated by a few stairs, is called a split level. I think Mordechai would have preferred what they call a ranch house, which doesn't have the levels, but he doesn't stick his nose into these things."

Rachel was taken to her bedroom, which was twice what she had in Bremen. The room was ornately decorated and seemed newly painted.

Supper was sumptuous. Every delicacy imaginable was served

from overflowing platters. Before Rachel could comment, Mordechai said, "No, we don't eat like this every evening. This is a special occasion. What's left over we'll have for lunch for several days."

Later, over coffee in the living room, Mordechai said, "It will be a while before you adapt to being here, but I don't want you to feel like a guest who walks on eggshells. You're family. If at some time you'd like your own home, maybe downtown where there are more young people, we can help you find something suitable."

"I'm speechless," she said, awed by everything she'd seen and heard. "I can never thank you both enough."

"You don't have to. We're doing this for our benefit as much as yours. You're a lovely young woman like your mother was, and I'm proud to have you here with us."

"I'd like to ask you something a bit awkward and I'm a bit shy to bring it up. But what should I call you? I feel uncomfortable calling you Mordechai as it's presumptuous and maybe a bit too disrespectful, and Cousin Mordechai sounds odd."

"Everyone calls me Mordechai, but if you feel more comfortable, for now, you can call me Uncle Mordechai. Later you might want to drop the uncle part."

"Not for me," broke in Sonia. "I want to be just Sonia. Auntie Sonia will make me sound old."

"One more thing, Uncle Mordechai. I would like to change my last name to my mother's maiden name, Prager. I don't want to be disrespectful to my father's memory, but I feel strongly about this."

"Prager's, the family's department store, is on the main street," Sonia said. "It's very modern in every way, and we try hard to make our customers comfortable. They can reach different floors through elevators, but most people use the escalator. Different floors have cosmetics and other beauty and health products, men's and women's clothing, children's wear, shoes and boots, kitchenware, sports equipment, and various types of hardware supplies."

They spent their time selecting assorted women's clothing and shoes, as well as winter clothing, which was deposited in large bags that would be retrieved later. Sonia knew every employee by their first name and spent a few moments chatting with some, asking how they were doing.

"I ask them to call me Sonia, but they are uncomfortable doing so and call me Mrs. P," she said. "I like them and I think they like me, and they're very loyal to us."

Rachel was impressed and made note of how important these relationships were in running a business.

Mordechai joined them after an hour and showed them the administrative area at the top floor, indicating an office was available for Rachel when she was ready, which puzzled her. Was she going to be working there and what would she do? She had no relevant skills.

Anticipating this, Mordechai had arranged for English lessons and accounting classes in the evenings. The plan was for her to shadow him every day as he managed the business. He evidently had a plan for Rachel but wasn't divulging anything except to say, "Your mother had a brilliant business mind, and I'm sure you do, too," he said.

Rachel was like a sponge, absorbing everything Mordechai taught, and was particularly impressed by his social skills and his way with staff. Like Sonia, he knew every employee by their first name and chatted with them whenever possible. He introduced her to suppliers and demonstrated how to negotiate prices with them. Her accounting skills were extraordinary, and it wasn't long before she didn't need lessons. Her English was impressive and her Polish accent made her sound intriguing. Eventually, she began to take on the jobs Mordechai otherwise would handle, which made him especially pleased, allowing him more leisure time. Rachel was fatigued at the end of the day but always excited by what the next morning would bring.

After 14 months, Mordechai, Sonia, and Rachel sat down in the living room after supper to have their usual coffee.

"There's no question you're happy here, Rachel. Is there something more you would like from life?" Mordechai said.

"Of course, I'm happy," she said. "I never dreamed I could be so enthralled with anything. There's no place I'd rather be, although I could do without the bitter cold and the ferocious wind in the winter, and I can't stand the mosquitos in the summer."

Mordechai had another question for her. "Our business has been doing very well here in Winnipeg. Do you think we should consider opening a store in another city?"

After thinking for a lengthy period, Rachel said, "I'm not sure. You don't need the money or the aggravation of looking after a second location. It could also be a risk that could drag on our operations here."

"I've thought the very same thing, and yet doing what we've been doing seems monotonous and I'd like another challenge," Mordechai said. "If we decide to open another store, where do you think would be the best place?"

Again, giving considerable thought, she replied, "Montreal is the largest city in the country, so that would be the obvious choice, but I have serious reservations about opening there. The political climate there makes me nervous, and my gut tells me the situation will become worse. Toronto is smaller with a lot of room to grow, so I think it is a better choice. Ottawa and Vancouver are also options, but not just yet. Maybe in a few years, but not now."

"Your analysis is exactly like mine. My agent in Toronto contacted me earlier this week to inform me a building that would meet our needs is available. It would need a bit of work, but it could be obtained at a reasonable price."

After discussing the cost of the building, projected renovation expenses, taxes, and other expenses, Rachel said, "I've calculated our expenses as we've been talking. Amortizing them over ten years, and assuming that renovation costs realistically will be 50% higher than you expect, interest on a mortgage will be reasonable, staffing will be 10 percent more than you anticipate, and sales will be almost double that in Winnipeg based on relative population size, we should be fine. But it may take a year or two for the store to be profitable."

"You figured this out in your head as we've been talking?" Sonia asked, entirely surprised.

"Yes, it isn't difficult," Rachel said. "The unknowns are more difficult to figure into the equation. Of course, in the end, it will all boil down to sales and how much we'll need to advertise to reach our goal, which is why I believe a year or two will be needed to get where we want to be. Of course, this all is based on the presumption no major events occur that can destabilize the marketplace."

"Like what?" asked Sonia.

"There are too many to list. A recession or depression, war, or a major epidemic like the one in 1928. You know our expression, '*Mann tracht un Got lacht*' [Man plans and God laughs]."

"So, in the absence of a catastrophic event, do you think we should do it?" asked Mordechai.

"I'm frankly uncertain. There's no doubt it will be a risk, a calculated one, but nevertheless a risk. I guess I'm still stuck on whether we need to roll the dice when we don't have to. We don't need more money than we already have, so why take a chance?"

"Everything you've pointed to is manageable," Mordechai said. "The big question is having the right person to manage all the operations."

He paused for Rachel to absorb his statement, then patiently set his gaze on her.

"Me?!" she exclaimed. "I wasn't expecting that. I don't have the skills or experience. It would be terrifying. Uncle Mordechai, that certainly wouldn't be a wise decision."

"Your concerns are perfectly understandable. You don't have the experience, but you certainly have the skills, and you'll do very well if you have a good team working with you. Besides, I would spend a few months with you at the outset and return periodically as needed."

Mordechai and Rachel flew to Toronto, where they met with the real estate agent. He walked them through the building as Sonia made notes concerning needed renovations. Over the next few days, they inspected the surrounding area thoroughly and obtained information about traffic flow, parking availability, and population density in the area. Once they were satisfied with the viability of the site, a meeting was arranged with the building's owners, Mr. Merton and Mr. Cavendish, and their lawyer.

"It's a lovely building, and you've done a wonderful job in maintaining its ambiance," Mordechai said. "The price is consistent with the estimated market value, and I would love to be able to purchase it. Unfortunately, it's beyond our finances."

After negotiating the price for almost an hour, it was clear an agreement couldn't be reached. They were about to part ways when Rachel proposed a different approach.

"I suggest you reduce the cost of the building by, say, 20 percent, absorb a portion of the renovation costs, again 20 percent, and allow renovations to proceed without our being charged, meaning we wouldn't have an interest-bearing mortgage in place during this period."

"And in return?" Mr. Merton inquired, curious about this odd way of negotiating.

"In return, you will hold shares in our company. If our venture is successful, you can recoup the discounts and hopefully continue to reap a profit for years beyond what you envisioned from selling the building."

She turned to look at Mordechai, who indicated it was acceptable to him, and then the building owners, who seemed pleased as well. After the owners briefly consulted with their lawyer, everyone went through the details and came to an agreement. The new partners shook hands.

Mordecai, Sonia, and Rachel spent the next week meeting with several architects, and after selecting a knowledgeable firm with a good reputation, they met with several contractors and agreed on costs for renovations, including provisions that would prevent cost overruns exceeding 10%. Satisfied with their choices, Mordechai headed back to Winnipeg while Rachel stayed behind to work with the architects.

Rachel had maintained frequent contact with Mayim and let her know she was in town. Over supper that evening, Mayim was annoyed Rachel was living in a hotel and hadn't called earlier.

"You'll stay with me in my apartment," Mayim said. "It's much more comfortable than the small cabin we shared on the ship, and it's much quieter." They agreed Rachel would bring her belongings over the next day.

Rachel showed up carrying the US army-issued rucksack she had used in moving from Bremen to Halifax. Recognizing the rucksack, Mayim laughed and said, "They have an expression here that in a modified form applies to you – you can take the girl out of the shtetl, but you can't take the shtetl out of the girl."

That day, Rachel told Mayim in detail about the business ventures in Winnipeg that led to her coming to Toronto. Mayim was genuinely thrilled by how well Rachel had been doing, inquiring about every aspect of the business.

When Rachel asked what Mayim had been up to, her ebullient mood vanished.

"You might recall my uncle has a small music school, which I joined to teach children and adolescents to play violin and piano," Mayim said. "However, there weren't enough students to justify my being there, so I reduced my hours at the school and began giving private lessons at children's homes. I earn enough to get by, but the constant search for students has stolen my passion for music."

"I'm so sorry to hear that," Rachel said. Then after a lengthy pause, she added: "I had intended to bring something up I hoped would interest you. Now I'm hesitant to do so."

"That sounds ominous," replied Mayim. "If it's something bad, then it's best to pull the bandage off quickly."

"It's not bad at all, so I can pull the bandage off slowly. From your letters, I concluded that teaching music hasn't been as prosperous as you hoped, but I hadn't realized how it affected your love of music."

"Yes, but that's not what you intended to talk to me about," Mayim replied.

"For the project into which my cousin Mordechai has inveigled me, it will be necessary to form a strong team," Rachel said. "A trusted team willing to work hard."

Before she could go further, Mayim interrupted, shaking her head. "And you want me to join your team?" she asked. "I love you like a sister, Rachel, but I'm not a charity case and would rather succeed on my own. So, my answer is a flat-out no, although I'm grateful for the offer."

"I know you too well, which is why I said I was hesitant to raise this. The fact is the offer wasn't meant as charity but based on pure business sense. You're creative and motivated, and we'll always be loyal to one another. Who would be better than you? Who, Mayim, tell me?

Mayim still appeared skeptical, however.

Said Rachel, "When Mordechai was here, I told him of my intentions. Since I had spoken of you frequently earlier, he thought it was an excellent idea. You know what Mayim? Let's call Mordechai now and you can ask him yourself."

"That's not necessary. You wouldn't lie to me, not even a little lie. I suppose when you raised the subject right after I told you my troubles, I naturally assumed your goodness caused you to make the offer. Now that I know that it's genuine, I'll be happy to work for you."

"Oh, Mayim, that makes me so happy," Rachel said. "But let's be clear, you won't be working for me, you'll be working with me."

Meetings with the architects and contractor continued. In between, Mayim revealed she had some news.

"I met a young man several months ago and things have become very serious between us," she said. "Shmuel hasn't yet asked me to marry him, but I think it will happen once he has the courage to do so. I've told him about you, although he has no idea you're here. He was supposed to come this evening, but if you feel it's too soon to meet him, I'll put him off for another evening."

Rachel said absolutely not. When he knocked on the door early in the evening, he was surprised to see it was Rachel who answered, with a beaming Mayim standing several feet back.

"Only one person could make Mayim smile as she is," he said, after which he hugged Rachel, lifted her off the ground, and swung her around several times.

Laughing hysterically, Rachel said, "I've never been greeted like that before. It was fun."

Deciding this was a special occasion, they went out for supper. The two young women were in high spirits, laughing and sharing funny stories, and Shmuel tried his best to fit in, even if he felt like a third wheel. He made conversation with Rachel, asking about Winnipeg, what she did on a day-to-day basis, and whether she went out in the evenings.

Rachel clued in quickly and said, "Shmuel, are you planning to play *shidduch* [matchmaker]?"

"Now that you mention, I suppose I could do that," he replied, only partially suppressing a smile. "As it happens, I have a friend Ephraim who might be a good match for you. As I only met you today, I obviously haven't discussed this with him."

"That's fine. Tell me a bit about him."

"He's a third-generation Canadian whose grandfather came here years ago to escape the pogroms in Russia. He's nice-looking, average height, and very smart, and every mother wants him as a son-in-law. I think he would be a real catch."

"And why hasn't he been caught yet?" Rachel asked.

"I can't say since it isn't something we have discussed. I think he's too wrapped up in his work and is reluctant to share his time with another person."

"Being wrapped up in his work might be a good thing. What does his work involve?" she asked.

"He's a lawyer who works exclusively with the Canadian Jewish Congress [CJC]." Seeing her puzzled expression, he described the function of the CJC as an advocacy group for Jews in Canada. "Ephraim's work with the CJC focuses on human and civil rights as well as immigration reform."

"I'm impressed, truly impressed. Especially by his work," Rachel said. "Let's be realistic, how likely is it he and I will be compatible? Besides, if he's so dedicated to his work, which is understandable, there may not be any room for me."

"True enough. Yet meeting him wouldn't necessarily be for the purpose of marriage. You may end up simply being close friends, which can also be good. I'll tell you what, I'll contact him, and the four of us can have a nice dinner together so there won't be pressure on either of you."

Shmuel arranged for them to go to the theater and then have supper the next Saturday. Rachel was taken by Ephraim, who was witty and knowledgeable on numerous subjects. He spoke little about himself, instead taking an interest in Rachel's history, ranging from her current work to her war experiences, which caused his eyes to moisten noticeably. How he felt about Rachel wasn't clear to her, but the mystery was solved when he called the next day to ask her to join him for supper on Monday. He called her the following evening, inviting her to accompany him to a play, "The Dybbuk," which would be performed in Yiddish.

"The Dybbuk ... I heard it mentioned when I was in Poland. What's it about?" she asked.

"I can't tell you since it will ruin the suspense," he replied. "I've seen it before and, believe me, it's an amazing play."

"So, you've seen it before and want to see it again. Yet telling me what it's about in a general way will ruin it for me?"

"Fine, I'll only say it's a very mystical Kabbalistic experience about a young woman who is possessed by a malicious spirit, a *dybbuk*, that is, the incarnation of a potential suitor who died of heartbreak when the young woman's father prevented him from seeing his daughter. That's it. I've already said too much, and I won't say anymore."

Rachel was awed by the play.

"I could identify with the young girl," she said afterward. "Rather than an evil father who lied to prevent a marriage to a poor man, I imagined it was the Third Reich that prevented the marriage, and I hoped multiple dybbuks would haunt them for eternity."

"I'm glad you enjoyed it."

"Will you take me to other plays?" she asked coyly.

"As many as you would like. As long as you can stand being with me, I'll take you wherever you like," he replied, gazing at her.

They appeared to be the perfect couple, and even though he doted on her and tried to accommodate her every wish, at the back of her mind there were doubts. In a letter from Nela, she learned what happened to her charmed life even though Isaac had initially been smitten by Nela and catered to her every wish. Perhaps the Holocaust had made Rachel wary of anything she deemed an uncertainty. She knew she had to leave the past behind even if it was exceedingly difficult.

Mordechai returned to Toronto and was overwhelmed by the progress with the store that had been made in only a few months. He was extremely pleased by the look of the place. He was even more taken by Ephraim, who seemed to be with Rachel every free moment. "Uncle Mordechai," she said, "Ephraim wants to marry me after he asks for your consent."

"He wants my consent! Such a mensch. I would be honored to have him as a nephew. Sonia will want the wedding to be in Winnipeg so she can show him off to all her friends. Would that be agreeable to the two of you?"

"It is for me, but Ephraim has a large family and I'm not sure how we would work that out."

"That's not a problem. I'll rent a plane and provide hotel rooms for everyone. This will be an amazing wedding. If only your mother could be here to celebrate with us."

Four months later they were married, with both families and their friends in attendance. The wedding was joyous, with singing and dancing going on late into the night. After everybody had left, only Sonia and Rachel remained.

Sitting on a loveseat in the hallway, Rachel put her head on Sonia's shoulder and said, "It's good I don't call you Auntie Sonia because you're more like a mother. Thank you for tonight. I know you arranged every detail so it would be perfect."

"You're so sweet, Rachel. You'll be just as kind to my children. A daughter learns from her mother, even if she's an auntie."

They returned to Toronto three days later with Mayim and Shmuel at their side as always. Neither of them put much stock in honeymoons and promised one another that when the time was right, they would take a nice trip. Following Rachel's lead, Mayim and Shmuel married soon afterward, and Rachel hosted an immense wedding celebration. At the wedding, Mayim, together with her uncle and several of their former students, entertained the guest with a rendition of "Vltava, the Moldau," composed by Bedřich Smetana. The guests recognized the music as the precursor to the Hatikvah, the Israeli national anthem. The beautiful orchestration had them swaying in their seats as they envisioned the river Moldau gently coursing through the length of Czechoslovakia.

Prager's in Toronto, which opened only two months earlier, seemed very successful, drawing customers from across the city. Rachel was reluctant to predict a profit in the first year, yet she told Mayim it was possible. Having established an excellent team, every element of the business from purchasing to advertising functioned smoothly. Just as she had been able to lighten the burden for Mordechai, it was apparent Mayim was doing the same for Rachel.

Ephraim had an idea for Rachel. The CJC wanted him to go to Israel to coordinate efforts to convince the Soviet Union to allow Jews to emigrate. He hoped Rachel would come along.

"Can you get away for about ten days?" he asked. "My work will only require five or six days, and we can extend it to about ten days so we can take some vacation time."

She agreed. Ephraim made the arrangements, and they arrived in Israel a week later. It was the first time Rachel had visited the Jewish homeland and she was awed by everything she saw.

On the second day in Jerusalem, Ephraim was to meet with a woman with whom he'd had frequent contact over the years, providing her with assorted information about what he had discovered regarding possible infiltration of Nazi war criminals into Canada and elsewhere.

When the couple entered the office of the woman, whose desk was littered with file folders and loose sheets of paper, Rachel suddenly stopped walking and stared. Then the woman looked back for a long moment.

Finally, the woman said, "Rachel?"

Having recovered from her initial shock, Rachel rushed over to Zosha, who had stood to greet her, and hugged her tight. "Zosha, I never expected this," Rachel said. "It's been so long, and I have frequently thought of you."

"Believe me, I've thought of you and Nela frequently as well. This is so unexpected. What are you doing here?"

Motioning toward Ephraim, who had been confused by the scene playing out, she replied, "I'm accompanying this very handsome man who is my husband."

"Come, sit with us," Zosha said. "Ephraim and I have some business, and as we speak, you'll hear what I've been doing with myself, and then later you can tell me what you've been doing."

Over the next hour, Ephraim and Zosha planned ways of aiding several prominent politicians, including one in Canada, to work toward the release of Jews from the Soviet Union. Listening to them, Rachel became increasingly absorbed in their work and, concurrently, frustrated at how little she personally had been doing.

As the meeting came to an end, Zosha turned to Rachel. "So, I want to hear what you've been doing all these years," Zosha said. "Your pensive look, coupled with hints of dismay, tells me something interesting is going on in your sweet head I'd like to hear about."

"Nothing profound, only some vague ideas," Rachel replied. She and Zosha then spent some time filling each other in on their lives since they were last together.

"I'm very impressed with what you've achieved," Zosha said. "I never imagined that the young, quiet girl I met on an army transport truck had such an abundance of skills."

"I suppose I've done well if money is the measure of success," Rachel answered. "But as you and Ephraim spoke, I wondered whether there is any value to profits without a purpose."

"Profits without purpose. That's an interesting turn of phrase. And do you have any ideas to give your life greater purpose?" Zosha asked.

"Perhaps. I'm not sure. Some still not fully formed ideas are percolating in my brain. This is more complicated than spreadsheets and planning a business expansion. Once I've formulated some concrete plans, I'll contact you to see if they can be turned into reality."

Touring Israel, Rachel was struck by what had been achieved since it gained independence only a few years earlier in 1948. Repeatedly, as she and Ephraim toured, her mind kept coming back to how she could use her money to make meaningful contributions to the welfare of her fellow Jews in the Soviet Union and Israel. Many Jews were desperate to leave the U.S.S.R., and Israel was equally in need of immigration.

When Rachel fell into one of her pensive states, she would catch Ephraim looking at her quizzically. She promised to tell him everything once her thoughts turned from vague notions to concrete plans.

Not long after their return to Toronto, Rachel received exciting news. She was pregnant, which she took to be especially auspicious as she had conceived while in Israel. Ephraim was delighted and suggested they name the baby Tel Aviv, Jerusalem, or Kinneret, which she said were good choices depending on whether it was a girl or a boy.

That good news wasn't all. She and Mayim had developed workable plans to do something meaningful with their profits. They focused on sponsoring a film that could be widely distributed. It would comprise a history of what Jews throughout Europe experienced during the Shoah, including the reluctance of countries to admit Jews during and after the war. The film would culminate with the travails of Jews in the Soviet Union over the decades, leading up to their recent desire to return to the Jewish homeland.

Rachel unilaterally decided the music in the background would be Mayim and her ensemble playing the Moldau – the same music as at her wedding. It had brought Rachel close to tears when she heard it, and she felt audiences would be moved, too.

They phoned Zosha and shared their ideas with her. Zosha was excited and promised to provide whatever help she could.

"My files include well-documented historical information, film clips that could be useful, as well as filmed testimonials from survivors," Zosha said. "I also have numerous contacts within the film industry, and if you agree, I can contact an Israeli director and a producer whom I hold in high esteem. They can arrange for writers and screenwriters."

As she spoke, Zosha grew increasingly excited. It was infectious. "We can make sure the film is widely advertised, and when word goes out, Jews would fall over themselves to contribute financially to the production of the film," Zosha said.

Mayim was overwhelmed after speaking to Zosha. "She's amazing," Mayim said. "What a treasure. Is there anything she's left for us to do?"

"I'm not sure. Hopefully, she'll find something for us," Rachel replied happily. "This will happen. Now I'll let Ephraim know about our plans."

"You haven't told Ephraim?" Mayim asked in consternation.

"Why would I tell him something that was a maybe?" Rachel responded. "It's better to deal with realities than uncertainties."

When she was three months pregnant, she phoned Sonia to tell her the news.

"You couldn't let me know earlier?" Sonia asked.

"Well, I thought it would be inappropriate to tell anyone before three months."

"Anybody! Suddenly I'm 'anybody'! You're like my daughter, although nobody would guess given how young I look. Never mind, I'll come right away. There's lots to do."

Rachel didn't object, knowing once Sonia was in action mode, nothing would derail her.

Sonia and Mordechai arrived the next day. Ephraim looked at Mordechai quizzically, hoping he could explain what Sonia had in mind. Mordechai simply raised his hands, saying, "I have no idea. I simply do what I'm told. It makes life easier."

"You won't be able to live in this cramped apartment once the baby comes," Sonia said to Rachel. "We need to find a house in a nice area, maybe on the outskirts of the city where the air is better. There's no time to waste. I've already lost three months because I'm just an 'anybody.' Once we find a nice house, we'll have to remodel a few things because it must be just right. It will have to be repainted and we'll have to make sure the garden is nice. I'll take care of the decorations and furniture and design the baby's room."

Turning to Mordechai, she said, "You don't need to come with me. You'll just get underfoot."

He whispered to Ephraim, "You see? I don't know why she made me come. I have no function other than to hold her purse now and then."

While Sonia was off on her mission, Rachel described her plans for the film. Mordechai was more than impressed. He was awestruck.

"I keep saying the same thing over and over," Mordechai said. "How much I wish Channah could have witnessed and enjoyed what you created."

When Sonia returned, she announced, "Max Kornblum, the best real estate agent in the city, took me to several available houses and we'll do this again tomorrow. If nothing is to my liking, we'll continue the next day. Don't worry, I'll get us the right house. Once you see what I've selected, you'll be pleased."

Mordechai returned to Winnipeg, while Sonia stayed behind to complete her project. Only when it was done did she go home, promising to return when the time for the delivery approached.

On schedule, Rachel delivered a healthy daughter. They named her Channah after her grandmother. Two years later, she had a second daughter, Miriam.

During Rachel's brief time away from work, Mayim handled what was needed at the store, and when Mayim was away delivering her children, Rachel reciprocated. The business prospered and profits kept improving, although as the city grew, more stores appeared and the competition became ferocious, requiring continuous adjustments to their business plan. As Rachel became more involved in raising her daughters and other projects, she chose to step back from managing the day-to-day operations. Her management team was excellent and could handle everything.

The film was exceptionally well received. Ephraim was proud of its impact.

"The film may have helped persuade leaders of the Soviet Union to come to their senses and permit Jews to emigrate," he said. "It also had the effect of facilitating my civil rights work. That said, while the Shoah is embedded in the mind of most Jews, progressively more non-Jews seem to have forgotten history, and antisemitism is again rearing its ugly head. Right-wing groups have had an increasingly greater impact, and simply establishing hate laws isn't sufficient to curb the spread of vile propaganda."

Unexpectedly, Mordechai died in his 78th year after a brief illness. Rachel implored Sonia to come live with her family.

"I can visit often," Sonia replied, "but I want to cook in my own kitchen and sleep in my bed. Besides, my memories are here, and Mordechai, God bless his soul, is buried here."

Her daughters were very different from one another. That was evident when they were preteens and became progressively more pronounced over the ensuing years. Channah, who was always smiling and cheerful, took to playing violin and piano, tutored by Mayim, whereas Miriam was sour and caustic in her interactions with others, frequently becoming quarrelsome for no apparent reason. On the advice of a psychologist who suggested her behavior may have reflected youngest child syndrome, Rachel and Ephraim increased their attention to Miriam despite their concern her problem stemmed from being excessively coddled as a child. Channah attempted to serve as a protective older sister, but her efforts were repeatedly met with contemptuous rejection.

Her daughters were now both university students and she took pride in their accomplishments. Channah was intent on going to medical school. Miriam was drawn to political science. However, while Channah was happy and content, Miriam continued being dour, persistently bitter, opinionated, and cynical. Miriam's negativity became still more pronounced after entering graduate school and continued unabated after she completed a doctorate and obtained a position as a university professor.

Rachel voiced her displeasure to Ephraim: "I'm terribly upset with Miriam, especially as some of my friends have told me she has been making derogatory statements about Israel. I can't understand why she has chosen to vent her bitterness this way. Was it misdirected animosity toward us given how strongly we have supported Israel, or is she following the new left-leaning attitudes that have focused on castigating Israel?"

She confronted Miriam about her behavior, but the response was a lecture concerning all the horrible things Israel had done to the Palestinians. Finally, in frustration, Rachel said, "I doubt very much you're the free thinker you try so hard to portray."

Miriam's contrarian attitude became still more prominent when she began calling herself Miri, perhaps to diminish her Jewish identity. Rachel was frequently embarrassed when she would hear from acquaintances that Miri was widely disliked in the Jewish community not only because of her beliefs but for being a loudmouth. The community saw her as a self-hating Jew who would express the most ridiculous notions and seemed intent on espousing her views on any media forum that would have her. Disturbingly, she would share her disdain with students in her classes, disguising her opinions as a neutral exposition on the situation involving Israel and the Palestinians.

Whatever pride she had in Miriam's early accomplishments entirely dissolved, as did Ephraim's. "She's not a natural leader of the left as she would like to believe," he said. "Instead, she's a useful idiot."

Said Rachel, "I'm reminded of King Lear speaking of his daughter, 'How sharper than a serpent's tooth it is to have a thankless child.' I've experienced hardships and horror in my life, but this wound is the deepest and I'll never forgive it."

8

MOTTI AND ELIE: REEMERGENCE

In peace, sons bury their fathers. In war, fathers bury their sons.

– Herodotus

The presence of large Jewish communities within Russia can be traced back at least 15 centuries, and many of the Jewish cultural and theological traditions practiced throughout Europe and elsewhere were rooted in those established in Russia. Although the Jewish community had flourished for a lengthy period, increasing antisemitism and vicious pogroms resulted in more than two million Jews leaving Russia during the late 1800s and early 1900s.

Despite their small numbers, Jews had a substantial influence on Russia's political trajectory. Karl Marx, Leon Trotsky, Maxim Litvinoff, Grigory Zinoviev, Karl Radek, and Leonid Krassin, who were all born Jews, became central figures in the socialist and communist positions that were adopted. Even Vladimir Lenin, born Vladimir Ilich Ulyanov, was of Jewish descent, although his religious ancestry was concealed by the Soviet authorities. During his time as the leader of Russia, expressions of antisemitism were banned, many Yiddish schools were established, scores of Yiddish newspapers sprang up, and despite their population amounting to less than two percent of Russia, about 14 percent of university students were Jewish.

After his premature death from heart disease at the age of 54, his successor, Joseph Stalin, was able to transform the Soviet Union from a poor country that had been a peasant society into an industrial and military power. At the same time, the treatment of Jews became less tolerable, although as a group they still maintained high political positions and were well positioned within the Soviet Red Army. As Lenin feared before his death, Stalin's success came with an enormous cost. His brutality and the terror he created kept him in power, while he showed no remorse for his responsibility for the deaths of millions of citizens.

Stalin was without question just as duplicitous, cruel, and inhuman as Hitler. When the Nazis and Soviets initiated the Molotov-Ribbentrop Pact in August 1939, it brought together avaricious authoritarians who had illusions, or delusions, of dominance over most of Europe and beyond. For public consumption, the pact largely was a non-aggression treaty stating the two countries would not attack one another and would not aid any third party that might come into conflict with either of the two. Less well-known was that the pact also defined spheres of influence for the two countries, including Estonia, Latvia, and Bessarabia falling under Soviet purview. After a subsequent modification, the Soviet sphere included Lithuania and a portion of Poland.

Having decimated Ukraine by instigating the Holodomor, which killed five million people in 1932-1933, Stalin was prepared to help himself to other regions abutting Russia. Just 16 days after Germany attacked Poland from the west, Russia invaded from the east. It took only 20 days for Russia to achieve its goals, meeting weak resistance from the underequipped Polish army. Its success was abetted by segments of the Polish military believing the Soviets were entering the war to fight the Nazis and protect Ukrainians and Belarusians living in Eastern Poland.

They were soon disabused of these optimistic notions. At the first opportunity, the Soviets began eliminating major figures who might challenge their authority. More than 22,000 Polish military officers, political figures, police, members of the intelligentsia, and priests were executed. Many thousands of Polish prisoners of war also were killed, and between 1.2 million and 1.7 million Poles, including many Jews, were deported to labor camps in Siberia, where most died.

Despite an agreement of mutual assistance among France, Britain, and Poland, the help delivered to Poland after the German invasion was limited, and the little that was done was ineffectual and late in coming. Once Russia invaded Poland, neither Britain nor France had the temerity to continue any efforts to assist.

Emboldened by the efforts at appeasement of the British and French in the takeover of Czechoslovakia, coupled with their abject failure to come to the rescue of Poland, Hitler was prepared to take further steps toward making Germany the dominant country on the continent. In early April, Germany invaded Denmark and Norway with little resistance, assuring Germany access to iron ore supplies and access to various ports.

On May 10, 1940, Germany invaded France, Belgium, Luxembourg, and the Netherlands. The French and British commanders had expected if Germany attacked, it would do so through central Belgium as it had in World War I. Hitler's tacticians didn't follow the script. Instead, they adopted a rapid and overwhelming attack, or blitzkrieg, through the Ardennes Forest in southeastern Belgium and northern Luxembourg. The German generals outmaneuvered the Allies through rapid movements aided by superior communications, the French and British chaotically abandoned efforts to resist, and the British were lucky to be able to rescue most of their expeditionary force at Dunkirk. The vaunted Maginot Line fell like matchsticks, and within six weeks, France and the Low Countries were defeated.

As deceitful and duplicitous as Stalin was, Hitler's treachery was arguably even greater. Either from the desire for more *Lebensraum* [living space for the German people] or Hitler despising communists as much as Jews, Nazi Germany attacked the Soviet Union on June 22, 1941. In desperation, Russia permitted the Polish soldiers being held in Siberia to return, perhaps in hopes some of the 20 percent who had survived would fight the Nazis. Some Jews were able to leave Siberia, although many remained behind, feeling it was safer to remain there than face the Nazi onslaught or Stalin's intense enmity toward Jews. Ironically, Stalin's antisemitism was instrumental in assuring many Eastern European Jews who survived the war did so because they stayed in the unoccupied, barely habitable regions of the Soviet Union.

Przemyśl, which had been established in the eighth century, was a center of commerce due to its ideal location and the San River running through town. Like many other cities within Poland, it had repeatedly changed hands. For a time, it was a part of Moravia. Then it became incorporated into the Hungarian empire before being returned to Poland, only to become part of the Austrian empire. In the last part of the 18th century, Poland was divided among Russia, Prussia, and Austria and stayed that way until the end of World War I. At the time, Przemyśl was claimed by both Poland and Ukraine, but after a battle, the Ukrainians were ejected from the city.

For centuries, the Jews of Przemyśl had the right to settle there, buy houses from Christians and conduct trade freely. Moreover, the election of community leaders and the appointment of rabbis were left to the discretion of the Jewish community. This tolerant period remained during the early 1900s and even saw such acceptance grow. Schools that provided Jewish studies became common, and there was a Jewish cultural center and a sports club. The city became known as a home of authors and scholars and even had a Zionist organization. Unfortunately, during the few years preceding the Nazi invasion, antisemitism increased markedly as reflected by elevated propaganda and increasing violence.

Motti had lived on a farm several kilometers from Przemyśl with his parents and younger brothers Elie and Daniel. Before the quality of life of Jews declined, Motti's family had chosen to leave their farm to be among the Jews who lived in the city. As Jews made up about 40 percent of the population of Przemyśl, they felt the sheer numbers would buffer against antisemitic behavior. Motti stayed behind to attend to the farm, which he enjoyed immensely. His brothers would frequently return to help with assorted chores and remain for weeks during the harvest. He, in turn, often visited his family on weekends, and thus they remained close to one another.

Soon after the invasion of Poland, reports reached Przemyśl that the Nazis were exterminating Jews in western Poland, leading a large number to quickly leave the city. Even though they were aware of the attitudes of Poles and Ukrainians, the departing Jews were dismayed and humiliated by the contemptuous jeering of their countrymen who lined the roadside. Motti's family had remained in Przemyśl in hopes this behavior simply reflected mass hysteria and would prove fleeting. For two days after they entered Przemyśl, the Nazis behaved in a somewhat civilized fashion, leading Motti's family to believe they were right to remain. However, over the ensuing week, many Jews were selected, either randomly or based on a list obtained from community leaders, and summarily executed. Jews who had been sufficiently naive or foolish enough to believe their fate might not be as horrid as they had heard were quickly disabused of their pipe dreams.

The arrival of the Russians four days after the Nazi occupation was met with relief, and some Jews who had left earlier returned, hoping the Russians would save them. It didn't take long for the Russians to show their abject antisemitism. Most assets held by Jews were confiscated. Jews were removed from political positions, and Jewish-owned institutions such as schools, orphanages, and hospitals were nationalized. Even doctors and lawyers lost their right to work and could obtain only low-level positions. The impoverishment of Jews was just the start. Many were killed or deported to inhospitable parts of Russia, whereas others were imprisoned in overcrowded jails on charges of being spies.

After Germany attacked Russia in 1941, Przemyśl quickly fell, leading to a different and still more horrendous situation for Jews. It began with being broadly depicted as vermin and germs and being isolated from the rest of society. A campaign began in which Jews were forced from their homes. When the Jews were gone, their valuables were confiscated, and local Poles and Ukrainians as well as police looted whatever was left. Many Jews who had been imprisoned earlier were executed, as were those suspected of cooperating with the Russians, and many young people were transferred to work camps.

The Jews were forced into a ghetto, and those found outside its boundaries or who tried to escape were immediately shot. The overcrowded ghetto made it necessary for Jews to find living spaces wherever they could. Their previously comfortable homes were replaced by cellars, attics, and storerooms. The poverty, deplorable sanitary conditions, and food shortage took a physical and mental toll. The Gestapo took pleasure in severely beating Jews who committed the slightest transgressions. Many were killed for attempting to smuggle food into the ghetto. Others were executed for no apparent reason. Of course, the intelligentsia was viewed as a threat and thus were among the first to be rounded up and murdered.

As in other ghettos, the Gestapo required the creation of a Judenrat that had to strictly follow Nazi orders, and if any transgressions occurred, its members were held responsible. Jewish clerks were assigned the unenviable job of selecting those who would work at the most menial and degrading jobs, thereby further humiliating them. The Judenrat was required to provide lists of people who would be shipped to camps such as Janowska, ostensibly to work, although it also served as an extermination center. Unfortunately, there were biases concerning who was placed on lists or obtained preferred work, resulting in conflict. Distrust of the Judenrat was exacerbated because it was widely believed bribes could buy preferable jobs, including within organizations that used forced labor, which would preclude execution.

Progressively greater pressure was placed on the Judenrat to supply more Jews for transport to camps. Jews who attempted to hide were shot, with their bodies left in the street to be removed by other Jews nominated by the Judenrat. In some instances, the Gestapo forced certain Jews to burn the bodies of the dead, after which they, too, were killed. Other Jews were required to sift through the ashes to find any valuables that those cremated in the public square might have been holding, after which the ashes were thrown into the river.

Despite the hope many Jews could be saved from Nazi treachery, in July 1942, the Judenrat was informed they could expect *aktions* [mass deportations of Jews from the ghetto to concentration camps]. The Judenrat attempted to limit the numbers, but the decision of the Gestapo was unalterable. The Germans intended to remove 17,000 people over several aktions that would occur weeks apart. Not all the prisoners were taken to camps. The sick and elderly were transported to the local cemetery, where they were killed. The aktions depleted the number of ghetto Jews, and except for those used for labor or saved by the local Polish underground, virtually all were transported to Auschwitz or the Belzec execution camp. Motti's parents and brothers were among those who were shipped off and, he assumed, would be killed.

From his vantage point on a bluff on the family farm, Motti had seen the military arrive in the region only days after the German invasion of Poland began. Even from a distance, he could hear fighting, and from the sound, it was apparent Polish resistance fell quickly to the German onslaught. His neighbors informed him that the Einsatzgruppen that entered the city ruthlessly eliminated Jews, while the Gestapo began searching for Jews outside of Przemyśl. Although some of his Christian neighbors, most of whom he had known since childhood, had offered to hide him from the Nazis, information from the western part of Poland indicated anyone found hiding Jews was executed. Because of the dangers they would face, he chose to remain in the forests during the warmer months, often receiving food from his neighbors. He was able to create a makeshift shelter that protected him from the wind, but on bitterly cold winter days, he took shelter in outbuildings and barns of farms where he had the company of cows that he laid next to so he could keep warm. His Christian friends kept him informed about family members who had survived the initial Nazi takeover of the city but nonetheless suffered with the remaining Jews. He desperately wanted to contact them and even to attempt to smuggle them food but was dissuaded as it might place them in greater jeopardy. Nevertheless, he was able to send them the message he was in hiding and doing well.

Like everyone else, he was astonished when Germany attacked the Soviets a little more than a year and a half later and soon afterward occupied Przemyśl on both sides of the river. For Motti, it didn't matter which Jew-haters controlled the city until he discovered that while the Russians were satisfied simply shipping many Jews to Siberia, the Nazi goal was their utter destruction. With Przemyśl under German control, the ghetto that had been established held about 24,000 Jewish residents, which comprised those from the city and others brought from the surrounding area, including settlements in Bircza, Kazifshka, Nizhankovichi, and Dinow.

If the objective was to rid themselves of Jews, Motti wondered, why did the Gestapo bring more to Przemyśl? The answer came when he learned Jews in large numbers were being transported out of the ghettos to work or die either in concentration camps or to be deported to extermination camps. Przemyśl was being used as a node to coordinate the elimination of Jews. Aside from the aktions that eliminated the vast majority of the ghetto Jews, the Nazis relentlessly searched for Jews that were hiding, executing any that were found and blowing up buildings where it looked like their prey might be hiding. They went so far as to have Jews come out of hiding by guaranteeing their safety. Tired of hiding and near starvation, 900 of the remaining Jews of Przemyśl emerged, and as promised they were put to work rather than being killed immediately. In the end, however, they, too, were massacred.

Throughout the previous two years, the ghetto residents vainly hoped Allied armies might liberate them, and being rescued by the Red Army was considered preferable to the indiscriminate cruelty meted out by the Nazis. Rescue seemed ever more unlikely given how German forces had initially been able to overrun the Russians. What they hadn't expected was the resolve of the Russian army as well as the desperate tactics to which it resorted. The scorched-earth policy adopted by Russian forces deprived the Wehrmacht of needed supplies, and German tanks were bogged down as the spring rains turned the fields into quagmires. Eventually, the Russian forces mounted a counteroffensive at Stalingrad and were able to encircle a large component of the German army, inflicting many injuries and deaths and ultimately capturing almost 100,000 soldiers.

To weaken the Russian offensive, Hitler and his henchmen intended to destroy the opposing forces at Kursk. However, the Germans were slow in building up their reduced army and in obtaining new weapons. Thanks to intelligence provided by the Allies, Russia was prepared for the assault, and when Germany made its move, it faced counterattacks from multiple directions. The largest tank battles in history took place, and the vaunted Nazi tank brigades that had so easily trampled over the defenses of many countries proved vulnerable to superior strategy. The troops of Mother Russia had defeated the soldiers of the German Fatherland. With the defeat, and setbacks in other regions caused by Hitler's enormous greed for conquest resulting in his war machine being too widely dispersed, the end of the Third Reich was in sight.

The Soviet army forced the Wehrmacht out of Russia and Ukraine, and Przemyśl was liberated in July 1944. Jews who had successfully hidden came out of their shelters to find only about 200 had survived, all emaciated and weak. As unlikely as it was, they initially were hopeful of finding family members and regaining what was left of their lives. Instead, they were greeted with animosity by the Poles and Ukrainians of Przemyśl who didn't want them there. Such hate may have reflected antisemitism; perhaps, among some, shame and guilt for not having been more supportive of Jews fueled efforts to avoid the survivors. Whatever the case, it was clear Przemyśl wasn't a safe place for Jews, but most didn't have the resources or physical capacity to leave.

Fearing the Russians as much as the Nazis, Motti stayed hidden, but when the war ended, he tried to find his parents and brothers. He assumed his family had perished, as did neighbors who commiserated with him about their apparent deaths. After several weeks of fruitless searching, and with nothing left for him in Przemyśl, he opted to find his way out of Poland and establish a new life elsewhere. Another country in Europe, or perhaps America, Australia, or Israel. It didn't matter, so long as it wasn't Poland, Ukraine, or Russia. Still, he continued to be haunted by not knowing what had become of his family.

Having learned the best way out of Europe was to go where the Allied armies were, he took to the road carrying a few items of clothes and food in a knapsack he had found at the side of the road. It took several days and a series of rides to reach the main highway headed for Germany. After walking along the roadside for hours, he felt fortunate to find himself on an American lorry with other survivors heading for Germany – the center of the pit of hell.

As the truck moved on its way, he listened intently to the conversation between Ari, Zosha, and others on it. He spoke little and brooded silently, only answering questions directed to him. Unlike some of them, he didn't believe God had a plan for him. Indeed, as he said to his travel companions, he had begun to doubt whether their God had the power to save the Jews or even whether God was inclined to intervene in any human matters. Only a young woman, Nela, had agreed with him. It never dawned on him God would have interceded to save any of his family members. None of them was especially worthy of being saved, and he certainly couldn't imagine God had a plan for them or him.

"I don't think there will be many Jewish survivors," Zosha said. "Maybe 20 or 30,000. When I worked with the Americans interviewing survivors, it puzzled me how any of us at all survived. It certainly wasn't the most devout, the most intelligent, or the strongest. Largely it was having a specific skill the Nazis wanted or being lucky."

Motti considered that if the motley Jews on the lorry managed to survive the camps, then maybe members of his family had as well. These thoughts, coupled with intense guilt over not doing more to find out whether any of them were still alive, fostered his decision not to continue the journey to Germany.

The next time the truck stopped, he left the group without a specific plan other than heading back to Przemyśl. Although it was unlikely he would find any of his family alive, he couldn't tolerate the uncertainty. Carrying the tattered knapsack, he walked along the roadside heading east, hoping drivers of passing vehicles would offer to take him toward his destination. Within an hour, an old truck pulled over and the Polish driver, who seemed to want company, took him as far as Łódź, where he stayed overnight and ate the last of the food he had with him.

He reached Krakow the next day, where he found a Red Cross post that provided overnight shelter, some clothes, and a food parcel. With rest and food, he arose early and was soon on the road, reaching Rzeszow during the early afternoon. As luck had it, he obtained another ride from a farmer who lived only a few kilometers from his family's farm. The older man was prepared to drive him to his destination, but he chose to get off the truck at the farm. As he came closer to home, his anticipation and anxiety increased and he had to restrain himself from running the last few hundred meters. To his disappointment, the farmhouse was deserted, although it seemed it had been used recently. Finding nothing that informed him of his family, he continued to walk to the home of a close friend who had often hidden him and provided food and other necessities while he hid in the forests.

As he began to walk along the long path to the farmhouse, its door opened and his friend Karol jumped down the three steps to the ground, ran over, and hugged him. "You look terrible," Karol said. "Worse than when I last saw you. I hadn't recognized you from a distance, except your distinctive lopsided walk gave you away."

They went inside together, and Karol set about preparing some food and tea. He placed a bottle of vodka on the table, saying, "I'd offer schnapps if we had any."

"Thank you, good friend," Motti said. "Right now, the food and tea are more than enough. What I'd like most at this moment is to obtain information about my parents and brothers."

"Of course, of course, Motti. The last I heard they were imprisoned in the ghetto, and I suppose that like most of the people they had been transferred to the wretched concentration camps. I have no idea to which camp your family was transported. Nobody is speaking of these things – there is utter silence as if the ghetto had never existed."

"I had hoped that if any of my family survived, they would find their way to our farm, so I went there but found nobody," Motti said. "It seemed it had been occupied recently and then abandoned. So, I came here in the hope you had seen them."

"For a small period, only a few weeks, it seemed the Nazis had intended to use the farm, with slave laborers doing the necessary work," Karol said, his head bowed. "The SS officers suddenly disappeared just before the Russians arrived, leaving behind the bodies of the laborers whom they had murdered."

"I suppose they killed them because Jews were disposable, or they didn't want witnesses alive who could implicate them in their earlier crimes."

"The reason is immaterial," Karol replied, repulsed even by the mention of the Nazis. "To kill people that way and then leave the bodies to rot in the field is beyond comprehension. They've become so accustomed to death, killing a few more people had no meaning to them."

After they sat quietly absorbing what had occurred, Karol said, "Motti, it's too late to start our search today, and we're best off waiting early tomorrow morning."

"You'll help me?" Motti asked, unsure if that's what Karol had meant.

"Of course!" Karol exclaimed. "We've been friends since we were children. Your mother frequently took care of me, and my mother took care of you. How could you wonder whether I would help?"

Because of the shortage of fuel for Karol's truck, they used bicycles to reach the town. Other than Soviet army vehicles, there was little traffic on the road to Przemyśl. The city itself was relatively busy. Shops had reopened and people were out to obtain food and other necessities. As the goods on sale were limited, food rationing continued as it had during the war. Rationing cards had been distributed, which allowed individuals to obtain bread, flour, sugar, coffee, tea, potatoes, milk, salt, fat, kerosene, and even small quantities of gasoline. Unlike people within cities, those living in the countryside, like Karol, did not receive ration cards, as it was assumed they could feed themselves.

They walked their bicycles slowly through the city, stopping at shops to ask whether any of Motti's family had been seen, and acquaintances they encountered were asked the same questions. Nobody had seen or heard anything. They repeated their search on successive days within different parts of the city. On the fifth day, they met one of the survivors who had escaped the ghetto, and although he hadn't seen or heard anything about Motti's family, he took them across the river where several other survivors had taken shelter. Now there were four additional people who could help in the search for his family. Each survivor could contact others in their small circle, who would spread the word Motti had survived and was looking for any of his family who might have lived through the horror.

Nothing of significance was discovered that day or the next. Despite feeling dejected, Motti was determined to keep searching. Karol had believed from the outset the search would be unsuccessful, and the failures of the preceding days reinforced his belief, but he would stick with Motti until his friend decided it was time to stop. When they returned the next morning, one of the survivors came to them saying he had some news but couldn't say whether it would come to anything. Together they crossed to the west bank of the river and soon met another survivor who walked them down the street to a partially destroyed building, indicating a few survivors had appeared there in recent days, although he knew little about them.

They found several shabbily dressed, emaciated people huddled under blankets, none of whom resembled any of Motti's family members. As they walked about, survivors greeted them and Motti promised to return soon and bring food with him. A man leaning against the frame of a bombed-out window stood listlessly, blankly staring out, seemingly unaware of the people around him. Motti passed by the man, who was absorbed by the scene outside, then after a few strides, he paused and turned back. He pulled on the man's coat sleeve and turned him as easily as if he were a bag of feathers. Startled, the man almost lost his footing before coming face-to-face with Motti. They looked at one another for several seconds, and as Motti's eyes widened, he pulled the man toward himself, holding him with every ounce of strength he possessed, while the man wept soundlessly. It was his brother Elie.

They sat Elie on the back of a bicycle, strapped him to Karol, and took him back to the farmhouse. Elie remained mute, usually staring blankly at the surroundings. Over the next days, he began to eat somewhat more, typically broth containing well-cooked vegetables. As his system settled, his appetite increased. His sleep likewise improved, the early-morning awakenings and persistent rumination he experienced diminished, and his signs of depression declined. As his despondency seemed to wane, he began to speak. First only a few words, and then with his improved physical and mental health, he was able to recount what he had experienced.

"On the first day at Auschwitz, Daniel and I were separated from Tata and Mama," he said. "We were sent to the work camp but didn't know what had become of our parents. It was only when another inmate of the camp pointed to the smoke and ash coming from a tall chimney saying, 'There are my parents and yours as well,' that we understood their fate."

Hearing this, Motti who had been sitting in front of Elie, slumped over, his hand covering his face, while Elie gently stroked his head. "I'm sorry. I had forgotten you hadn't known this. I'm so sorry to have been so insensitive."

"No need to be sorry," Motti said. "While I knew they were gone, it hadn't dawned on me they had been cremated and their ashes spewed about like industrial waste."

"Not that it's much consolation, but at least they hadn't been subjected to further horror. The squalid conditions in the camp were intolerable. The unheated buildings were overcrowded, and we slept three or four on wooden berths that were stacked three levels high. We received only enough food to barely survive, and many died of hunger. Prisoners were frequently beaten by SS guards and by kapos who had been appointed by the Gestapo. Every morning a cart arrived at each barracks, and those who died overnight were stacked on it and taken away."

"Elie, please tell me what became of Daniel."

Collecting himself, he said, "Our filthy clothes were infested with lice and fleas that caused a typhus outbreak, and within several weeks Daniel became infected. There were no medicines available, so his symptoms quickly became severe. He developed a very high fever, delirium, chills, muscle aches, and extreme fatigue to the extent he could hardly lift his head. He developed a bright red rash on every part of his body. I tried to help him as best I could, but he died after about eight days of misery. Eight miserable, horrible days."

"How did you manage to survive those conditions?" Karol asked, horrified.

"How? I'm not sure how or why. I did the work to which I was assigned, stayed as far away as I could from the SS guards and the kapos, and miraculously I never became ill. Every day of horror was like every other day of horror, only varying in intensity, and I somehow adapted. When the soldiers of the Red Army liberated the camp, many inmates greeted them as saviors. I had already witnessed the ruthlessness of Stalin's soldiers, so I kept a distance from them, remaining as unobtrusive as possible. I met several other survivors from this region who had decided to return to their homes, and I went along with them. The rest you know."

With time, rest, and food, his strength returned, and the two brothers began to work the farm to assist Karol in any way they could. The labor was good for their physical health and diminished the signs of anxiety and depression that had persisted. They gained weight and muscle began to appear on their thin frames.

The brothers frequently returned to Przemyśl carting various foods they delivered to the Jewish survivors they had met, and whenever they acquired clothing, they brought it along. In town, they would use their ration cards to obtain supplies that couldn't be obtained by Karol. While they were in a shop to obtain a few items, Elie suddenly moved behind Motti, and in a whisper instructed him to act naturally and make his way out. Once they had left, Elie took his bicycle and walked about 100 meters, crossed the street, and pulled Motti into the alcove of a building.

"What's going on? What spooked you?" Motti asked, not understanding what had suddenly set off his brother's behavior.

Without taking his eyes from the shop they had been in, Elie, who had turned pale, said, "I saw a man in the shop who had been a kapo in Auschwitz. He was the worst of the kapos — more vicious than the SS guards. He found a new victim every day and took pleasure in beating them. His bitterness and every failure in his miserable life, every frustration he encountered, was taken out on us. On one occasion I saw him beat a man to death for no apparent reason. He had come into the barracks in a foul mood and found a target to whom he could express his venom."

The man, who was large and quite strong judging by his frame, soon left the shop carrying a sack that contained supplies. Walking casually, he headed along the street, looking through several shop doors before he entered a bake shop, coming out soon afterward with a loaf of bread protruding from his sack. He continued to saunter along the street unaware Elie and Motti had been discretely following him. The brothers walked on opposite sides of the street, and when one fell back, the other moved forward. The kapo, confident and full of himself, showed no caution and never turned around. After walking for a while, he turned onto a side street just off Kolasa and entered a three-level building about 60 meters away. Shortly afterward, they were able to see him walk by a window on the top level.

The brothers moved to the corner less than 100 meters away and looked at one another, uncertain of what they ought to do. Elie broke the silence, saying, "We should kill him. Beat him to death!"

"Kill him?!" Motti exclaimed. "We're not killers. Besides, he may well kill us."

"Fine, then let's report him to the Russians," Elie said. "They'll know what to do with him."

"Really! What would they do?" Motti replied sarcastically. "They don't care about kapos and are more interested in capturing Ukrainian nationalists who pose a threat to them. They will respond that it's an issue between Jews who should take care of their own problems."

As they considered their options, a voice several meters away said,

"It's good to see you both again, especially as you seem much healthier now."

The young man, Natan, who was one of the men who had helped find Elie, said, "What are the two of you doing standing here, whispering conspiratorially?"

The brothers looked at one another, unsure of what to say, until Motti took the initiative and pulled them around the corner out of sight of the building they had been watching. Briefly, he indicated they had been following a man whom Elie recognized as a kapo at Auschwitz.

"A kapo! Are you sure?" Natan asked. Receiving a nod from Elie, he continued: "Are you absolutely sure? One hundred percent certain? For something like this, there is no room for error."

"Yes, I'm 100 percent certain. How can I forget the face of a fellow Jew who brutalized us in the camp simply because he had the authority to do so? How can I forget the man who ate well while the rest of us starved? Is it even remotely possible to forget the face of a man who simply shrugged his shoulders and walked away as I cried over my dead brother's body?"

Nodding, Natan said, "Which apartment is he in?" After they pointed it out, he muttered venomously, "We can take care of this. You go home and stay away from here."

"What are you planning to do? Elie asked, astonished at Natan's response.

"You don't need to know. Don't ask any more questions. Just go home and don't return here under any circumstances. There are always eyes on us. Please, just go and don't return."

Reluctantly, the brothers headed off, turning back to see Natan motioning them away.

Throughout that day and evening, they wondered what plan Natan had and whether he would be successful. The next day, their curiosity was too great, and after some debate, they returned to the city. As they reached the side street just off Kolasa, they saw a large crowd gathered in front of the house that was their destination. Hanging by his feet from the window on the third level was a man with his throat slit from ear to ear and the word "kapo" painted on his forehead.

As they rode their bicycles toward town several days later, a black car stopped in front of them and another came up from behind. Russian army officers confronted them, saying they had been spotted on two successive days in the vicinity of a place where a murder had been committed. Before the brothers could say anything in their defense, they were placed in one of the cars and driven to the Russian headquarters.

A colonel who steepled his fingers in front of him interviewed them. "Only a Jew would kill another Jew who was a kapo at Auschwitz," he said. Pointing at Elie, he continued, "As you were at Auschwitz, it follows you are his murderer, probably with the help of your brother. I have no option other than to sentence you both to ten years of hard labor in Siberia."

They objected but to no avail. The colonel simply said, "Be thankful you're not being shot. We need people working in Siberia to replace those who died. You'll be in good company with the many other Jews who have been sent there, so they may welcome the likes of you."

They knew that between the bitter cold, malnutrition, and hard labor, being committed to Siberia was likely a death sentence – a slow death rather than a more merciful end by simply being shot in the back of the head.

"You saved me once," Elie said to his brother. "Maybe you'll be able to do it again."

"I think this will be different from anything we've known, and we'll have to save one another," Motti replied, not fully realizing how much it shook Elie to have been unable to save their youngest brother.

While jailed, they tried to mentally prepare themselves for what they would face. Dismally, Elie said, "One day I was afraid of being incinerated and now I'm worried about freezing to death."

"The Nazis and the Bolsheviks have much in common in their attitudes toward Jews," Motti replied. "They differ primarily in how they kill us."

To their astonishment, fate took them on a different path. The day before they were due to be transported to Kolyma, the worst of the Gulag labor camps, their sentences were changed. They were to take up residence in Birobidzhan. They had no idea where it was and why the decision to send them to Kolyma was rescinded, but they were grateful for the reprieve.

They learned from a writer who was also being sent to Birobidzhan that the city and surrounding region were a strange place. The city was situated along the Trans-Siberian Railway, close to the border of China. The city had been established in the early 1930s, with many Jewish communists intending for the Birobidzhan oblast – the region surrounding the city – to ultimately become the Jewish homeland.

The original settlers proselytized to various agencies within and outside Russia to have Jews move there. During its early years, several Jewish intellectuals and Yiddish writers pushed hard to have other Jews join them in the region in hopes their writing would finally have an audience. One of them, David Bergelson, had survived the Bolshevik revolution and moved to Germany and then in 1933 was sufficiently astute to leave and return to Russia. He was enlisted to promote Birobidzhan, which he did rather successfully.

From the perspective of Soviet government officials, Birobidzhan could be used as a place to relocate Jews who were unwanted in Russia, Belarus, Ukraine, or Crimea but could be useful in exploiting the many natural resources in the region. For several reasons, the Birobidzhan Experiment, as it came to be known, was doomed not to become a Jewish homeland. The area had already been inhabited by a substantial number of Russians, Cossacks, and Ukrainians who had been granted land, making it difficult for Jewish immigrants to find a place to live. Many Jews had to be housed in shoddy barracks that allowed the winter weather to enter unhindered. Lastly, there were no cultural connections for Jewish settlers to the Birobidzhan area other than Yiddish becoming the common language.

Motti and Elie were surprised by the number of Jews there. They couldn't conceive of it becoming the homeland of Jews. Nonetheless, they were content to be in a place that was safer than other Soviet-occupied regions.

"I've been told there are more than 30,000 of us here, maybe even 40,000," Motti said.

"Maybe we ought to approach other Jews to help us get settled here," Elie replied.

"Perhaps they'll be welcoming," Motti said. "At the same time, my feeling is we should only count on ourselves."

They had been uncertain what they would do for a living. Nonetheless, together they were a formidable team with varied farming skills that could be applied despite the cold environment.

Soon, Motti arrived at their shack with good news. "I met with a resident of Ukrainian origin who has reasonably good land outside of the city, and he's willing to rent it to us," he said.

"Excellent, and how will we pay the rent?" Elie asked sarcastically. "The shirts off our backs won't be enough."

"This fellow, Demchuk, seemed very reasonable, and since he isn't using the land, he agreed we can pay him at the end of the year with a portion of crops we grow," Motti said.

During the warm, humid summer they grew assorted agricultural products such as wheat, oats, rye, soybeans, sunflowers, and assorted vegetables. At the end of the season, they were able to pay the agreed-upon rent and feed themselves as well as to sell at market.

Clapping his brother's back enthusiastically, Elie said, "Next year, we'll grow even more crops and we'll be able to raise some farm animals."

As hoped, the following year, their produce was more substantial, and they obtained farm animals that cooperated by producing offspring whose meat they sold to local residents.

"I think we should approach Pan Demchuk to buy this land," Elie suggested.

"I do, too, although I doubt he'd be willing to sell it," Motti responded.

"Finally, for once you're wrong, Motti. I've often spoken to Pan

Demchuk when I bring him vodka that I make from our grain and potatoes, and he's confided he hates living here. He would have left long ago but lacks the money. If we continue to provide him with crops, meat, and vodka and offer him enough money to emigrate, I believe he'll be glad to sell."

Demchuk agreed to sell. Having their own land was satisfying and reinforced their identity as citizens of Birobidzhan. They prospered and were able to expand their land holdings and hire workers to increase their agricultural production.

Unfortunately, in the late 1940s, just as their business enterprise had begun to expand, Stalin started his campaign to get rid of "rootless cosmopolitans," which was code for Jews. The campaign was undertaken throughout the Soviet Union, and although Birobidzhan was far off, it didn't escape the widespread antisemitism.

Speaking to members of the Jewish community, Mottie said, "We hadn't realized when we first came here that shortly after the creation of Birobidzhan, attempts had been successful in eliminating Jews in this region. Now, we're seeing the very same thing. Again and again, we seem to be fooled. Just as we come to believe that life is finally good and we are safe, tyrants appear who want to remove us from the face of the planet. We were seduced to come here where the Yiddish language could be fostered, and now we're being targeted for speaking our language and having to hide our identity as Jews."

"We may be far from the heart of Russia and largely irrelevant to the country's goals, but they'll come for us as they always do," Elie added. "They started with the intelligentsia, our writers, our poets, murdering some and sentencing others to ten years of hard labor. Even our friend David Bergelson, who had repeatedly escaped the clutches of antisemites, was executed by Stalin's goons. It's only a matter of time before they come for the rest of us."

Luckily, after several years of fear and uncertainty, God gifted the Jews with Stalin's death in 1953. The persecution of Jews soon abated. The duration of prison sentences meted out to intellectuals was shortened and life slowly returned to the way it had been a few years earlier.

"I think the worst is over," Elie said.

However, Motti responded, "You're just not a realist. You look at storm clouds above our heads and look kilometers away hoping to see a small break you can interpret as the rain ending soon."

"Better that than feeling a few sprinkles and rushing to build an ark," Elie laughed.

"Whatever the case, we need to believe we're safe for the moment but be ready to leave when things turn sour again."

They chose to pursue the projects they had previously planned so they could live comfortably. As usual, by cooperating, they were able to achieve more than they would have on their own. Elie successfully acquired the rights to log Mongolian oak and fir trees in nearby forests and subsequently fashioned a lumber mill to produce wood that could be used for different products, including assorted types of furniture.

Meanwhile, Motti focused on establishing a company to mine tin and iron ore that could be shipped to steel mills in nearby China. Using the lumber from the forest and the metals from mining operations, they were able to build respectable homes for new immigrants to the region, and they built themselves a comfortable house, which included an efficient fireplace Motti had designed to keep them warm.

Not only did they earn enough to live well but were able to help the needy in their community. As it turned out, the recipients of their philanthropy opened small shops that sold food items, hardware, footwear, and various textiles, and they typically made purchases from the products farmed and manufactured by the brothers. As the city modernized and grew, the brothers supplied materials for larger industrial projects.

Through it all, they worried about antisemitism and the region's ability to survive. As leaders in the community, Motti said, they had to step up to convince Jews to remain.

"I know," Elie said, "but I'm afraid this won't be achieved easily. The lawyer Mendel Mayerovich told me that since 1946, Jewish emigration had outstripped the number that arrived. Half of new immigrants left within a year or two, and many more would have if they could. The way things are now, others will soon follow. He projects in just a few years our population will be seriously reduced."

Working with others, they did what they could to make the area more welcoming for Jews. They established a small *cheder* [Jewish school] where Torah could be studied. The small nondescript building also served as a synagogue for Jewish holidays and a place for mourners to light candles for those who died. Afternoons were reserved for studies of secular subjects including science, mathematics, literature, and trades of various forms that would be of practical value. Children were educated about the history of Jews, focusing on the heroes who fought against Jewish oppression in olden times, martyrs who perished protecting Jewish identity, and those who generated pride in being a Jew. Students were taught about Russian literary giants such as Chekhov and Dostoyevsky and were similarly introduced to Jewish literature, including that of the poets and writers who had been tortured and killed in Lubyanka prison on what became known as the Night of the Murdered Poets. In fear of being discovered by authorities, Jewish history and religion and the works of Jewish writers were studied in secret, just as their Spanish-Jewish forebears had celebrated Jewish customs more than four centuries earlier amid the Inquisition.

The brothers believed Jews would flourish with proper education and were gratified by the success of their students. They hoped the young people who left the community for more advanced training might prosper and return for the benefit of those who remained. But they rarely did.

Fear of antisemitism and the hard life in the region spurred continued population declines. Eventually, Motti and Elie gave up on trying to stem the tide. Given the Birobidzhian life expectancy was markedly lower than in the rest of Russia and worsening, especially among men, they turned their efforts to promoting the health of the population. They promoted healthy lifestyles, provided healthy foods, and helped establish parks where children and adults could exercise. Their efforts to reduce consumption of alcohol, in contrast, were a dismal failure. Likewise, they struggled to establish walk-in clinics because few doctors and nurses would come to this isolated place.

While the Jewish population diminished, the overall population began to surge, surpassing 70,000.

"Have you noticed how Birobidzhan has changed?" Elie asked.

"How could I not?" his brother answered. "Large buildings have been constructed, and there are a few industrial centers. It's no longer a Jewish region.

"But," Motti continued, "I see the flavor of our people everywhere. On municipal buildings, Russian and Yiddish appear, signposts pointing to Moscow 6,000 kilometers in one direction, and 8,000 kilometers to Tel Aviv in another direction. A large menorah stands in front of the fancy new railway station, there's a kosher restaurant, and a shul that may soon receive a Torah. Although the experiment to make this a Jewish homeland was unsuccessful, we have left a mark."

The inseparable brothers grew old together, never wanted for anything, and lived humbly in the house they had built years earlier. They reached their mid-eighties and died days apart, content in the knowledge that from the ashes they had been able to find meaning in their lives.

EPILOGUE

With all memory and fate driven deep beneath the waves. Let me forget about today until tomorrow. – **Bob Dylan**

Chaviva followed in Zosha's footsteps, frequently leaving Israel to provide lectures in other countries. On this day, she was in a lecture hall at a New York university accompanied by several elderly survivors to inform the audience about the lives of those who hadn't perished during the Shoah.

After a moment of silence to commemorate the martyrs, Chaviva said, "Over the years, numerous scholars have attempted to identify what might have led to the Shoah. Social and political scientists have pointed to factors such as endemic racial discrimination, capitulating to social norms, the need for power or wealth, collective jealousy, and festering political and religious grievances that were allowed to emerge. I suppose understanding the causes of such hatred might offer a way to prevent the killing of large swaths of people. For most of us, unbridled, irrational hatred of others makes little sense, and finding ways to curb it will certainly be difficult. Indeed, can logical arguments sway the attitudes and behaviors of illogical people, especially as these hatreds have been bred for generations?"

The audience could sense she was building up steam as the tenor of her voice changed and her words became more vehement.

"Of course, you'd be correct in asking me if I can offer approaches to diminish racial hatred, and more specifically, the hatred directed at Jews," she said. "I freely confess I don't. Perhaps Jews should be herded together and allowed to live quietly on a remote island or somewhere in Northern Siberia, which, incidentally, had been tried but was unsuccessful. Theodor Herzl, who was known as a writer and political activist, had taken the position that in the end Jews couldn't survive without having a safe place, and we aspired to establish, or more accurately, reestablish, Eretz Yisrael as our homeland. Yet, this bred animosity, and the term Zionism, which simply refers to the development of a Jewish national state, has been repeatedly castigated and become a dirty word equated to racism. Go figure!"

Most of the audience appreciated the comment, smiling broadly or nodding in agreement. Others sat dourly, arms crossed, clearly disagreeing with anything she had to say.

"What annoys me terribly is the common conception I've heard far too often that the creation of Israel was in repayment for what Jews experienced during the Shoah," Chaviva said. "Let's look at the realities of the situation. The British initially offered us Uganda or Kenya as a place for Jews, which was rejected by early Zionists who wanted to return to our ancient homeland. We Jews weren't handed Israel on a silver platter. We were the indigenous people for millennia and our Israel was recreated despite considerable efforts to stop us. We got rid of the British colonialists, and we fought repeated wars with Arab countries. We turned a desert green through our science and technology, and we are a free and democratic society.

"So when I'm confronted with the assertion Israel was a concession made to us because of the collective guilt of other countries, my response is the Yiddish expression '*Ti mir nisht kein toyvehs* [don't do me any favors].' We can take care of ourselves. Of course, like most countries we benefit from good relations with others, but don't be mistaken, these countries have and will continue to receive benefits from our science, our agricultural formulations, and even our armaments industry. In any sphere you choose to look –

science, medicine, biotechnology, computer technology, and many others – we've contributed to the world as much as we've received."

The statement brought loud and lengthy applause. Raising her hands to quiet the audience, she added: "If we could, if we were allowed, we would do much more for the world. The concept of tikkun olam is with us all the time, but too often we don't have the opportunity to practice this precept."

This brought still greater applause, and again she raised her arms for the audience to quiet so she could continue.

"As Herzl indicated repeatedly, for millennia, Jews had nowhere to stay and nowhere to go," she said. "Yet, diaspora Jews always faced east when saying our daily prayers, and always hoped for 'Next year in Jerusalem.' To be sure, the United States has become a safe haven for many of our brethren, but it wasn't always so. Some of you may not be familiar with the Jewish-American activist and writer Emma Lazarus. However, I'm sure you know of at least one sentence of her monumental poem "The New Colossus," which is inscribed on the base of the Statue of Liberty. 'Give me your tired, your poor, your huddled masses yearning to breathe free.' That sentiment may have been true in 1883 when the poem was written, but this sentiment no longer held at the time of the Holocaust, when entry of Jews was severely curtailed."

At this comment, an indignant audience member rose, saying, "I'm here to listen to your perspective of the Holocaust, not be preached at about how bad the US has treated anyone. We have been and continue to be the bastion of survival for many immigrants!"

This was hardly the first time Chaviva had encountered aggressive comments. She knew how to handle them deftly, but this attack got under her skin. Her natural inclination was to respond forcefully. But she had learned from Zosha that diplomacy was the best route to take to change minds.

"Almost six million Jews are living here today, which is far more than the number of Jews in Israel," Chaviva said. "I agree America is a wonderful country that has hosted many Jews. But I repeat, this wasn't always so. Please, ask yourself where the US was when it could have saved thousands of children through Kindertransports. What was the US attitude during the war when shiploads of Jews arrived here? Had they been welcomed or were they turned away? After the war, the US had no problem taking in Nazi scientists for their expertise in building missiles while at the same time not opening its doors to Jews maintained in displaced person camps in Germany. I'm sorry you feel offended by my comments. That certainly wasn't my intention. What I want to do is make America a better, more welcoming country.

"We need to be realistic about human behavior. Anybody can be fooled, and the retelling of historical events can be altered to suit specific situations. For example, most of you have heard of Charles Lindbergh, who was initially hailed as a great hero for his achievement as the first person to fly solo across the Atlantic. However, how many of you are aware he became a Nazi sympathizer who even received a medal from Hermann Göring on behalf of the Führer? He was a proponent of eugenics, preached antisemitism, and was instrumental in trying to keep the US out of the fight against the Nazis. When this first became widely known, his star faded, and he was forced out of the US Army Air Corps. Like too many others, he was eventually reinstated, his reputation sanitized, and it was as if his bad deeds had never happened. Despite his malevolent attitudes and behaviors, most of you assumed Lindbergh was an American hero, someone to be admired."

Turning to the man who had been critical of her, she added: "My point is most people can be made to believe almost anything. This doesn't make them bad people, just naive."

"It wasn't just Charles Lindbergh who was rehabilitated and then lionized," added another audience member. "I'm sure you're aware that the former SS officer, Wernher von Braun, who was instrumental in the Nazi V-2 ballistic missile program, has been made into a hero for his work on sending a man to the moon. Furthermore, Alfred Krupp whose industrial organization used more than one million people as slave laborers and who was found guilty of war crimes at the Nuremberg trials, has been able to rehabilitate himself through generous donations to institutions such as Harvard and Stanford

University. How is this possible? Do university presidents and NASA officials have terribly short memories?"

"I doubt that. I'm sure they have very good memories," Chaviva responded, "good enough for officials to have taken pains not to mention Krupp and von Braun were Nazis who were responsible for the deaths of many innocents. What they choose to remember overtly boils down to what's in their best interests at the moment."

After a pause to let the comments sink in, Chaviva continued. "Now, as the gentleman requested, I'll get to the heart of my lecture, namely the persistent impact of the Shoah," she said. "For a time, there had been a focus on understanding the long-term negative mental health consequences on survivors of the Shoah. Some survivors indeed experienced signs of PTSD, and periods of depression frequently overtook them. But these outcomes weren't the rule, and most survivors did not experience these mental health conditions. Like many of my current Jewish friends, I went through the Shoah. I'm not damaged ... at least I don't think I'm damaged. Most of my friends and their children don't appear to be damaged either, certainly not visibly so. Scholars like Viktor Frankl have maintained that to get through unimaginable trauma, people need to rise above themselves to find some form of meaning from what they went through. I admired Frankl and think his insightful views applied to many people during the Shoah and for some afterward. But here again, this doesn't apply to all people."

A young woman asked, "So what do you think made some people resilient in overcoming trauma while others were not so fortunate?"

Chaviva replied, "Frankly, I'm not at all sure. It's easy to explain why a vase that falls from a shelf breaks apart. It's more difficult to explain why a nearby second vase didn't incur any damage. I've looked into the lives of dozens of people who survived the Shoah and I've yet to understand why some people fared relatively or extremely well, whereas others carried their horrors with them to the extent it even affected their children and their children's children. What struck me as especially telling was that for many people, having social support and a community to rely on preserved their well-being. In other instances, resilience among some survivors seemed to be tied to a sense of reality and understanding. They seemed to be able to accept the stressors they experienced, almost as if they had been saying, 'I can't do anything to change events, so I have to accept the reality of what I confronted and move on.' It very much reminds me of a clinical strategy – acceptance and commitment therapy – that has become relatively useful in treating psychological conditions such as depression."

When asked to expand on this comment, Chaviva said, "I can do better than that."

She turned and walked to one of the elderly survivors who had accompanied her, and they had a brief private conversation. Together, they walked to the podium, Chaviva having placed her arm through Elisha's to support her.

"I'd like to introduce you to my friend Elisha, who went through the war hidden from the Nazis by Christian Poles," she said. "Please give her your attention."

Speaking hesitantly, the older woman relayed her experience. "My family had been hidden by my sister's friend throughout the war," Elisha said. "It was an awful time. We were afraid every moment of every day, which was far worse than the hunger we experienced. Being kept in deprived conditions eats at your brain and your *nefesh* [soul]. I had my children with me, and I was afraid the experience in a cellar would damage them. As my youngest daughter had very light blond hair, we felt she wouldn't be identified as being Jewish, so I allowed her out of the shelter to go outdoors and play. However, one awful day she failed to return. We searched for wherever we could, risking our lives going outdoors where Nazi sympathizers might see us. Our search for her was fruitless."

Slightly nodding her head repeatedly, and sighing heavily, she continued: "A neighbor subsequently informed us my beautiful daughter had been taken by two Nazi officers. We were told blond children were often abducted perhaps to be adopted by a childless German couple. I had my doubts about this, especially as the Nazis perceived Poles to be inferior people. I mourned the loss of my child terribly, but with no options open to me, I had to accept the reality I wouldn't ever see my sweet daughter again, and with time I was able to move on."

A young student unable to restrain her curiosity raised her hand and asked, "Did you ever find out what had become of the child?"

"Yes, I did," she said. "After the war, I stayed in touch with the kind Christian family that had hidden us during the war. I would often send them money to help them. It wasn't much and I would have liked to do more for them. In 1963, I received a letter and a newspaper clipping from the woman whose family had been our savior. The clipping, which came from the personal section of the newspaper, had been posted by a young woman who indicated she believed her family had lived in Poland during the war, but she came to be adopted by a Russian couple. The notice in the newspaper suggested that after the war, a Russian couple had purchased the child through a black-market exchange, although I believed it was more likely the child was abandoned by the fleeing Nazis and was taken by the Russians. It really didn't matter since the most interesting thing was that the picture of the woman in the clipping resembled one of my daughters, Syma, who had survived the war.

"As you can imagine, we were excited by the information, and shortly afterward, Syma and I obtained a visa and negotiated with the Soviet embassy for us to travel to Moscow where we would meet the young woman. We brought 20,000 US dollars to be used in case we needed to use *vzyatki* [bribes]. Our Soviet contact played games until we passed over several thousand American dollars, after which we were introduced to a young woman named Katia. Her resemblance to my daughter Syma was remarkable, absolutely remarkable. She even had a small birthmark on her left wrist I recognized. What little she recalled of her early life resembled what we had endured while hidden from the Nazis."

Elisha was aware of the rapt attention of the audience as they anticipated the ending of the story. "Well," she said, "the reunion seemed to be going well and I was intent on taking my newly recovered daughter with me to Canada, and Katia was excited to emigrate. The Russians had made emigration easier, especially when dollars were part of the arrangement. Everything had been going as if it were ordained to come to a very good ending. Unfortunately, when Katia learned we were Jewish, she rejected further overtures of a reunion and made clear her strong antisemitic views. She behaved as if we disgusted her."

The audience was shocked by this revelation, and it was clear no comments would be made until an ending was provided to this captivating story. Elisha sighed deeply, quietly said to herself, "*Ribono shel olem* [God in heaven]," and went on.

"Realizing the depth of Katia's feelings, I chose not to appeal to her," Elisha said. "Just as Katia couldn't abide Jews, I couldn't think of having an antisemite under my roof. In the end, I just handed her an envelope containing the remaining US dollars I intended to use as bribes. About 12,000 dollars remained, which was a fortune in Russia at the time. Katia opened the envelope and immediately put it in her purse without thanking me. She behaved as if she was entitled to the money. On the plane trip back home, Syma and I were desolate, but after considerable thought, I said to Syma, 'I've now lost the same daughter twice. What is, is, and I can't look back.' Other than recounting the story to the rest of our family, the issue of my lost daughter was never mentioned again."

As the audience absorbed there wouldn't be the happy ending they anticipated, Chaviva accompanied the older woman to her seat and then took the podium and continued her lecture, addressing the unasked questions.

"You see, Elisha didn't persistently focus on this apparent loss," Chaviva said. "She didn't persistently dwell on what could have been but never would, she didn't blame herself, and she didn't raise her fist to the sky blaming God. She only shrugged her shoulders sadly, accepted reality, and went on with her life."

After a lengthy quiet, an older man in the audience thanked her for her insights and said, "The story you told is both very sad yet also inspiring. I'm curious about what your experiences have been concerning the religious beliefs of survivors. With all they experienced during the Shoah, do they still believe in a merciful God?"

"That's a good question," she said. "I can't speak for all survivors.

My interviews indicated some survivors tended toward religion and continued to believe the God to whom they pray is a merciful one. Others have taken a different view. Some have abandoned religion, and a few hold a grudge against God, so to speak. Several survivors had rejected God after the war, only to resume their religiosity later in life. One of the women with me today can describe her feelings on the matter."

Nela, who was then in her early fifties, approached the podium, and it was soon evident she was highly intelligent and well-spoken.

"A few years ago, our mutual friend Zosha had asked me to accompany her to one of her lectures," Nela said. "I wasn't comfortable doing it at the time and rejected her request. Now, I feel more ready to share my experiences, which in some ways have been positive, whereas others, well, not so much."

Without wasting words, she described her experience being enslaved in work camps, how she and Rachel had survived, her blessed reunion with her father after the war, the joy she felt being able to leave Europe and come to America, her marriage and life in Chicago while her husband was training in medicine, the birth and death of her child, the dissolution of her marriage, and her positive and negative experiences in New York.

"You see," she said, "my life has encompassed more ups and downs than the roller coaster here at Coney Island. The ups were very high, and the downs were very, very low. Before the war, my parents were observant Jews and my father had been well-trained in Talmudic studies. Following the lead of my parents, I was religiously observant, and during my first year in a work camp, I prayed every day God would rescue us. Eventually, I stopped doing it since it was clearly having no effect. I had been needlessly banging my head against a wall. I hadn't disavowed God; I had simply stopped thinking of God at all. As humans, we have several basic needs, with simple survival being the most cogent, so my focus was on day-to-day survival and God no longer was useful in this regard. My attitude in later years followed in the same way. Things happen that are out of our control, and when we do have control, we might inadvertently make mistakes, which I did."

An audience member asked, "Did you abandon God, or did you feel God abandoned you?"

Taking a few moments to think about how to respond, Nela said, "Honestly, neither applies. I haven't given the issue much thought. I was happy when I experienced good luck and unhappy when things turned out badly. Perhaps I was too self-focused, so I attributed the good experiences to my cleverness, and except for losing my child, I took responsibility when things didn't work out as I had hoped.

"I expect you're aware of Einstein's famous quote, 'God doesn't play dice with the universe.' This often-misunderstood statement should be taken in the context of other notable comments he made, specifically something akin to God might well reveal Himself in balances and harmonies that exist throughout the universe, but it's unlikely this God is concerned with the behavior and fate of humankind. It's not a matter of whether God is merciful or malicious. If anything at all, if there is a God, then what he might do is open a crack in a wall for us to go through. However, God doesn't dictate whether we do or don't go through that crack. That's mostly up to us."

ABOUT THE AUTHOR

Shimon and Chana Anisman, and their two-year-old son Chaim (Hymie) reached Halifax, Canada on December 31, 1950, after attempting to emigrate from Europe for more than four years following the Shoah. They settled in Montreal, where Hymie attended a Yeshiva and subsequently obtained university training, and then received his doctorate at the University of Waterloo (Waterloo, Ontario) in 1972. He accepted a position at Carleton University in Ottawa, Ontario, in the Psychology Department and subsequently the Department of Neuroscience where he continues to be a faculty member. He was a Fellow of the Ontario Mental Research foundation, held a Canada Research Chair in Behavioural Neuroscience, and was elected as a Fellow of the Royal Society of

Canada. His research was ranked as being in the top two percent of medical and psychological research in Canada and worldwide.

Hymie's research has focused on the neurobiological and immunological effects of stressors and the impact of these processes on psychological and physical health disturbances. Much of his research has concerned the multiple factors that increase an individual's vulnerability to the adverse effects of stressful events and those that imbue them with resilience. These have included the interplay between genetic factors and environmental experiences that can affect diverse pathologies. Adverse experiences comprise events encountered during childhood, chronic discrimination and stigmatization, the distress created by immigration, the consequences of unsupportive social interactions, and the impact of collective historical trauma on the transmission of stressor effects across generations. He is the father of Simon, Rebecca, Jessica, and Max, and grandparents of Aoife and Shep.

These two books about his family history have been published by Hymie Anisman. Both books are part of the series Holocaust Survivor True Stories (Amsterdam Publishers).

Before the Beginning and after the End (2023)

From One Generation to the Next. Unbroken Resilience (2026)

AMSTERDAM PUBLISHERS HOLOCAUST LIBRARY

The series **Holocaust Survivor Memoirs World War II** consists of the following autobiographies of survivors:

The Dead Years. Holocaust Memoirs, by Joseph Schupack

Hank Brodt Holocaust Memoirs. A Candle and a Promise, by Deborah Donnelly

Rescued from the Ashes. The Diary of Leokadia Schmidt, Survivor of the Warsaw Ghetto, by Leokadia Schmidt

My Lvov. Holocaust Memoir of a twelve-year-old Girl, by Janina Hescheles

Remembering Ravensbrück. From Holocaust to Healing, by Natalie Hess

Wolf. A Story of Hate, by Zeev Scheinwald with Ella Scheinwald

Save my Children. An Astonishing Tale of Survival and its Unlikely Hero, by Leon Kleiner with Edwin Stepp

Holocaust Memoirs of a Bergen-Belsen Survivor & Classmate of Anne Frank, by Nanette Blitz Konig

Defiant German - Defiant Jew. A Holocaust Memoir from inside the Third Reich, by Walter Leopold with Les Leopold

In a Land of Forest and Darkness. The Holocaust Story of two Jewish Partisans, by Sara Lustigman Omelinski

Holocaust Memories. Annihilation and Survival in Slovakia, by Paul Davidovits

From Auschwitz with Love. The Inspiring Memoir of Two Sisters' Survival, Devotion and Triumph Told by Manci Grunberger Beran & Ruth Grunberger Mermelstein, by Daniel Seymour

Remetz. Resistance Fighter and Survivor of the Warsaw Ghetto, by Jan Yohay Remetz

My March Through Hell. A Young Girl's Terrifying Journey to Survival, by Halina Kleiner with Edwin Stepp

Roman's Journey, by Roman Halter

Beyond Borders. Escaping the Holocaust and Fighting the Nazis. 1938-1948, by Rudi Haymann

The Engineers. A memoir of survival through World War II in Poland and Hungary, by Henry Reiss

Spark of Hope. An Autobiography, by Luba Wrobel Goldberg

Footnote to History. From Hungary to America. The Memoir of a Holocaust Survivor, by Andrew Laszlo

Farewell Atlantis. Recollections, by Valentīna Freimane

The Courtyard. A memoir, by Benjamin Parket and Alexa Morris

The Mulberry Tree. The story of a life before and after the Holocaust, by Iboja Wandall-Holm

The Boy in the Back. A True Story of Survival in Auschwitz and Mauthausen, as told to Fern Lebo by Jan Blumenstein

Beneath the Lightless Sky. Surviving the Holocaust in the Sewers of Lvov, by Ignacy Chiger

From Sorrow to Joy. From Hitler's Darkness to the Sunlight on Mount Carmel, by Dr. Yakov Adler

Memories of a Subhuman. A Jewish Teenager's Journey of Survival. From Riga to Buchenwald and Back, by Aleksandr Bergman

Mendel Run, by Milton H. Schwartz

The Kapos of Auschwitz, by Charles Liblau

The series **Holocaust Survivor True Stories**
consists of the following biographies:

Among the Reeds. The true story of how a family survived the Holocaust, by Tammy Bottner

A Holocaust Memoir of Love & Resilience. Mama's Survival from Lithuania to America, by Ettie Zilber

Living among the Dead. My Grandmother's Holocaust Survival Story of Love and Strength, by Adena Bernstein Astrowsky

Heart Songs. A Holocaust Memoir, by Barbara Gilford

Shoes of the Shoah. The Tomorrow of Yesterday, by Dorothy Pierce

Hidden in Berlin. A Holocaust Memoir, by Evelyn Joseph Grossman

Separated Together. The Incredible True WWII Story of Soulmates Stranded an Ocean Apart, by Kenneth P. Price, Ph.D.

The Man Across the River. The incredible story of one man's will to survive the Holocaust, by Zvi Wiesenfeld

If Anyone Calls, Tell Them I Died. A Memoir, by Emanuel (Manu) Rosen

The House on Thrömerstrasse. A Story of Rebirth and Renewal in the Wake of the Holocaust, by Ron Vincent

Dancing with my Father. His hidden past. Her quest for truth. How Nazi Vienna shaped a family's identity, by Jo Sorochinsky

The Story Keeper. Weaving the Threads of Time and Memory - A Memoir, by Fred Feldman

Krisia's Silence. The Girl who was not on Schindler's List, by Ronny Hein

Defying Death on the Danube. A Holocaust Survival Story, by Debbie J. Callahan with Henry Stern

A Doorway to Heroism. A decorated German-Jewish Soldier who became an American Hero, by W. Jack Romberg

The Shoemaker's Son. The Life of a Holocaust Resister, by Laura Beth Bakst

The Redhead of Auschwitz. A True Story, by Nechama Birnbaum

Land of Many Bridges. My Father's Story, by Bela Ruth Samuel Tenenholtz

Creating Beauty from the Abyss. The Amazing Story of Sam Herciger, Auschwitz Survivor and Artist, by Lesley Ann Richardson

On Sunny Days We Sang. A Holocaust Story of Survival and Resilience, by Jeannette Grunhaus de Gelman

Painful Joy. A Holocaust Family Memoir, by Max J. Friedman

I Give You My Heart. A True Story of Courage and Survival, by Wendy Holden

In the Time of Madmen, by Mark A. Prelas

Monsters and Miracles. Horror, Heroes and the Holocaust, by Ira Wesley Kitmacher

Flower of Vlora. Growing up Jewish in Communist Albania, by Anna Kohen

Aftermath: Coming of Age on Three Continents. A Memoir, by Annette Libeskind Berkovits

Not a real Enemy. The True Story of a Hungarian Jewish Man's Fight for Freedom, by Robert Wolf

Zaidy's War. Four Armies, Three Continents, Two Brothers. One Man's Impossible Story of Endurance, by Martin Bodek

The Glassmaker's Son. Looking for the World my Father left behind in Nazi Germany, by Peter Kupfer

The Apprentice of Buchenwald. The True Story of the Teenage Boy Who Sabotaged Hitler's War Machine, by Oren Schneider

Good for a Single Journey, by Helen Joyce

Burying the Ghosts. She escaped Nazi Germany only to have her life torn apart by the woman she saved from the camps: her mother, by Sonia Case

American Wolf. From Nazi Refugee to American Spy. A True Story, by Audrey Birnbaum

Bipolar Refugee. A Saga of Survival and Resilience, by Peter Wiesner

In the Wake of Madness. My Family's Escape from the Nazis, by Bettie Lennett Denny

Before the Beginning and After the End, by Hymie Anisman

I Will Give Them an Everlasting Name. Jacksonville's Stories of the Holocaust, by Samuel Cox

Hiding in Holland. A Resistance Memoir, by Shulamit Reinharz

The Ghosts on the Wall. A Grandson's Memoir of the Holocaust, by Kenneth D. Wald

Thirteen in Auschwitz. My grandmother's fight to stay human, by Lauren Meyerowitz Port

The Jewish Woman Who Fought the Nazis. Bep Schaap-Bedak's life during the Holocaust in Holland, by Eli Schaap

Little Edna's War. A True story of Resistance and Hope. A Gripping WWII page-turner, by Janet Bond Brill, PhD

Voices of Resilience. An Anthology of Stories written by Children of Holocaust Survivors, Edited by Deborah (Devora) Ross-Grayman

Was it just a matter of luck? A Family, the Holocaust, and the Founding of a Museum, by Dr Charles Kaner

Dreaming of the River. A Mother and Daughter's Fight for Survival during the Holocaust, by Pauline Steinhorn

From One Generation to the Next. Unbroken Resilience, by Hymie Anisman

Irmgard. The Girl from Dresden. A Memoir of Survival and Legacy, by Fiona Kelmann

The World has Caught Fire, by Leah Grisham PhD

The series **Jewish Children in the Holocaust** consists of the following autobiographies of Jewish children hidden during WWII in the Netherlands:

Searching for Home. The Impact of WWII on a Hidden Child,
by Joseph Gosler

Sounds from Silence. Reflections of a Child Holocaust Survivor, Psychiatrist and Teacher, by Robert Krell

Sabine's Odyssey. A Hidden Child and her Dutch Rescuers,
by Agnes Schipper

The Journey of a Hidden Child, by Harry Pila and Robin Black

Out of the Woods, by Aliza Levy Erber

The series **New Jewish Fiction** consists of the following novels, written by Jewish authors. All novels are set in the time during or after the Holocaust.

The Corset Maker. A Novel, by Annette Libeskind Berkovits

Escaping the Whale. The Holocaust is over. But is it ever over for the next generation? by Ruth Rotkowitz

When the Music Stopped. Willy Rosen's Holocaust, by Casey Hayes

Hands of Gold. One Man's Quest to Find the Silver Lining in Misfortune, by Roni Robbins

The Girl Who Counted Numbers. A Novel, by Roslyn Bernstein

There was a garden in Nuremberg. A Novel, by Navina Michal Clemerson

The Butterfly and the Axe, by Omer Bartov

To Live Another Day. A Novel, by Elizabeth Rosenberg

The Right to Happiness. After all they went through. Stories, by Helen Schary Motro

Five Amber Beads, by Richard Aronowitz

To Love Another Day. A Novel, by Elizabeth Rosenberg

Cursing the Darkness. A Novel about Loss and Recovery, by Joanna Rosenthall

The series **Holocaust Heritage** consists of the following memoirs by 2G:

The Cello Still Sings. A Generational Story of the Holocaust and of the Transformative Power of Music, by Janet Horvath

The Fire and the Bonfire. A Journey into Memory, by Ardyn Halter

The Silk Factory: Finding Threads of My Family's True Holocaust Story, by Michael Hickins

Winter Light. The Memoir of a Child of Holocaust Survivors, by Grace Feuerverger

Out from the Shadows. Growing up with Holocaust Survivor Parents, by Willie Handler

Hidden in Plain Sight. A Family Memoir and the Untold Story of the Holocaust in Serbia, by Julie Brill

The Unspeakable. Breaking my family's silence surrounding the Holocaust, by Nicola Hanefeld

Eighteen for Life. Surviving the Holocaust, by Helen Schamroth

Four Survivor Grandparents. Run. Rely. Rebuild, by Jonathan Schloss

Austrian Again. Reclaiming a Lost Legacy, by Anne Hand

Never Fitting In. My Journey with Parental Trauma, Addiction, Healing, by Sonia Claire Ascher

Divine Corners. In the Shadow of the Holocaust on a Catskills Chicken Farm, by Michelle Friedman

Milk in an Eggshell. A WWII story of hiding in plain sight, by Miryam Sas

The series **Holocaust Books for Young Adults** consists of the following novels, based on true stories:

The Boy behind the Door. How Salomon Kool Escaped the Nazis. Inspired by a True Story, by David Tabatsky

Running for Shelter. A True Story, by Suzette Sheft

The Precious Few. An Inspirational Saga of Courage based on True Stories, by David Twain with Art Twain

Dark Shadows Hover, by Jordan Steven Sher

The Sun will Shine Again, by Cynthia Goldstein Monsour

The Memory Place. How My Parents Survived Nazi Hell, by Monica van Rijn

The series **WWII Historical Fiction** consists of the following novels, some of which are based on true stories:

Mendelevski's Box. A Heartwarming and Heartbreaking Jewish Survivor's Story, by Roger Swindells

Brave Face. The Inspiring WWII Memoir of a Dutch/German Child, by I. Caroline Crocker and Meta A. Evenbly

When We Had Wings. The Gripping Story of an Orphan in Janusz Korczak's Orphanage. A Historical Novel, by Tami Shem-Tov

Jacob's Courage. Romance and Survival amidst the Horrors of War, by Charles S. Weinblatt

A Semblance of Justice. Based on true Holocaust experiences, by Wolf Holles

Under the Pink Triangle. Where forbidden love meets unspeakable evil, by Katie Moore

www.ingramcontent.com/pod-product-compliance
Lightning Source LLC
LaVergne TN
LVHW091708070526
838199LV00050B/2303